ALSO BY ERICA BROWN

Happier Endings

Seder Talk: The Conversational Haggada

Leadership in the Wilderness

Return

In the Narrow Places

Confronting Scandal

Spiritual Boredom

The Case for Jewish Peoplehood

Inspired Jewish Leadership

TAKE YOUR

SOUL

TO WORK

365 MEDITATIONS
ON EVERY DAY LEADERSHIP

ERICA BROWN

SIMON & SCHUSTER

New York London Toronto Sydney New Delhi

Simon & Schuster
1230 Avenue of the Americas
New York, NY 10020

First Simon & Schuster hardcover edition December 2015

SIMON & SCHUSTER and colophon are
registered trademarks of Simon & Schuster, Inc.

Ellen Bass, excerpt from "If You Knew" from *The Human Line*, copyright © 2007
by Ellen Bass, reprinted with the permission of The Permissions Company, Inc.,
on behalf of Copper Canyon Press, www.coppercanyonpress.org.
David Whyte, poem "On Faith," copyright © 2007, reprinted with
permission from Many Rivers Press, Langley, WA 98260 USA.

For information about special discounts for bulk purchases,
please contact Simon & Schuster Special Sales
at 1-866-506-1949 or business@simonandschuster.com.

The Simon & Schuster Speakers Bureau can bring authors to your live event.
For more information or to book an event, contact the
Simon & Schuster Speakers Bureau at 1-866-248-3049
or visit our website at www.simonspeakers.com.

Manufactured in the United States of America

1   3   5   7   9   10   8   6   4   2

Library of Congress Cataloging-in-Publication Data

Brown, Erica, date.
Take your soul to work : 365 meditations on every day leadership /
Erica Brown.—First Simon & Schuster hardcover edition.
pages cm
1. Work—Religious aspects—Meditations. 2. Leadership—
Religious aspects—Meditations. I. Title.
BL65.W67B76 2015
204'.32—dc23
2015013653

ISBN 978-1-4767-4341-7
ISBN 978-1-4767-4343-1 (ebook)

"Not by power not by might but by spirit," says the Lord.
—ZECHARIAH 4:6

This book is dedicated to our veterans.
Thank you for teaching us what sacrifice and service mean.

CONTENTS

INTRODUCTION:
LEADING FROM
THE INSIDE OUT

How do you know if you are leading from the inside out, from the depths of your soul and your humanity?

You'll know in your work when you can . . .

Listen with your eyes as well as your ears.

Stretch yourself and others.

Forgive with a full heart.

Be fully present for yourself and others.

Cultivate quiet.

Practice simplicity.

Walk with tenderness and curiosity.

Respect others.

Attune your senses to the world around you.

Remember the good.

Pay careful attention.

Make gratitude a daily habit.

Find holiness in shared laughter.

Feel purpose in collaborative work.

Work to bring more justice to the world.

Acknowledge that there are forces far greater than yourself that operate within you.

Give voice to the needs of those who do not think or act like you.

Use language at work that elevates conversations.

Have the trust of others.

Smile at strangers.

Actively create time to rest and time to reflect.

Know to whom you really answer in life.

Value self-improvement as a daily and welcome challenge.

Reflect on both your current state of being and the opportunity
of becoming.

Sound good?

Now the question is how you get there. How do you lead spiritually, from a place of abundance, where goodness spills over into all realms of your life? You need personal discipline to bring greater depth and humanity to your leadership. You need reminders, especially in the darkest hours, to help you remember what leadership is ultimately about: the capacity to stretch yourself and others, to envision something larger, brighter and bigger than yourself, to transcend the ordinary and achieve deep meaning and purpose, and even, on a really good day, to touch eternity.

You also need a plan.

Most leaders have no plan when it comes to soul-building at work. It is not for lack of heart or compassion that leaders don't make one. As leaders, we let go of reflection or sometimes default on integrity loans because we have no time—or make no time—to cultivate the spirit. This is not helped by the fact that our followers usually expect very little of us in the realm of virtue. The bar is so low morally, you can practically step over it. No one expects leaders to be nice or kind. And when so little is expected, you may deliver even less and betray your best self. We're often short on moral, spiritual and ethical language in the corporate sector.

Enter this book.

Take Your Soul to Work is essentially a prayer book for leaders. Prayer and meditation are not only for religious people with a particular faith commitment and tradition. A meditation is a spiritual pause, an act of reflection and a chance to renew our emotional and intellectual commitments, blending the house of worship with the corner office. When you ask for a little daily grace, you can make every space just a little bit more sacred because of the way you lead.

This is essentially a book of hours. In the spiritual world of medieval Christendom, a book of hours referred to a special prayer book of the Roman Catholic Church—a breviary or primer—that contained the service for every day of the year with adjustments for holidays and seasons.

We have surviving books of hours from this period. Some owned by the wealthy were ornate and illuminated. Some were personalized with the names and faces of their owners. Others were plain and simple. Grooms gave them to brides as wedding gifts. Parents gave them to children. A book of hours was more than a special keepsake; it was a small, precious compass that both anchored your day in transcendence and affirmed your core beliefs.

Take Your Soul to Work is a modern book of hours for leaders. It offers one brief meditation a day on leadership, followed by a personal challenge in the form of a question or assignment. It's a short daily read because (1) leaders who are working at their peak can rarely afford the time to immerse themselves in books but need many more opportunities for self-reflection, evaluation and challenge. You need to build spiritual capacity daily, not quarterly or in a few hours at an annual conference. (2) We become better by making goodness a habit. Goodness does not emerge out of one retreat on spirituality or one robust conversation on morality and ethics. It emerges from the daily habit of centering ourselves. Why a question a day? Transformation rarely occurs because of a statement. We change because of a question. You may also want to use a page of this book and a question in a department or staff meeting to stimulate a group conversation.

For the purpose of this book, we'll define spirituality as an inner platform for insight, mindfulness and intention regarding self and others. The spiritual life calls us to lead and serve others with tenderness and generosity. In a world where the self often comes first, spiritual leadership acknowledges both the presence of others and also our profound need to live in greater harmony. At the same time, growing a healthy spiritual practice requires us to spend time alone, integrating what we know about good leadership with who we are. If your leadership is a service, then serve others as best you can: from a place of strength, authenticity, integrity and wholeness. Spiritual leadership thrives on attentive listening, compassion, optimism and hope. It requires an understanding that humility is more important than ego.

When you feel strong, inspired and well-supported, you can transcend the politics and pettiness of organizational life and realize the best in yourself and others. You can lead with more grace and greater competency, forgiveness and love.

Make no mistake. This is difficult work. You have to work at it every day.

With each page ahead, embrace discomfort. Let it stretch you to places you have not been before. Try, for a few minutes a day, to live your most important questions. Every meditation on the pages ahead offers a promise of reflection and prayer because a tender moment of prayer can be generative and inspiring. Try to read only one page a day, ideally at the start of your day, to carry the day's charge with you. Prayer is a reminder of all that is important to us. It puts us in a posture of gratitude to receive the day and its blessings and challenges. It steadies us and readies us to be our best selves every day.

John Quincy Adams, sixth president of the United States, once defined effective leadership this way: "If your actions inspire others to dream more, do more and become more, then you are a leader." Yes. You are a leader. Yes, you can inspire people to dream more and be more when you lead from the inside. And when you truly lead from the inside, you won't ultimately become just a better leader. You'll also become a better person.

ON THRIVING

The book of Psalms opens with the words "Happy is the person . . ." We begin *this* book with what it takes to flourish as a human being.

"One is like a tree planted besides streams of water, which yields its fruit in season, whose foliage never fades, and whatever it produces thrives" (Psalms 1:3).

A person who thrives yields fruit and can see what he or she has grown. The foliage never fades; the leaves are evergreen. At every natural cycle, the thriving tree embodies the activity of the season and shows productive results. Every part of the tree is achingly alive.

But there is something else that is extraordinary about this tree that, on the surface, may seem very ordinary. It is planted beside streams of water. Given its placement, success seems likely.

Often we fail to thrive as leaders because although we have the requisite skill-sets or talents, we place ourselves in situations or among people who get in the way of our flourishing. They diminish us or stunt our growth. We forget that thriving is also about creating conditions for success: the sun, water and soil of our leadership. We put ourselves in the shade with an inadequate water supply and wonder why we are not flourishing.

**What can you do right now in your leadership
to create the conditions to thrive?**

ON INTIMACY

Henri Nouwen was a Catholic priest who wrote close to forty books on spirituality. Despite his academic training and positions at major intellectual centers, he spent the last years of his life caring for a disabled adult in a special community in Ontario, Canada, giving up the prestige of theology to live in compassionate, sacred space with another human being.

Creating intimacy, especially with those who are distant physically, intellectually and spiritually from us, was what Nouwen wrote about, and it embodied the way he lived. He once wrote a note to God saying, "I am so afraid to open my clenched fists!" Intimacy scares us, yet we live for it. We avoid intimacy, as Nouwen wrote:

"The world says: 'Yes, I love you if you are good-looking, intelligent, and wealthy. I love you if you have a good education, a good job, and good connections. I love you if you produce much, sell much, and buy much.' . . . The world's love is and always will be conditional. As long as I keep looking for my true self in the world of conditional love, I will remain 'hooked' to the world—trying, failing, and trying again. It is a world that fosters addictions because what it offers cannot satisfy the deepest craving of my heart."

The deepest craving of humanity is for intimacy.

In what ways has your leadership gotten in the way of achieving intimacy with others?

✦ DAY #3 ✦

ON WONDER

"Never once in my life did I ask God for success or wisdom or power or fame. I asked for wonder, and he gave it to me." These are the famous words of the rabbi and scholar A. J. Heschel (1907–1972). They are a powerful reminder that as a leader it is so easy to become jaded, to believe that there is nothing new under the sun. Been there. Done that. Heard it all before. It is hard to invite wonder into life. You must ask for it.

"Our goal," Heschel wrote, "should be to live life in radical amazement . . . get up in the morning and look at the world in a way that takes nothing for granted. Everything is phenomenal; everything is incredible; never treat life casually. To be spiritual is to be amazed." Walk in the world with your eyes wide-open. Expect amazement and then see it everywhere.

Heschel wasn't simply looking at nature and beauty. He also looked at the great ugliness of human nature and tried to reform it. He marched at Selma right beside Martin Luther King Jr. and said it was like praying with one's feet. And as he aged, he took on a different universe of concerns: "When I was young, I admired clever people. Now that I am old, I admire kind people."

Wonder surfaces in curiosity, amazement, celebration, social justice and kindness.

**When did you last have a sense of
radical amazement as a leader?**

✦ DAY #4 ✦

ON PRAYER

Prayer can be a few words woven together with vulnerability that sings to the human condition. As leaders, we unknowingly pray all the time, offering up small supplications for help and wisdom in times of confusion. Say a little prayer for me, we think, before entering a boardroom or a corner office. Prayer is a ladder upon which our aspirations climb higher and higher.

Because we so often associate prayer with institutions or organized religion, we may cut off our own capacity to pray extemporaneously, to give expression to the deep longings and feelings of the soul.

Mahatma Gandhi (1869–1948) wrote: "Prayer is not asking. It is a longing of the soul. It is daily admission of one's weakness. It is better in prayer to have a heart without words than words without a heart." Gandhi's surroundings perhaps helped him understand the power of simple prayer. He lived modestly, wore a shawl and a loincloth that he sewed himself and ate a vegetarian diet. He lived in community, not separated as a leader from those he led.

Gandhi did not grow up a religious man and only encountered religious texts later in life when studying to be a barrister in London.

His experience reveals that prayer is not a function of words on a page that someone else wrote. It is an expression of the heart that admits failure and asks for strength.

**Write a prayer about your leadership that
is no more than three sentences long.**

✦ DAY #5 ✦

ON POWER

Power changes people. Abraham Lincoln once wrote: "Nearly all men can stand adversity, but if you want to test a man's character, give him power." Lincoln had the largest shoe size of any American president—a size 14—but those shoes were hard to fill, not because of their size but because of his personal humility.

When Lincoln died, he had in his pocket a news-clipping of unrest in the Confederate army. His very last day on this earth, he carried the news of his detractors close to his side. The power of the presidency mattered, but the power of equality mattered much more. It was a vision of justice worth living for, but he had to die for it instead.

When you have power, it is hard to remember not having power.

As a leader, it can be easy to confuse power with influence. You are powerful when you exert authority over those who are powerless to disagree. You are influential when people want to follow you out of admiration, respect and inspiration. People *want* to be led by you. They do not *have* to be led by you. Leading to serve others helps us reevaluate power while growing influence.

As a leader, you will be changed by power.

Strive instead for influence.

If you want to test someone's leadership, Lincoln told us, give that person power.

**Holding up a mirror to yourself, how
have you been changed by power?**

ON HUMILITY

Frank Wells was a Rhodes scholar, an athlete, a mountain climber and the vice chairman of Warner Brothers when Disney approached him and asked him to partner in running the company. In the ten years he ran Disney, the company's market value went from $2 billion to $22 billion. Usually people recognize Wells's more famous partner, Mike Eisner. But Wells was much more comfortable outside the spotlight, doing the quiet work and giving others the credit. That's why you may not recognize his name. On April 3, 1994, Wells was in a helicopter crash while on a ski trip. He died at the age of sixty-two. When his belongings were collected, his family found a note that he had carried for thirty years in his wallet: "Humility is the final achievement."

It was his final achievement.

To be humble, you must remind yourself of your deficiencies. Think about where you came from and how far you still have to go. You have to remind yourself with a note in your pocket. A famous piece of Hasidic wisdom states that you should always carry two notes in your pockets. In one pocket, carry the words, "For me, the world was created." In the other, carry the words, "I am but dust and ashes." Your leadership lies between these pockets of power and humility.

Enter each day with your head bowed.

Every day. Remember the note in your pockets.

Identify a powerful leadership quote that keeps you humble. Copy it and carry it in your wallet.

ON TRUST

There are two types of followers: those whose first instinct is to trust others and then be proven wrong, and those who distrust others and

must be proven wrong. Leaders must convince both types of followers to trust them.

Trust is the most important and fragile of commodities among
human beings. We need to trust leaders, believe that they are credible, reliable and fair. Break that trust, and it will be very difficult to
recapture. Not impossible, just much harder. Followers resent leaders they cannot trust, waiting for confirmation of their suspicions
and receiving it.

Ernest Hemingway once wrote this: "The best way to find out if
you can trust somebody is to trust them." Otherwise you will never
know. Sometimes people withhold trust because they have been
badly scarred before, and here Hemingway's wisdom comes back
at us again. "The world breaks everyone, and afterward, some are
strong at the broken places." When we can be strong in our broken
places, we can begin to trust people until we are proven wrong. Let
trust be the default.

Do people trust you?
How would you know?

✦ DAY #8 ✦

ON PRAISE

"Blessed is he who has learned to admire but not envy, to follow but
not imitate, to praise but not flatter, and to lead but not manipulate."

William Arthur Ward (1921–1994) named the fine lines between
emotions that, pulled slightly in one direction, are destructive and, in
another, constructive. Ward was a popular author and inspirational
speaker who, as a Methodist and religious man, recognized the importance of inspiration in building character.

Insecure leaders hang on the praise of others.

Secure leaders give praise to others.

Secure leaders enjoy praising others. They feel good—not when
others tell them how good they are, but when they can tell others
how good they are.

We enjoy being with people who make us feel special, who notice our distinctiveness, who compliment our uniqueness. We shrink in the presence of those who make us question ourselves, who make us feel insignificant and small. With our praise we create light and buoyancy.

We may follow leaders, bosses and supervisors who need praise but cannot give it, but we will never truly believe in them because they do not believe in us.

When we praise others often, it is easier to critique them when necessary because they feel respected. We have put enough deposits in their emotional bank to make an occasional withdrawal. They understand that we are invested in the relationship and are trying to grow us, not diminish us.

Who needs your praise today?

✦ DAY #9 ✦

ON MENTORING

Andrew Carnegie was a steel magnate in the nineteenth century. He was also a great philanthropist grown from the crucible of poverty and hard work. He propounded in his article *"The Gospel of Wealth"* the thesis that those who earn more than others need to take greater responsibility for the welfare of others. And he did. In the arts. In the sciences. In the building of libraries and great academic halls. But perhaps Carnegie's greatest contribution is revealed in the words chiseled on his tombstone:

> *Here lies a man*
> *Who knew how to enlist*
> *In his service*
> *Better men than himself.*

When the last words said about you speak of others, your leadership has spilled into the world. In addition to all the buildings and endowments that live beyond you are a troop of people who value what you valued and live in the spirit of your generosity and expansiveness.

Seeing what is great in another is a mark of greatness within the self. Being able to compliment, nourish and challenge someone else demonstrates that you are never alone in your work. Pay attention to growers. They're the people who step away from their own desks when you come into view. They're the people who ask challenging questions, not to show how smart they are, but to show you how talented you are. They're the ones who suggest next steps and help you get there and beyond.

**Identify someone for greatness and take
the first step in mentorship.**

◆ DAY #10 ◆

ON TENSION

"There is not one aspect of life where tension doesn't have critical value," said Reggie Joiner, the founder and CEO of Orange, a company that helps ministries maximize their spiritual influence. Joiner offered examples of the value of tension:

Tension among the parties and branches of a government creates a needed system of checks and balances.

Tension in science can lead to remarkable insights and discoveries.

Tension in a family provides an opportunity to demonstrate commitment and unconditional love.

Tension within a team pushes its members to better perspectives and deeper relationships.

Joiner invited us to observe Jesus's relationship with his disciples. "Too many Christians have an image of twelve best friends sitting in a circle on a peaceful hillside, listening to their teacher tell inspirational stories. It's just too easy to miss the point that Jesus almost always made his point in the middle of some extremely tense moments."

When a rope has tension, it is being stretched to capacity. When we're tense, we're often being stretched to capacity. Leaders do not cower in the presence of tension. Tension is confrontation. Confrontation means that you are facing a challenge directly rather than turning away from it. Tension grows us.

All growth begins with discomfort. Without it, there is no reason to change. We mature when we finally realize that life is not about achieving peace but about effectively managing tension.

Think of a very tense moment in your leadership. How did you grow from it?

✦ DAY #11 ✦

ON EMPTINESS

A professor once went to visit a Zen master to find out the secrets of his faith. The master made the professor a cup of tea. Even though the cup was full, he kept on pouring. Finally the professor yelled at the Zen master: "Why do you keep pouring into a cup that is full?" The master explained, "I wanted to show you a picture of yourself. You want to understand something new when your mind is still full. Empty your mind and you will have room." The Buddhist master Suzuki Roshi wrote: "If your mind is empty, it is always ready for anything; it is open to everything."

We tend to think pejoratively of emptiness, believing it to signal a void or hole within ourselves where our energies are drained or lost. As leaders bearing the brunt of responsibility for the success or failure of others, it is easy to see emptiness with a capital E, the way it appears on a dashboard—a signal that we are about to run out of fuel. Fuel propels us and keeps us going.

Emptiness is really fullness. Emptying the self of egotistical needs creates space for others. When something is empty, it is not a void. It is waiting for possibility.

Leaders who are full of themselves cannot make room for others.

**Consider a project or relationship that is
dominated by your presence. How can you
empty yourself to lead more effectively?**

✦ DAY #12 ✦

ON PATIENCE

Aristotle taught us: "Patience is bitter, but its fruit is sweet." What a relief. Someone as wise as Aristotle validated that patience is bitter. It does not taste good, but it will turn from bitter to sweet if we can wait. In his *Nicomachean Ethics*, Aristotle helped us understand that the word *ethos* or *ethics* comes from the Greek for "character." In character development, nothing beats patience.

Many leaders fault themselves for being impatient, wanting results more quickly than they are delivered, beating themselves up for not working better or smarter, expecting more from those who answer to them. Rather than view this form of impatience as a deficiency, view it as a strength. It is sacred. It is the fire that moves us and the drive that pushes us forward, even when surrounding conditions and people resist change.

Some leaders have too much patience for mediocrity. It shows.

Just as there is sacred or holy impatience, there is destructive impatience, which judges others as inferior because they are not us. They do not work like us. They do not think like us. And, therefore, they are not worthy of us.

Achieving the balance of just the right amount of patience and impatience may be the leader's single greatest daily challenge.

Be impatient with outcomes. Be patient with people.

**What project/idea needs a dose of your impatience today?
Who would benefit from your patience right now?**

ON REST

Repose repositions us for work.

Like a muscle that is worked hard, you cannot forever sustain heavy lifting. Leadership is not an endurance test to demonstrate your limits or a competition to see who can work harder. No one ever wins that competition.

Leadership is about stretching people to where they never thought they could go. This aspiration will be merely ephemeral if you are worn-out, burned-out or too distracted to think straight.

Maya Angelou in *Wouldn't Take Nothing for My Journey Now* advised us to take it easier:

"Every person needs to take one day away. A day in which one consciously separates the past from the future. Jobs, family, employers, and friends can exist one day without any one of us, and if our egos permit us to confess, they could exist eternally in our absence. Each person deserves a day away in which no problems are confronted, no solutions searched for. Each of us needs to withdraw from the cares which will not withdraw from us."

For some leaders, a vacation is not a rest. It is merely an opportunity to work in a more scenic location.

In some languages, the word for *rest* is related to the word for *soul*. A true rest reconnects us with our true selves, needs and desires. It gives expression to our sense of wonder.

Decompress. Recharge. Nurture the soul.

When was the last time you had a real rest?

ON INFLUENCE

"Few will have the greatness to bend history itself, but each of us can work to change a small portion of events. It is from number-less diverse acts of courage and belief that human history is shaped. Each time a man stands up for an ideal, or acts to improve the lot of others, or strikes out against injustice, he sends forth a tiny ripple of hope; and crossing each other from a million different centers of energy and daring, those ripples build a current which can sweep down the mightiest walls of oppression and resistance."

Robert F. Kennedy (1925–1968) was taken from us too young to exert his full influence, but he understood a great deal about how small acts build energy and power.

What is your sphere of influence?

How many people have you changed?

What idea have you introduced to the world?

In how many places has this idea taken root, shaped a culture, changed our language?

Too many leaders look at the wrong numbers to evaluate impact and, therefore, never really expand their sphere of influence. Spiri-tual leadership evolves, expands and deepens over time. It is like the unsheathing of a snake's skin. In order to grow, the snake has to shed its outer layer. Not once but several times.

**What is the next step in expanding
your sphere of influence?**

ON ROUTINE

Routines can wound our creativity with their sameness. The novelist Dave Eggers warned us: "We've reached the end of pure inspiration, and are now somewhere else, something implying routine, or doing something because people expect us to do it, going somewhere each day because we went there the day before, saying things because we have said them before, and this seems like the work of a different sort of animal, contrary to our plan, and this is very, very bad."

Leaders need certain routines for themselves and their followers to anchor good habits that need reinforcement. We may complain about leaders who are predictable, yet secretly they model stability for us in a world that can feel untethered and insecure. It is hard to work under someone who constantly changes his or her mind, especially if those changes happen abruptly and without sufficient warning. When work defeats us, we find comfort in routine.

When your schedule is well-ordered and well-known, you can afford the luxury of pockets of unpredictability. Novelists, composers and artists often lock themselves into a schedule not to diminish creativity but to liberate it. Ideas flow not when the muse makes a random inspired visit but because we set aside regular time for her appearance.

The muse may arrive. She may not. Be ready.

What part of your routine currently needs to change?

✦ DAY #16 ✦

ON FORGIVENESS

There is no act more emotionally generous or difficult than forgiving someone else. A genuinely open heart can embrace contrition. A closed heart repels it. There is nothing harder than having an open heart.

"I am sorry" are the three most important words that show your humanity to those you serve, because, as a leader, you can always get away with silence.

Leaders who can ask for forgiveness are not timid. They reveal immense inner strength. They demonstrate to those who look up to them the honesty to confront mistakes, to take the blame, to own the mess.

When you make a mess, clean it up. Then apologize.

You may think that your apology is worth little because words do not speak the same volume as actions. This may be true in the ultimate sense, but it is rarely true in relationships. We need to know that those with power can recognize when they have hurt us, when they have shut us down, when they have exploited their authority.

The apology—when sincere—tells followers that you have the moral grit to learn from error. Your humility is not a sign of weakness. It is a sign of your greatness. Mahatma Gandhi, in *All Men Are Brothers: Autobiographical Reflections*, wrote: "The weak can never forgive. Forgiveness is the attribute of the strong."

What do you need to say sorry for right now?

✦ DAY #17 ✦

ON PERFECTION

Perfection is a sophisticated way to name unrealistic expectations of self and others. It suggests being free from flaws or defects, the way that we might describe a highly crafted object made at the hands of a master. Objects are inanimate. They cannot make mistakes. They cannot lie. They cannot deceive. They cannot cry.

It is hard to let go of this ideal, the notion of being perfect. The author Anna Quindlen wrote: "Nothing important, or meaningful, or beautiful, or interesting, or great ever came out of imitations. The thing that is really hard, and really amazing, is giving up on being perfect and beginning the work of becoming yourself."

We are not static. The minute you can move, you can bump into someone else. You bruise. You bully. You laugh. You love and hate. You are imperfect—gloriously so.

To be a perfectionist as a leader is not a label of praise but one of danger. Perfectionists believe admitting to being one is a badge of self-praise, but it actually tells others that you are impossible to satisfy. To be a perfectionist is rarely to see the totality of humanness; it is to spot where there is a shortfall and an error.

Oh, and one more thing. Quindlen also said: "A finished person is a boring person." So stop calling yourself a perfectionist. It scares people. *And* it's boring.

Is your definition of the perfect leader ever achievable?

✦ DAY #18 ✦

ON AMBIGUITY

It's hard to forget comedian Gilda Radner (1946–1989), an original member of the cast of *Saturday Night Live*. She loved ambiguity. It worked in every comedic routine:

"I wanted a perfect ending. Now I've learned, the hard way, that some poems don't rhyme, and some stories don't have a clear beginning, middle, and end. Life is about not knowing, having to change, taking the moment and making the best of it, without knowing what's going to happen next.

"Delicious Ambiguity."

Radner did not get the perfect ending she wanted. She died young of cancer and kept jumping off the gurney when they brought her for her final hospital stay. She wanted desperately to live, to make more people laugh.

Many leaders disdain ambiguity. They want order and control. They want to know the answer and clarify the options. It feels wrong to say the three words:

"I don't know."

Yet ambiguity keeps us tensile and open. Somewhere in the land of doubt lies an answer. The wiser we get, the less we know.

There is arrogance in too much knowing. When we explore possibilities, there is an inexactitude to it. Do not be afraid to dwell in that liminal place of the amorphous, where many directions are possible. Stay there for a while before possibilities narrow.

Our biggest leadership mistakes can come from committing too quickly for the sake of certainty.

Name a complex decision before you now that would benefit from a less definitive approach.

✦ DAY #19 ✦

ON REJECTION

Jia Jiang stood up at a World Domination Summit and told thousands of people his story of rejection. As a young man whose start-up company failed, he spiraled into a deep depression. He then invited rejection closer, engaging in a hundred days of rejection therapy. He told an emotional audience at the Summit:

"I depended on blind faith and was rejected. That rejection taught me to not give up. When I see something very negative now, instead of running away from it I think 'Let's dance with it, play games with it, blow it up and see how negative it really is.' Then it turns out not to be negative after all. It becomes positive, really."

The audience hearing his story did not reject him. They gave him a long and emotional ovation, admiring his courage.

When we are rejected, the door before us becomes a wall. At that moment—that sad, pensive, crushing moment—we have four choices.

We can *push* on the wall, pretending it is a door, telling ourselves that those who rejected us made a mistake.

We can *cry* on the wall and bemoan our lack of talent, connections or gumption.

We can *try to scale* the wall, realizing that it is tall, hard and unyielding, but we must get over it nonetheless.

Or we can *walk away* and look for another door.

Leaders find others doors. Those doors are called resilience.

Give an example of rejection and resilience in your leadership.

ON CURIOSITY

Curiosity is the capacity and desire to learn; it has a hungry quality. It is more than having to know something to serve a need. It is wanting to know something with your entire heart and mind, swallowing that knowledge in big gulps. Albert Einstein, a man of great imagination, told us: "The important thing is not to stop questioning. Curiosity has its own reason for existing."

Curiosity can produce outstanding scientists and philosophers, inventors and physicians. What if we tried something this way? Or that? Curiosity produces questioning minds. When the object of curiosity is efficiency or function or sustainability, the curious mind wants to know how to make an object better, faster and more reliable.

Curiosity can produce great friendships or marriages among colleagues and lovers when the direct object of one's curiosity is another human being. It tells someone else that we want to know them better, more profoundly. We want to exist in relationship to them with greater intimacy. We want to *learn* them, putting our mental and emotional capacities into high gear but making our communication slower and richer.

Spiritual leadership requires curiosity about things, but it requires greater curiosity about people. Take your time. People are not an easy study.

**Who would benefit from a powerful dose
of your curiosity at this moment?**

ON SERVICE

Where there is hatred, let me sow love;
Where there is injury, pardon;

Where there is doubt, faith;
Where there is despair, hope;
Where there is darkness, light;
Where there is sadness, joy.
O divine Master, grant that I may not so much seek
to be consoled, as to console;
to be understood, as to understand;
to be loved, as to love;
For it is in giving that we receive,
In pardoning, that we are pardoned,
It is in dying that we are born to eternal life.

— The Prayer of Saint Francis, quoted in *In the Heart of the*
World: Thoughts, Stories & Prayers by Mother Teresa

Mother Teresa was prepared to use every part of herself to serve those she cared for, and she was prepared to serve every day. She asked God for strength to do what she believed God expected of her.

Service requires that we make ourselves smaller so that we can build capacity. You cannot serve someone else when you believe that they should be serving you. Those who want to serve are served by others in the grace of reciprocity.

When you make the chambers in your heart large enough, your heart always makes more room than you expect.

When you feel diminished by someone else you can lash back or you can ask yourself: Can I serve this person in some small way right now? Open the window of compassion, and it will open much wider.

How has your leadership enabled
you to serve someone today?

✦ DAY #22 ✦

ON DISCIPLINE

Discipline is the art of reaching desired goals through a patient and deliberate routine of repeated acts and behaviors. It is a muscle that must be exercised regularly in order to achieve outcomes.

On May 13, 1940, Winston Churchill gave his first address as prime minister to the House of Commons about national discipline; it was among his most memorable and influential speeches: "I would say to the House, as I said to those who have joined this Government, I have nothing to offer but blood, toil, tears and sweat. We have before us an ordeal of the most grievous kind. We have before us many long months of toil and struggle."

Churchill did not pretend that circumstances were easier than they were or that the future looked promising. He was painfully honest about the problems facing his people and their need for discipline and determination. Such outcomes emerge incrementally as a result of constant and unwavering commitment.

We all have goals, but not all of us have the commitment to follow through on those goals and achieve success. We get sidetracked. We discover obstacles. Our minds imprison us in negative thinking so that we begin to believe that we are incapable or unworthy.

Leaders cannot model genius to others; they can merely exhibit it. Leaders can always model hard work to others for their emulation.

Are you working hard at the *right* things in your leadership?

✦ DAY #23 ✦

ON BEING STUBBORN

The writer Anthony Liccione observed: "Some people would rather die in their pride, than live in their humility." Leaders can become easy victims of their own stubbornness. They can hold on to false ideas, judgments and first impressions. This can determine the fate of other lives and a company's future.

Remember Captain Ahab? Ahab steered a ship. He had a personal vendetta against a whale. As a result, he was willing to compromise the lives of other men and his professional duties. "From hell's heart I stab at thee; for hate's sake I spit my last breath at thee. Ye damned whale." But it was not only Ahab's last breath expended on revenge for the loss of his leg. His crew all followed him into the abyss of revenge and hatred. When Ahab bellowed, "I'll follow him around the Horn, and around the Norway maelstrom, and around perdition's flames before I give him up," he was taking others with him.

When his stubbornness got the best of him, he stopped caring. Who else could utter these words and mean them:

"I don't give reasons. I give orders!"

We all own a little piece of Ahab, and it comes out sometimes. We have to catch it before it grows and gets out of control and sinks a ship.

Think of a time when your stubbornness came at too high a cost. Why did you hold on and not let go?

✦ DAY #24 ✦

ON AUTHENTICITY

Remember the scene from *The Velveteen Rabbit* when the Rabbit asks the Skin Horse how to become Real?

"Real isn't how you are made," said the Skin Horse. "It's a thing that happens to you. When a child loves you for a long, long time, not just to play with, but REALLY loves you, then you become Real."

"Does it hurt?" asked the Rabbit.

"Sometimes," said the Skin Horse, for he was always truthful. "When you are Real you don't mind being hurt."

"Does it happen all at once, like being wound up," he asked, "or bit by bit?"

"It doesn't happen all at once," said the Skin Horse. "You become. It takes a long time. That's why it doesn't happen often to people who break easily, or have sharp edges, or who have to be carefully kept. Generally, by the time you are Real, most of your hair has been loved off, and your eyes drop out and you get loose in the joints and very shabby. But these things don't matter at all, because once you are Real you can't be ugly, except to people who don't understand."

Authenticity can hurt. It's who we are when no one is looking.

The problem, when you are a leader, is that everyone is looking. It's no wonder the toys in *The Velveteen Rabbit* came alive only at night, when no one was looking.

**What does your authentic self look
like when no one is looking?**

✦ DAY #25 ✦

ON WAITING

In life and leadership, there is a lot of waiting.

We wait for results.

We wait for promotions.

We wait for change.

We wait for wisdom.

We wait for our lives to begin.

Shauna Niequist shared this sentiment in *Cold Tangerines: Celebrating the Extraordinary Nature of Everyday Life:* "I have always, essentially, been waiting. Waiting to become something else, waiting to be that person I always thought I was on the verge of becoming, waiting for that life I thought I would have. In my head, I was always one step away."

One step away is not close enough. We wait in line. We wait our turn. Good things come to those who wait. But so much waiting can produce tedium and lethargy. It can wear us down. It can create hopelessness.

We wait for the next position or the next life stage or the next level of material success because we believe that it is then when life will *really* start. We will be kind, but only later. We will work harder, but only later. We will control our anger, but only later. Niequist continued: "And through all that waiting, here I am. My life is passing, day by day, and I am waiting for it to start. I am waiting for that time, that person, that event when my life will finally begin."

Life started long ago. Why wait?

In your leadership, what are you waiting for right now?

ON CALM

Friedrich Nietzsche, in *Twilight of the Idols, or, How to Philosophize with a Hammer*, observed that a state of inner peace can be constructed only through inner discipline:

"To learn to see—to accustom the eye to calmness, to patience, and to allow things to come up to it; to defer judgment, and to acquire the habit of approaching and grasping an individual case from all sides. This is the first preparatory schooling of intellectuality. One must not respond immediately to a stimulus; one must acquire a command of the obstructing and isolating instincts."

Maintaining a state of calm allows what you work on and who you work with to ripen to maturity. No one is rushing the process, which may compromise the outcome.

Calm is not a state of being; it is a response to what is happening that surrounds one's leadership. The frenetic leader creates a storm of energy. The calm leader combines visible concern and compassion with optimism and a clearheaded strategy for problem solving. Leaders wittingly or unwittingly set the emotional barometer in a culture.

How can you maintain calm in your next leadership storm?

ON BEAUTY

Leaders can be easily seduced by beautiful people, luxury goods and status items. Things of beauty are a mark that a leader has arrived.

We think that beauty demonstrates excellence. Beauty gives us hope that we can approximate perfection at times. Hold up a single flower or a piece of fruit and look at it carefully. But don't make the false leap that that which is beautiful is also good. Beauty is not goodness. The two are often confused.

Ansel Adams (1902–1984) spent a lifetime capturing beauty through a camera lens. But he did not see beauty as something to observe passively, nor did he see it as a moral good. Beauty is both more and less than that. Beauty is transactional:

"Art is both the taking and giving of beauty; the turning out to the light the inner folds of the awareness of the spirit. It is the re-creation on another plane of the realities of the world; the tragic and wonderful realities of earth and men, and of all the interrelations of these."

For us as for Adams, beauty slowly unfolds as we deepen our knowledge of that which is outside of ourselves, until almost everything can have the capacity for beauty.

When is the last time you shared something of beauty with those who work with you?

✦ DAY #28 ✦

ON PRESENCE

In *Authenticity*, James Gilmore and B. Joseph Pine argued that to create genuine presence you have to take an inventory of what you say about yourself and offer five ways that a person/business can talk about its "self" (italics in original):

Assigned *names*: Who you call yourself
Expressed *statements*: What you articulate you are
Established *places*: Where and when you're encountered
Declared *motivations*: Why you say you are in business
Displayed *appearances*: How you show what you are

This combination as a whole creates presence, an enduring sense of identity that is visible to others.

In the Bible, prophets answered the call to service with one simple Hebrew word, which means, "I am here." I will be here to accomplish any task you set before me. My work is only to serve. And in this admission, they created an enduring presence.

I am *fully* present.

But our plethora of electronic devices suggests to others that we may be snatched away by a call or an e-mail at any moment.

There are individuals so present that even in their absence they are present. We see their image in the periphery of our vision. We hear their voices advising us or judging us. We feel them hovering close to us to guide us.

Leaders can be absent but present, and present but absent.

**How can you make yourself more present
today for those you serve?**

✦ DAY #29 ✦

ON HUNGER

There is so much hunger in the world that we have not yet sated. There is emotional hunger, the profound desire to fill in the huge, gaping holes caused by abandonment, neglect, insecurity and abuse.

John Piper, Baptist preacher and chancellor of Bethlehem College and Seminary, wrote in *A Hunger for God*: "If you don't feel strong desires for the manifestation of the glory of God, it is not because you have drunk deeply and are satisfied. It is because you have nibbled so long at the table of the world. Your soul is stuffed with small things, and there is no room for the great." Hunger for the important things.

Be careful about hunger. All of our emotional needs cannot be met in an office. Work is not the place for love. It is the place for results. It is the place where healthy, functioning, professionally ma-ture people can express their talents and expertise, where these gifts should be valued.

Your work is not your family. Your work cannot take the place of satisfying personal relationships. We need both to make us and keep us whole.

This is not a matter of lowering your expectations. No one wants to do that. Adjust your expectations so that they are realistic to what work should provide. Expecting too much emotional gratification from your job will get in the way of serving others with a full heart and mind.

What hunger does your leadership satisfy?

ON ALTRUISM

Every day we can give of ourselves unconditionally.

We tend to think of altruism in big, world-saving gulps, but as the writer P. J. O'Rourke reminded us: "Everybody wants to save the Earth; nobody wants to help Mom do the dishes." Our altruism should come in helping those around us in all the small ways.

Nick Hornby explored the limits of altruism in his novel *How to Be Good*. David Carr, the novel's protagonist, is a bitter and sarcastic person. And it is killing him. He is told by his spiritual adviser, DJ GoodNews, that he can help himself only by learning to be altruistic. David's wife, however, does not find this helpful when her husband gives away their Sunday dinner and their son's computer. And this is just the beginning. He visits people on the street and encourages others to use spare bedrooms to take in the homeless. His role reversal becomes challenging to his family members. They wanted him to be good but not this good. Hornby provokes us. Is there a limit to goodness? Is altruism ever wrong?

Leaders can afford to give more of themselves because they have been endowed and trusted with the ability to make decisions that change lives. An affirmation of goodness from a person in power has the capacity to heal and validate another human being precisely because that other person will not be able to reciprocate in kind.

But leaders can also give too much. Beware.

What is the last truly altruistic thing you did as a leader?

ON INSPIRATION

"Most people don't know there are angels whose only job is to make sure you don't get too comfortable and fall asleep and miss your life," observed American artist and writer Brian Andreas.

Some people spend a lifetime with the express purpose of inspiring others. Andreas created StoryPeople, a collection of books and digitalized snippets to record why people want to be alive. He called his project the Hall of Whispers, after rooms in ancient Babylonian ziggurats that were so highly polished that they could keep a whisper alive forever.

In days of old, muses gathered within your soul and pushed out ideas with force and passion. That was yesterday. And also today. Inspiration is not only about the huge, extraordinary moments in life. As Andreas tells us: "Time stands still best in moments that look suspiciously like ordinary life."

Leaders need not only be inspired themselves to maximize their influence. They also have to inspire others. Inspiration has the strength to move the intellect and the emotions, to keep leaders energized and to reenergize. As a leader you cannot be inspired once. Inspiration wears thin. The need calls again and again.

To be inspired is to touch the sacred. To inspire is to share the sacred.

"Anyone can slay a dragon," Andreas cautioned, "but try waking up every morning and loving the world all over again. That's what takes a real hero."

When was the last time you were truly inspired?

ON TRUTH

Once upon a time, a man who was struggling with personal inadequacies came to Muhammad. "O prophet of Allah, I have many bad habits. Which one of them should I give up first?" The Prophet replied, "Give up telling lies first and always speak the truth." The man pledged to give up lying and left.

The next time he was about to steal something, he thought about his conversation with the Prophet. "If tomorrow the Prophet asks me where have I been, what shall I say? Shall I say that I went out stealing? No, I cannot say that. But nor can I lie. If I tell the truth, everyone will start hating me and call me a thief. I would be punished for stealing." So the man decided not to steal that night.

The very next day, the man was about to drink wine—a practice forbidden by Muslims—and then asked himself the same question: "What shall I say to the Prophet if he asks me what I did during the day? I cannot tell a lie." He did not drink that day.

Eventually, he understood that telling the truth would prevent him from engaging in all of his bad habits.

Leaders know that lying is convenient. It is much harder to tell the truth when you do not have to in order to be successful. It takes extraordinary courage to lead and not lie.

When was your last temptation to lie?

ON MISTAKES

Jim Morrison said that some of the worst mistakes in his life were haircuts. Hair grows back.

You are not your mistakes.

Every mistake is a little piece of failure. Every piece of failure mounts. Every error injures self-confidence. Each stumble hurts, especially in the presence of others. Leaders' mistakes get magnified, sometimes to the point where one mistake can topple a long list of achievements.

In the aggregate, the list of our mistakes looks like a mountain of shame. Or maybe it is just one mistake, a very, very large one.

Mistakes have consequences, often irreparable ones. Every once in a while a mistake is easy to correct.

The confrontation with error puts every leader at a crossroads. You can admit or you can blame. Admission may cost you a title. Blame will only save you in the moment. Admission will prepare you to do better next time. Blame will prepare you for another, greater fall.

The mistake will never matter as much as your reaction to it. The wise playwright George Bernard Shaw offered this advice: "Success does not consist in never making mistakes but in never making the same one a second time."

Shaw had an acerbic tongue and, no doubt, made many a mistake as a result. But he was also the only person to win both an Oscar and a Nobel Prize for literature, so he took his mistakes seriously enough to overcome them.

What is your most prized mistake?

✦ DAY #34 ✦

ON IMPERMANENCE

We cannot hold on to anything forever: not our children, not our titles, not our comforts, not our dreams.

Sometimes we grow people and expect they will stay with us out of loyalty and gratitude. When they leave us, we feel the initial stab of betrayal. We feel a false pride of ownership. We do not own anyone else's success. We must let them go with our blessings. If we bless their growth, they may return when they are ready. If we shun them, they will be gone to us always.

When you embrace the reality of impermanence, you begin to acknowledge the constant changes in the universe: its dynamism and its grief. The Japanese Buddhist master Dōgen Zenji (1200–1253), in *A Primer of Soto Zen*, warned: "One must be deeply aware of the impermanence of the world." If you are unaware, you can suffer great and unexpected loss.

But impermanence is not the same as loss. Impermanence helps us appreciate wonder precisely because it does not last. Leaders can see through change, but it is not invisible. It is a slight turn of reality, and in order to adjust to it, you have to let go of the known world. You never really held it in the first place. You just think you did.

Let go. In the surrender will come new freedoms.

In the relinquishing will come the strength.

**What do you have to let go of now that
will make you a better leader?**

◆ DAY #35 ◆

ON VULNERABILITY

In *Daring Greatly*, Brené Brown put forward the thesis that when others make themselves vulnerable, they are being courageous; yet, when we make ourselves vulnerable, we believe we are showing weakness. "Vulnerability sounds like truth and feels like courage. Truth and courage aren't always comfortable, but they're never weakness." Vulnerability requires bravery. Our capacity to be vulnerable helps open others up; it creates our joint humanity.

Nothing requires more courage than vulnerability. Leaders are afraid of revealing what we all know: We are so very human; we are continuously prone to error. We are inadequate. We feel we are imposters. We are terrified of exposure. We do not want to make ourselves susceptible. We cannot afford to lose our credibility.

We damage easily. We tear. We are malleable. But we will not allow the past that damaged us to damage others. We do that not by creating a tower to defend and hide a scarred past. We do that by making a small hole in the heart that lets others see what we have overcome.

Your vulnerability as a leader makes you brave. It gives those you lead the courage to overcome the hurt and reinvent themselves. It empowers as it creates bonds of compassion. We are fragile. But we do not break from our fragility. We learn from it. It makes us alive.

Our vulnerability makes us stronger than we will ever know.

How can you share your vulnerabilities as a leader?

✦ DAY #36 ✦

ON COLLABORATION

Individuals maximize chances of survival when they reach out to others. Charles Darwin wrote: "It is the long history of humankind (and animal kind, too) that those who learned to collaborate and improvise most effectively have prevailed."

The biblical book of Ecclesiastes praises this utilitarian mindset: "Two are better than one, in that they have greater benefit from their work. For should they fall, one can lift up the other. But woe to him who is alone and falls with no companion to lift him. And when two lie together they are warm, but how can he who is alone get warm? Also, if one attacks, two alone can stand up to him."

Collaboration is efficient and a great way to keep a bed warm! Thomas Stallkamp, founder of Collaborative Management, said: "The secret is to gang up on the problem, rather than gang up on each other."

Isaac Newton had a different take: "If I have seen further it is by standing on the shoulders of giants." This was a humble way to approach new thinking and innovation. Those who preceded us are giants and we are small, but on the shoulders of giants we see further than giants alone.

When we rest on the shoulders of giants, we can see just a little bit further. And that kind of vertical collaboration can make all the difference.

Name your greatest collaboration.

ON CONNECTION

"All life is interrelated. We are all caught in an inescapable network of mutuality, tied into a single garment of destiny. Whatever affects one directly, affects all indirectly. We are made to live together because of the interrelated structure of reality."

We are all connected—even if we don't see it—into a single garment of destiny. Martin Luther King Jr. understood that not everyone sees the deep connections shared by all of humanity—and he paid the price for this understanding with his life. Instead, people are trapped in the brutal force of hate and its attractions. Here is what King said as he continued his Christmas sermon on December 24, 1967:

"I've seen too much hate to want to hate, myself . . . and every time I see it, I say to myself, hate is too great a burden to bear. Somehow we must be able to stand up before our most bitter opponents and say: 'We shall match your capacity to inflict suffering by our capacity to endure suffering. We will meet your physical force with soul force. Do to us what you will and we will still love you.'"

How many of us, in our own leadership, could say "We will still love you" to those who oppose us, diminish us or use us?

Think of something hateful in your organizational culture. How can you lead others to a place of light?

ON LIMITATION

The late eighteenth century in literature is known as the Age of Johnson: Samuel Johnson (1709–1784), that is. His wise and pithy writing gained him renown as one of the greatest literary men of letters. But Johnson knew about limitations. He went to Oxford University until his funds ran out, and then he left to pursue a career in teaching and then writing. He likely suffered from Tourette's syndrome, before people knew what it was. He knew limitation.

Here's what Johnson wrote about limitation in *The Rambler*, the journal in which he published his reflections on art and life:

"The uncertainty of our duration ought at once to set bounds to our designs, and add incitements to our industry; and when we find ourselves inclined either to immensity in our schemes, or sluggishness in our endeavors, we may either check or animate ourselves by recollecting, with the father of physic, that art is long and life is short."

Human life itself is our greatest limitation. We will live and then we will die, and this stark reality may instantly "set bounds to our designs." Life is short. Art is long. "Add incitements to our industry"—get moving.

Let your leadership be your art, because although life is short, we only limit ourselves when we don't squeeze out every possibility.

Name one area where you are limiting your leadership, then create a strategy to challenge this limitation.

ON CONTROL

Leaders are used to being in control, particularly in ambiguous situations where no one else steps forward. The moment of daring belongs to the leader who steps into hazardous places and exerts control.

The problem with this from a spiritual point of view is that, to live a life of higher calling, we often have to surrender to mystery, to things we do not understand and will never comprehend.

In *Life, the Truth, and Being Free*, Steve Maraboli wrote: "Incredible change happens in your life when you decide to take control of what you do have power over instead of craving control over what you don't." He asks us to shift our energy to projects where we can detect progress and advancement.

Life requires submission to forces far greater than ourselves. Maraboli observes that this submission does not come naturally or easily. We have to teach it to ourselves: "You must learn to let go. Release the stress. You were never in control anyway." And then Maraboli challenges us with a question:

"How would your life be different if . . . you stopped worrying about things you can't control and started focusing on the things you can? Let today be the day . . . free yourself from fruitless worry, seize the day and take effective action on things you can change."

Let go of your control over one thing today.

◆ DAY #40 ◆

ON SELFLESSNESS

Can we ever be truly selfless if we are a self? It would seem not.

One rainy day, Gretchen Rubin thought about this on a city bus. "The days are long, but the years are short." Given the time constraints of her mortality, she decided she had better focus on the important things. She spent a year finding bliss and writing about it in *The Happiness Project: Or, Why I Spent a Year Trying to Sing in the Morning, Clean My Closets, Fight Right, Read Aristotle, and Generally Have More Fun.*

She arrived at many conclusions, like:

"Never start a sentence with the words 'No offense.'"

"What you do every day matters more than what you do once in a while."

"The things that go wrong often make the best memories."

"Look for happiness under your own roof."

And:

"The belief that unhappiness is selfless and happiness is selfish is misguided. It's more selfless to act happy. It takes energy, generosity, and discipline to be unfailingly lighthearted, yet everyone takes the happy person for granted. . . . And because happiness seems unforced, that person usually gets no credit."

Our happiness is an expression of selflessness. "One of the best ways to make yourself happy," Rubin concluded, "is to make other people happy. One of the best ways to make other people happy is to be happy yourself."

Can we ever be truly selfless if we are a self? It would seem so.

How has your happiness helped you become more selfless?

✦ DAY #41 ✦

ON DISTRACTION

"If you get stuck, get away from your desk. Take a walk, take a bath, go to sleep, make a pie, draw, listen to music, meditate, exercise; whatever you do, don't just stick there scowling at the problem. But don't make telephone calls or go to a party; if you do, other people's words will pour in where your lost words should be. Open a gap for them, create a space. Be patient."

These are the words of author Hilary Mantel in a newspaper interview about distraction. An artist once captured writer's block as a ceramic old-fashioned typewriter in a cage. Mantel advised distraction. Get up. Get out. Julio Cortázar, in *Around the Day in Eighty Worlds*, offered similar advice: "All profound distraction opens certain doors. You have to allow yourself to be distracted when you are unable to concentrate."

In *A Place of Greater Safety*, Mantel wrote how tiring it is to shuffle papers and shuttle opinions. We've all been there. Our lives become tiring, and we seek relief in the form of distractions.

Distraction takes our focus away but sometimes just enough to help us gain it back. Learn how to leverage distraction, and it will achieve the opposite of what it sets out to do.

**When in your leadership does
distraction actually help you?**

✦ DAY #42 ✦

ON EGO

The plays of Tennessee Williams (1911–1983) have graced the stage for decades with their subtle tensions and explosive conflicts. He was himself a weak and sickly child. He had a schizophrenic sister, an overprotective mother, an abusive father, and he struggled for years with alcoholism and drug use.

Williams knew about pain and its temporary alleviation. Yet he believed that human beings put on a veneer of dignity to hide the mess of tangled emotions and anguish. He shared this thought in all its rawness in *The Milk Train Doesn't Stop Here Anymore*:

"We are all civilized people, which means that we are all savages at heart but observing a few amenities of civilized behavior. We all live in a house on fire, no fire department to call; no way out, just the upstairs window to look out of while the fire burns the house down with us trapped, locked in it."

We are trapped, trapped by desire, trapped by personal history, trapped by ego. But there is one release, love, as Williams wrote in *A Streetcar Named Desire*:

"Nobody sees anybody truly but all through the flaws of their own egos . . . except when there is that rare case of two people who love intensely enough to burn through all those layers of opacity and see each other's naked hearts."

We break through the preoccupation with our own self-importance when we love another person enough to have a naked heart.

**When has your leadership ego
been chipped away by love?**

+ DAY #43 +

ON ABSENCE

Many corporate leaders have become road warriors, constantly in flight, traversing the world. Their presence is felt everywhere. But their absence is also felt everywhere.

The office is dark. The desk is clean. The chair is empty. There is a hovering sense of emptiness in the spaces the leader occupies.

Sometimes absence is presence. Sometimes absence is just absence. Technology has fed us the delusion that we can be there but not there simultaneously. We cannot.

Everything will not collapse without you. Go fill up and nourish yourself, because otherwise you will not have the strength to be present for those who constantly need you. But don't forget to come back.

Sometimes determining presence or absence is a matter of discovering who needs us most. We want to be needed, but we also have to tell ourselves who needs us least.

As a leader, when are you present but absent?

ON SELF-CONTROL

"Among my most prized possessions are words that I have never spoken." Orson Scott Card explained he has a filtering mechanism that tells him not to say everything he thinks, not to send every e-mail he writes, not to express every feeling he has.

Card is a writer, mostly of science fiction, who teaches writing. Among his most famous works of fantasy is *Ender's Game*. Card also happens to be the great-great-grandson of Brigham Young, a leader and shaper of the Mormon faith, or the Church of Jesus Christ of Latter-day Saints. He did his mission service in Brazil.

"I tell students that suspense comes, not from knowing almost nothing, but from knowing almost everything and caring very much about the small part still unknown."

The small part still unknown speaks to desires that can destroy or debilitate us. When we act without self-control, it is not because we do not know ourselves. It is because we know ourselves too well. "One mind can think only of its own questions; it rarely surprises itself," Card told us.

We know we will eat that last piece of cake, share that gossip or buy something we shouldn't. Self-control is not only about self-knowledge. It is that discipline, self-possession, willpower and composure that gives us self-restraint. It makes us more powerful than we will ever know.

In the spirit of self-control, Card did confess his own weakness: "I buy way too many books."

**Where is your self-control most
exercised in your leadership?**

ON CLARITY

Malcolm Gladwell wrote: "The visionary starts with a clean sheet of paper, and reimagines the world." Gladwell's blank piece of paper is an invitation to clarity. Confusion looks like a page of scribbles, dense formulas, thick notations leading nowhere.

In his best-seller *Blink*, Gladwell challenged some of our most deeply held beliefs about thought and instinct. To achieve clarity, sidestep some of the analysis that can weigh you down and trust your gut when you have enough expertise and experience to do so.

"What do we tell our children? Haste makes waste. Look before you leap. Stop and think. Don't judge a book by its cover. We believe that we are always better off gathering as much information as possible and spending as much time as possible in deliberation."

We make an assumption that the outcome or quality of a decision is "directly related to the time and effort that went into making it," because, as Gladwell wrote: "We really only trust conscious decision making. But there are moments . . . when our snap judgments and first impressions can offer a much better means of making sense of the world.

"The key to good decision making is not knowledge. It is understanding. We are swimming in the former. We are desperately lacking in the latter." Clarity can come from the heart. It can come from the soul.

**What is the best leadership decision you made
from instinct rather than analysis?**

ON TRANSCENDENCE

"One resolution I have made, and try always to keep, is this: 'To rise above little things.'"

John Burroughs (1837–1921) believed that transcendence was not always about the larger ways we put ourselves above our environment but how we "rise above the little things."

Burroughs was called the Grand Old Man of Nature, and he believed in protecting and preserving it as stewards and custodians: "To learn something new, take the path that you took yesterday."

For Burroughs, nature was its own religion: "Communing with God is communing with our own hearts, our own best selves, not with something foreign and accidental. Saints and devotees have gone into the wilderness to find God; of course they took God with them, and the silence and detachment enabled them to hear the still, small voice of their own souls, as one hears the ticking of his own watch in the stillness of the night."

To achieve transcendence, don't only look up.

"Look underfoot. You are always nearer to the true sources of your power than you think. The lure of the distant and the difficult is deceptive. The great opportunity is where you are. . . . Every place is the center of the world."

The intricacy of a spider. The smell of loam. The industry of an ant. The great subterranean universe of insects and plant life beneath us is enough to create reverence.

"Leap and the net will appear."

Name the last time communing with nature
created transcendence for you.

ON TRANSITION

Imagine that you are on a train. You decide to change cars. As you change cars, you notice that the platform is much shakier than the car you just left. Standing on that platform between cars, you suddenly feel vulnerable. The movement no longer feels secure and comforting; it feels perilous, menacing. But you do not stay on the platform long. You soon move into the next car, and the shadow of that moment of fear fades instantly.

Liminality is from the Latin word for a threshold, the place where we hang a door, the space in between rooms. We use it to describe the ambiguity of in-between spaces or times where we may experience confusion or disorientation. We know that we have begun a journey, but we also know that we are, at the same time, unsure where this journey will take us and what status we will secure by the journey's end. Most religions place rituals at transitional times: birth, adolescence, marriage, death. Rituals provide comfort at these anxious junctures.

Leaders must be able to recognize the tension of transitions. With our fast pace of change, we are always in motion. Sometimes that motion accelerates and feels dangerous—like that platform that we won't stay on but have to cross to get to the next place. Articulate and ritualize those times for yourself and others.

Lead well in liminal moments.

Describe the last time you were on that train platform.

ON BROKENNESS

When Laura Hillenbrand wrote *Unbroken: A World War II Story of Survival, Resilience, and Redemption*, its subject—Louis

Zamperini—was ninety-three years old. Hillenbrand found his story while researching an earlier book, *Seabiscuit*. Zamperini was a troublemaker turned Olympic runner; the war almost broke him, and then he foundered in the years after his amazing rescue. Hillenbrand was able to re-create Zamperini's frightening plane crash, sea journey and time in a POW camp, bringing to life the anguish, the starvation, the isolation and pain.

Hillenbrand had a phone relationship with Zamperini for seven years. They never met. Zamperini had no idea why. After the book came out, he read an interview about her and discovered she was ill and had written the book largely confined to her bed. Then, he said, "I sent her one of my Purple Hearts. I said you deserve this more than me."

Hillenbrand described her struggle with Chronic Fatigue syndrome in "A Sudden Illness." The article described what saved her: "I'm looking for a way out of here. I can't have it physically, so I'm going to have it intellectually."

In *Unbroken*, she wrote: "Dignity is as essential to human life as water, food, and oxygen. The stubborn retention of it, even in the face of extreme physical hardship, can hold a man's soul in his body long past the point at which the body should have surrendered it." Zamperini did not surrender. Hillenbrand did not surrender.

Think of a time you were really broken. What saved you?

♦ DAY #49 ♦

ON STRENGTH

"I am still far from being what I want to be, but with God's help I shall succeed."

We might have thought these words came from a struggling artist with little acclaim. But Vincent van Gogh (1853–1890) painted thousands of works and shook the art world with his primitive bursts of color.

Van Gogh wrote extensively to his brother, Theodore, about

rejection and his inner demons. "I put my heart and my soul into my work, and have lost my mind in the process."

He had a strategy for managing those demons: "If you hear a voice within you say 'you cannot paint,' then by all means paint, and that voice will be silenced."

But the voice was not quieted. As his talent evolved, he struggled more: "As we advance in life it becomes more and more difficult, but in fighting the difficulties the inmost strength of the heart is developed." Proximity to greatness makes you more aware of the distance.

Van Gogh's strength did not fail him.

"Even the knowledge of my own fallibility cannot keep me from making mistakes. Only when I fall do I get up again."

And he did.

"In spite of everything I shall rise again: I will take up my pencil, which I have forsaken in my great discouragement, and I will go on with my drawing."

**Van Gogh said, "Great things are done by
a series of small things brought together."
What small victories give you strength?**

◆ DAY #50 ◆

ON MERCY

Goswami Tulsidas (1543–1623) was a poet, revered Hindu spiritual leader, founder of a temple and writer of hymns. He summed up the fundamentals of spirituality in one *doha*, or couplet: "The root of religion is embedded in mercy, whereas egotism is rooted in love of the body." Mercy is always outer directed. Egotism is always inner directed.

In Latin *merces* is a price paid.

Think for a moment of one night in the life of Bishop Myriel in *Les Misérables*. Ex-offender Jean Valjean went to the church, asking to stay the night. He was given food, a bed and mercy. When everyone went to sleep, Valjean took many silver objects and ran away, only to meet the police yet again. After his capture, the police took him to confront the bishop. But the bishop saw something in Valjean: the possibility of repentance. Myriel told the police that he had given Valjean the silver and then added silver candlesticks to further emphasize the point, telling Valjean to use the silver to become an honest man.

Valjean never forgot this act of mercy. It transformed everything about his life, even after he learned of the bishop's death. When Valjean was nearing his own end and was asked if he wanted a priest, he pointed heavenward and said, "I have one."

**Extend your mercy to someone who
does not really deserve it.**

◆ DAY #51 ◆

ON LUCK

Imagine the Bard and the Boss in conversation about luck and fortune. In *King Lear*, Shakespeare belittled the way we naively think a star can change everything.

"This is the excellent foppery of the world, that when we are sick in fortune (often the surfeits of our own behavior) we make guilty of our disasters the sun, the moon, and stars: as if we were villains on necessity; fools by heavenly compulsion; knaves, thieves, and treacherous by spherical predominance; drunkards, liars, and adulterers by an enforced obedience of planetary influence; and all that we are evil in, by a divine thrusting on."

And yet Bruce Springsteen used to visit Madam Marie Castello, who told fortunes at the Temple of Knowledge on the Asbury Park boardwalk in New Jersey. Bruce Springsteen immortalized her in "4th of July, Asbury Park (Sandy)." Springsteen played at the Stone Pony, a nightclub across from the boardwalk. In an interview about the song, he wrote: "I'd been evicted from my apartment above the beauty salon, so I . . . was living with my girlfriend in a garage apartment, five minutes from Asbury Park. . . . I used the boardwalk and the closing down of the town as a metaphor for the end of a summer romance and the changes I was experiencing in my own life." A struggling musician played in dives waiting for a lucky break. One day, his luck morphed into success.

The saying goes, "The harder I work, the luckier I get." Name your lucky break.

✦ DAY #52 ✦

ON LAUGHTER

"Laughter is the sound of the soul dancing."

Jarod Kintz's words help us imagine the buoyancy and lift we experience in the simple joy of laughter, a primal and exhilarating release of happiness.

Laughter has a life-affirming quality. We seek out those who can join us in mirth, as W. H. Auden said of his closest companions: "Among those whom I like or admire, I can find no common denominator, but among those whom I love, I can; all of them make me laugh." He was joined by Audrey Hepburn: "I love people who make me laugh. I honestly think it's the thing I like most, to laugh."

Do you laugh enough? Probably not. Do you make others laugh enough? Probably not. "Laughter and tears," Kurt Vonnegut wrote, "are both responses to frustration and exhaustion." Vonnegut preferred to laugh because "there is less cleaning to do afterward."

Something sad happens as we age. We laugh less. Research tells us children laugh dozens of times more than adults every day. Why did we stop?

Fyodor Dostoyevsky said: "If you wish to glimpse inside a human soul and get to know a man, don't bother analyzing his ways of being silent, of talking, of weeping, of seeing how much he is moved by noble ideas; you will get better results if you just watch him laugh. If he laughs well, he's a good man."

Think of someone who makes you laugh and schedule time for a visit. Laughter heals.

ON FAME

Andy Warhol (1928–1987) gave us more than permission to enjoy our fifteen minutes of fame. He told us to ignore it at the same time.

"Don't pay any attention to what they write about you. Just measure it in inches."

Fame can be extremely destructive. The need for constant acknowledgment, recognition and pampering attention can have a morally corrosive effect. It becomes an addiction, and, like any addiction, it seems necessary all of the time. Fame inures leaders to truths about the world and about themselves.

Warhol wrote from experience. He came from humble roots. His father was a coal miner from Slovakia who died when Warhol was thirteen. Youngest of three sons and a fragile, ill child, he thought he would spend his life as a schoolteacher. In university he found his inner artist, dropped the *a* from his last name, *Warhola*, and created images that are iconic today. Fifteen minutes of fame grew into more than fifteen years of fame, and it continues growing.

As success shined brightly on his career, he found himself seeking the spotlight more and more. "I have to go out every night. If I stay home one night I start spreading rumors to my dogs."

Warhol understood, however, the most fundamental truth about fame:

"As soon as you stop wanting something, you get it."

**Try to let go today of what other people
think about. Is fame important to you?**

ON TAKING

Life is filled with givers and takers. Adam Grant offered us another category in *Give and Take*: matchers. A matcher balances getting and giving, operating with fairness while protecting and defending himself. He gives favors and expects them in return.

Givers experience true pleasure in sharing contacts, gifts, wisdom, suggestions and time without expecting anything in return. They are surprised when they get something, like thanks or acknowledgment. It's easier to give if you have no expectations of getting.

Takers, on the other hand, need to get as much as they possibly can from every opportunity and situation, even and often at the expense of others. Grant described these approaches to the world: "If you're a taker, you help others strategically, when the benefits to *you* outweigh the personal costs." Givers, he said, use a different cost-benefit analysis: "You help whenever the benefits to *others* exceed the personal costs."

Push takers out of their comfort zone, Grant advised, by starting a love machine.

"Givers," Grant wrote, "go unrecognized. To combat this problem, organizations are introducing peer recognition programs to reward people for giving in ways that leaders and managers rarely see. A Mercer study found that in 2001, about 25 percent of large companies had peer recognition programs, and by 2006, this number had grown to 35 percent—including celebrated companies like Google, Southwest Airlines, and Zappos."

Manage takers by rewarding givers.

As a leader, are you a giver or a taker? Honestly?

ON SUCCESSION

"The CEO succession process is broken in North America. . . . Almost half of companies with revenue greater than $500 million have no meaningful CEO succession plan, according to the National Association of Corporate Directors. Even those that have plans aren't happy with them," bemoaned Ram Charan in an *HBR* article titled "Ending the CEO Succession Crisis."

"A CEO or board that has been in place for six or seven years and has not yet provided a pool of qualified candidates, and a robust process for selecting the next leader, is a failure. Everyone talks about emulating such best practitioners . . . but few work very hard at it."

In the Bible it is rare for one leader to die without the next put in place. If you love what you have created and want it to live beyond you, then create the structures for its endurance. "Moses said to the Lord, 'May the Lord, the God of the spirits of all mankind, appoint someone over this community to go out and come in before them, one who will lead them out and bring them in, so the Lord's people will not be like sheep without a shepherd.'"

We are often in denial about the long-term health of our organizations. We live and work for today. We know tomorrow is coming, but there is no sense in getting there too quickly.

Tomorrow is here. What now?

What are you doing now to groom a successor for later?

ON OPTIMISM

The strength of optimism lies in finding it where it's least expected. During the Nazi occupation of the Netherlands, Anne Frank was hidden in an attic with her family in Amsterdam. They were discovered and transported to concentration camps. Anne died in Bergen-Belsen in 1945, just before liberation. Anne's father published her diary two years later, as *The Diary of a Young Girl*. Often it sounds like the scribbles of an ordinary adolescent, but its two-year record of events and emotions is a chronicle of optimism:

"How wonderful it is that nobody need wait a single moment before starting to improve the world."

"Think of all the beauty still left around you and be happy."

"I can shake off everything as I write; my sorrows disappear, my courage is reborn."

"I don't think of all the misery, but of the beauty that still remains."

"Where there's hope, there's life. It fills us with fresh courage and makes us strong again."

"Look at how a single candle can both defy and define the darkness."

"I don't want to have lived in vain like most people. I want to be useful or bring enjoyment to all people, even those I've never met. I want to go on living even after my death!"

Anne, know that you have gone on living through your optimism, helping us have a broader, more beautiful and embracing perspective on humanity.

Thank you for this gift.

Circle the quote above that resonates with you most.

✦ DAY #57 ✦

ON PRODUCTIVITY

What do the most successful people do before breakfast?

Laura Vanderkam, in *What the Most Successful People Do Before Breakfast*, wrote that people with a high-achievement orientation often wake up before others. If you want to get more done, create more time. Once you use up the time you have, it's not coming back.

Many religions have special prayers for the dawn hours to infuse the day with ambition.

"Time passes whether or not you make a conscious decision about how to use it," said Vanderkam. "Since there's no chance to pause," she added, "not choosing is still a choice." This may seem obvious to us until we are lying in a nice, warm bed on a cold winter morning and the snooze button has gone off for the third time.

Vanderkam recommends making short lists with time limits to work off the momentum of crossing off what you've done. If a list is too long, it can be psychically overwhelming. Increasing productivity also requires building in rest and recovery time: "If you don't rest, you will not be able to manage your energy." Part of using your time well is managing your energy and being strategic about taking breaks so you can feel productive enough to get things done.

Productivity is ultimately not about lists and time. It is about how we see our purpose in this world.

What is your most productive hour of the day, and how can you leverage it better?

✦ DAY #58 ✦

ON PUNISHMENT

In Greek mythology, Sisyphus was a corrupt king of Ephyra who took pleasure in deceit, murder and violently injuring people in high places. Zeus punished him. Sisyphus was made to push a boulder up a mountain only to have it roll back on itself. The gods thought that "there is no more dreadful punishment than futile and hopeless labor."

The French philosopher and journalist Albert Camus (1913–1960) wrote a book on futility based on the story: *The Myth of Sisyphus*. Camus, famous for his existential posture—"Should I kill myself, or have a cup of coffee?"—believed that, without purpose, there is no purpose in living. "Nobody realizes," Camus wrote, "that some people expend tremendous energy merely to be normal."

"When the soul suffers too much, it develops a taste for

misfortune." This is an apt description of the pain some people experience in leadership. After a while, they believe that leadership can never be a source of pride or pleasure. Like Sisyphus, they feel that they repeat tasks and never advance.

In *The Stranger*, Camus confronted the punishment of Sisyphus in a different voice: "For it says that no matter how hard the world pushes against me, within me, there's something stronger—something better, pushing right back." As a result of this progress, Camus left us with a beautiful thought:

"In the midst of winter, I found there was, within me, an invincible summer."

Describe a leadership role that makes you Sisyphus. How can you change it?

✦ DAY #59 ✦

ON MODESTY

"I want to do something splendid. . . . Something heroic or wonderful that won't be forgotten after I'm dead. . . . I don't know what but . . . [I] mean to astonish you all someday. I think I shall write books."

These are Jo's words in *Little Women*, when the March girls are busy discussing dreams for the future. Louisa May Alcott (1832–1888) did write books, possibly dozens of them, but she was most known for *Little Women*. Alcott grew up in New England and she empowered young women to think of themselves in bold, creative terms. She set out to astonish us.

Yet, as she achieved fame, she tempered the youthful exuberance of her splendid dreams. She learned to seek beauty in small details rather than large, heroic gestures: "The power of finding beauty in the humblest things makes home happy and life lovely." To conquer the world is to conquer the self:

I ask not for any crown
But that which all may win;

Nor try to conquer any world
Except the one within.

When Amy gets in trouble in school for rule breaking, her mother, Marmee, gives her advice: "You have a good many little gifts and virtues, but there is no need of parading them, for conceit spoils the finest genius. There is not much danger that real talent or goodness will be overlooked long, and the great charm of all power is modesty."

When you have everything going for you, you can afford a little modesty.

Spend today being more self-deprecating than usual.

✦ D A Y # 6 0 ✦

ON IDENTITY

How many times did someone sign your high school yearbook, "Never change a thing," as if you had nothing to learn and develop in the years ahead? Philosopher Charles Taylor wrote that we have a thick identity and a thin identity. We have identities that are temporal and situational—who I am on a cruise or in a particular job or in a specific role or relationship —and then a core or thick identity that I carry with me and inhabit no matter where I am.

Identity is tricky for leaders because the way we see ourselves often differs from the way others see us. In *Against Identity*, Leon Wieseltier suggests that identity is "a euphemism for conformity," because it "announces a desire to be subsumed, an eagerness to be known primarily by a common characteristic." In leadership, we assume the identity of an organization until we move to another organization. "It is never long," Wieseltier observed, "before identity is reduced to loyalty."

Who are we really?

"We call ourselves what we are, but also what we wish to be. This is inspiring and this is corrupting. For the ambiguity allows us to see the one in the other, to mistake what we wish to be for what we are. . . . A good rule is: We are never already what we should be."

What are five words that describe your thick identity—who you are, no matter where you are or who you are with?

✦ DAY #61 ✦

ON AUDACITY

Audacity is believing you have something to offer the world that no one has yet given it.

Audacity is believing that you are an original and that what you create has the capacity for novelty and innovation.

Audacity is the valor and pluck to speak up when others are silenced.

Audacity is the fearless grit to get things done when others stagnate and make excuses.

Audacity is the nerve to find wisdom where others see only folly.

Audacity is the daring willingness to take risks and fail.

Audacity is the bold, brash, fierce, courageous, brazen gall we use when we demand moral excellence from ourselves and others.

Audacity is acting on all these beliefs.

Belief itself is an act of audacity.

Desiderius Erasmus (1466–1536) was a Dutch Catholic priest and theologian with a sharp mind and an equally sharp tongue. He knew quite a bit about spiritual audacity, and he used his chutzpah to reform the Church from within.

So just in case you were losing your nerve to change the world— or at least your little corner of it—because it suddenly feels too risky, remind yourself of four of the most important words that shape all leadership—given to us by Erasmus:

"Fortune favors the audacious."

Use today to do something absolutely, unforgivingly bold.

ON RESILIENCE

"Resilience is accepting your new reality, even if it's less good than the one you had before. You can fight it . . . or you can accept that and try to put together something that's good."

These fighting words are from Elizabeth Edwards (1949–2010). She had a lot of fight in her but not enough. In 2010, breast cancer took her life. She knew a thing or two about accepting new and unexpected realities. "Nothing ever stays the same."

In *Resilience*, Edwards shared the heartache of being a parent who lost a teenager in a car accident. "If you know someone who has lost a child, and you're afraid to mention them because you think you might make them sad by reminding them that they died—you're not reminding them. They didn't forget they died. What you're reminding them of is that you remembered that they lived."

Her approach to life's misfortunes was simple.

"The days of our lives, for all of us, are numbered. . . . I have found that in the simple act of living with hope, and in the daily effort to have a positive impact in the world, the days I do have are made all the more meaningful and precious. . . . You cannot stand back and hope for the best. You have to act."

Resilient people need good company: "Leave me if you must, but be faithful to me if you are with me."

**How resilient are you—on a scale of
1 to 10, with 10 being outstanding?**

ON GOSSIP

Which verse from Proverbs best describes your feelings about gossip?

"A dishonest man spreads strife, and a whisperer separates close friends" (16:28).

"Whoever keeps his mouth and his tongue keeps himself out of trouble" (21:23).

"Whoever goes about slandering reveals secrets; therefore do not associate with a simple babbler" (20:19).

"The words of a whisperer are like delicious morsels; they go down into the inner parts of the body" (18:8).

Gossip separates us from friends. Sure, it's tasty. It's like a delicious morsel that goes down smooth, but then it reaches our insides and rusts our core goodness. It spreads strife and anger and embarrassment. The momentary pleasure we get from saying or hearing gossip is drowned out by the shame, guilt and hurt that gossip brings in its wake. Leaders can be shamefully guilty of gossip because they often know more about the private lives and foibles of others.

The wisdom of Proverbs is echoed by the wisdom of Benjamin Franklin (1706–1790): "A slip of the foot you may soon recover, but a slip of the tongue you may never get over." The price of gossip may be a changed relationship forever.

So try a morsel of information that is less tasty but better for you—and others. Spread more love and ditch the gossip. You'll be a better leader. You'll like yourself more.

**What can you do to reduce gossip in
your work and in your life?**

ON TRANSFORMATION

"As Gregor Samsa awoke one morning from uneasy dreams he found himself transformed in his bed into a gigantic insect." We've all had Franz Kafka mornings, when we wake up cramped and insectlike, trapped in a hard outer shell that we have difficulty breaking.

From our earliest years, we were fed on transformation tales: princes turn into frogs and a reporter turns into Superman in a phone booth. Talent and strength always came from the capacity to transform.

Donald Miller, a Christian spiritual writer, observed in *A Million Miles in a Thousand Years: What I Learned While Editing My Life*: "If the point of life is the same as the point of a story, the point of life is character transformation. . . . In nearly every story, the protagonist is transformed. He's a jerk at the beginning and nice at the end, or a coward at the beginning and brave at the end. If the character doesn't change, the story hasn't happened yet."

In *Through Painted Deserts: Light, God, and Beauty on the Open Road*, Miller left us with a blessing:

"My hope is your story will be about changing. . . . We get one story, you and I, and one story alone . . . It would be a crime not to venture out, wouldn't it?"

We don't always choose that which changes us most. We react and respond. "It is always the simple things that change our lives. And these things never happen when you are looking for them to happen."

Describe a major life transformation you didn't expect.

ON COMMUNITY

"No man is an island, entire of itself; every man is a piece of the continent, a part of the main . . . any man's death diminishes me, because I am involved in mankind, and therefore never send to know for whom the bells tolls; it tolls for thee."

John Donne (1572–1631), poet and Anglican priest, understood the importance of not living in isolation. He struggled mightily with poverty and relied upon his friends for basic support.

The cement of a community is essentially the belief that we cannot live alone. We are all part of the organism called humanity. Any death diminishes us all because it is not someone else's fate. It will soon enough be ours. Every interaction impacts our capacity to build community.

Donne advised us to use the most basic brick that builds community: "We give each other a smile with a future in it." A smile given to others invites a nod into our future together.

The bell will toll for us all. Since we will all die—we hurtle closer each day to our final day—we also must take better care of each other. This makes the prospect of our mortality more bearable. There are also side benefits; Donne once said, "Death is an ascension to a better library."

Does your organization feel like a community of intention? Do one thing now to make it so.

✦ DAY #66 ✦

ON PERFORMANCE

"What does it take to be good at something in which failure is so easy, so effortless? When I was a student and then a resident, my deepest concern was to become competent . . . lives are on the line. Our decisions and omissions are therefore moral in nature. We also face daunting expectations. . . . The steps are often uncertain. The knowledge to be mastered is both vast and incomplete. . . . It's not only the stakes but also the complexity of performance in medicine that makes it so interesting, and at the same time, so unsettling."

Atul Gawande wrote this in *Better: A Surgeon's Notes on Performance*. Gawande is a surgeon, writer and the recipient of a

MacArthur grant. He seems, at times, obsessed with human error. He challenges his readers to be more disciplined, more safety conscious, more careful, more methodical. "We always hope for the easy fix: the one simple change that will erase a problem in a stroke. But few things in life work this way."

There is a moment when the hard work pays off, when it all begins to click and runs like clockwork. Gawande wrote in *The Checklist Manifesto*: "We are by nature flawed and inconstant creatures. We can't even keep from snacking between meals. We are not built for discipline. We are built for novelty and excitement, not for careful attention to detail. Discipline is something we have to work at."

**Identify one skill you need to master
through enhanced discipline.**

✦ DAY #67 ✦

ON AUTHORITY

In Walter Isaacson's biography *Einstein: His Life and Universe*, the young Einstein is depicted as a student with high marks. This is contrary to many myths about Einstein not doing well in school, particularly in math. He did write a letter to a young girl in 1943 saying, "Do not worry about your difficulties in Mathematics. I can assure you mine are still greater." (Contrast this with advice he received from a six-year-old girl in 1951: "I saw your pictures in the paper. I think you ought to have a haircut, so you can look better.")

His teachers, however, did criticize him for resisting authority. He believed in curiosity and imagination above conventional governing structures. "I speak to everyone in the same way, whether he is the garbage man or the president of the university." You weren't worth more by virtue of your intelligence.

Einstein's humility and childlike sense of fun shaped his learning. "I have no special talents. I am only passionately curious." He told others: "It is not that I'm so smart. But I stay with the questions much longer."

Einstein raises a paradox that many leaders experience. "Good" students follow the rules. Excellent students often break them. What makes a good leader may get in the way of making a great leader. "To punish me for my contempt for authority, fate made me an authority myself."

Describe a moment of resistance to authority that defined your leadership.

ON GENDER

"Ah, well, do I wish that we lived in a world where gender didn't figure so prominently? Of course. Do I even think about myself as a woman when I go to make art? Of course not." But that is not entirely true: "I go to make art as who I am as a person. The fact that I am a woman comes into play maybe in the kinds of things I'm interested in or in the way I structure a canvas."

Judy Chicago was born in Chicago. She changed her name upon the death of her father and husband and took the name of a place. She began making art as a child. As she matured, her passion for art grew, as did her commitment to feminism.

"There's no question that many more women artists are showing worldwide now than they were when I was a young woman, and that's really great." But that wasn't always the case. Chicago suffered for her art. "With my early work I got eviscerated by my male professors, and so you learned to disguise your impulses, as many women have done. And that's definitely changed."

Chicago wrote in the introduction to *The Dinner Party*: "Exercising authority does not necessarily have to be a domineering process." She concluded that leadership for her was about "personal empowerment rather than power over others."

In your leadership, how have you created greater gender equality?

ON EXAGGERATION

"Never exaggerate."

So admonished Baltasar Gracián y Morales (1601–1658), Spanish Jesuit and philosopher, in *The Art of Worldly Wisdom*, a collection of Gracián's aphorisms with commentary that has been translated and reprinted for centuries. His sharp tongue was wrapped in delicious prose.

Gracián felt that exaggeration did a disservice to the person who employed it. "It is a matter of great importance to forgo superlatives, in part to avoid offending the truth, and in part to avoid cheapening your judgment. . . . Err in understatement rather than overstatement."

Gracián advised minimalism as a route to wisdom. Don't use words that overpromise and underdeliver. Don't reveal too much of yourself either. Conceal more than you reveal: "Keep the extent of your abilities unknown. The wise man does not allow his knowledge and abilities to be sounded to the bottom, if he desires to be honored at all. He allows you to know them but not to comprehend them."

We love a good story, an unexpected flourish, a tall tale told with detail and richness to keep us laughing, but—although we may amuse—the listener becomes suspect, and we compromise credibility.

"Do not enter where too much is anticipated. It is the misfortune of the over-celebrated that they cannot measure up to excessive expectations. . . . You will make a better exit when the actual transcends the imagined, and is more than was expected."

Try not to exaggerate today. If this is difficult, think of Gracián's words: "Be first the master of yourself."

ON CHANGE

"I found over the years that any momentary change stimulates a fresh burst of mental energy," said Woody Allen. "So if I'm in this room and then I go into the other room, it helps me. If I go outside to the street, it's a huge help. If I go and take a shower it's a big help."

Change can be positively disruptive when offering a shift of perspective or thinking or a slight irritation that stimulates mental activity.

Allen wrote that when he is deep in the creative zone, his stories benefit from obsessive thinking. "I think in the cracks all the time." The story line dominates his mental landscape, filling every fissure. "I never stop."

Mason Currey captured Allen's habits—along with those of hundreds of other writers, composers and painters—in *Daily Rituals: How Artists Work*: Martin Amis believed two hours of writing a day was a good output; Umberto Eco found his ideas while swimming in the sea or sitting in the tub; after writing, P. G. Wodehouse never missed his three-thirty soap opera; Twyla Tharp wakes up every day at five thirty and hails a cab to the gym: "A dancer's life is all about repetition."

Currey quoted V. S. Pritchett: "Sooner or later, the great men turn out to be all alike. They never stop working. They never lose a minute. It is very depressing."

**Invite change into your routine today so
that your ideas don't grow stale.**

ON DEPENDENCE

There are only so many people you can
carry in your small boat before their
weight sinks you.
A hundred you can carry whom you love.
But barely one you wish to harm.

Shams-ud-din Muhammad, or Hafiz (c. 1320–1389), was a beloved Persian poet from Shiraz. Hafiz is a name typically given to someone who knows the Koran by heart, and this Hafiz did. Ralph Waldo Emerson called him a poet for poets, and Goethe said that he had no peer.

In the poem above, Hafiz offers us a visual of dependency. He shows us the way that we often carry others, relying upon the buoyancy of the water and the strength of the skiff to assist us. But a small boat can hold only so many before it begins to sink.

And Hafiz cleverly linked the small boat to the holder our hearts make. The heart has a capacity for many when our emotions are expansive and loving. But if there is one antagonizing person in the boat, then even two will be too many.

Overreliance does not enable people. It disables people. Others stop carrying their own weight because it is easier for someone else to do the heavy lifting. A leader may be able to do it faster, better or more efficiently, but remember: There are only so many people you can carry in your small boat. Make sure they are truly the important ones.

Who are you carrying in your small boat?
Who needs to leave your small boat?

ON CIVILITY

P. M. Forni is an unlikely civility advocate. He teaches Italian litera-ture at Johns Hopkins University, specializing in Dante—who was not particularly well-known for his manners as he was for his poetry. Forni has said that he spent the first half of his life concerned with beauty and he plans to spend the rest of it concerned with meaning. He would teach Dante and realize that his students were usually not changed by it.

Today he directs the Civility Project at Johns Hopkins Uni-versity. He hasn't given up his day job at the Academy. In *Choos-ing Civility*, Forni wrote: "*Courtesy* is related to *court* and evoked in the past the superior qualities of character and bearing expected in those close to royalty."

Forni ends his exploration with a rhetorical question: "What is civility if not a constant awareness that no human encounter is without consequence? What is it if not sharing with intention the best that is in us?" Civility for Forni is not merely a matter of saying *please* and *thank you* but an approach to living that makes constant acknowledgment and room for others.

**How can you leverage your leadership to
strengthen civility in your organization?**

ON INCLUSIVITY

Leaders often play favorites. This can leave followers feeling hurt, left out or rejected. There are only a certain number of hours in the day and a limit to our patience and energy, so maybe we just don't have enough love to go around. But then we would be betray-ing what love is. In *Everyday Ethics: Inspired Solutions to Real-Life*

Dilemmas, Joshua Halberstam, a professor of philosophy, cited cartoonist Charles Schulz on this problem: "I love mankind; it's people I can't stand."

Halberstam questions the way people often make grandiose statements about the global community while forsaking basic human kindness and decency. "In general, the devotion to humanity is often a mask for an inability to connect to other people on a personal level. Some of the greatest 'lovers of mankind' have downright ugly histories when it comes to their personal relationships." He cited Karl Marx, who is said to have neglected one of his surviving children; and Rousseau who—with his mistress—left five illegitimate babies on the steps of an orphanage. Both opinion shapers were too busy saving mankind to save or nurture specific members of the species.

Why does this matter? the philosopher asks.

"Our emotions are directed to individuals, not abstractions." Loving humanity, therefore, in Halberstam's view is loving no one at all. If you want to be truly inclusive, let go of the proclamations of your goodness. Show your love, one relationship at a time.

How might Halberstam's observations on loving humanity impact your own leadership today?

+ DAY #74 +

ON RESTLESSNESS

"If you haven't found it yet, keep looking. Don't settle. As with all matters of the heart, you'll know when you find it." These are not the words of a spiritual master. They are the words of Steve Jobs (1955–2011). His restlessness stirred him to create innovation after innovation.

His biographer Walter Isaacson wrote that Jobs did not experience this restlessness episodically. He experienced it daily: "For the past thirty-three years, I have looked in the mirror every morning and asked myself: 'If today were the last day of my life, would I want to do what I am about to do today?' And whenever the answer has been 'No' for too many days in a row, I know I need to change something."

"Remembering that I'll be dead soon is the most important tool I've ever encountered to help me make the big choices in life." On another occasion, Jobs harked to this same sentiment that provided him with a good night's sleep: "Being the richest man in the cemetery doesn't matter to me. Going to bed at night saying we've done something wonderful, that's what matters to me."

Jobs may just be the richest man in his cemetery, but that was not his objective. "I want to put a ding in the universe," he told the world. And he did.

How will you put a ding in your universe?

✦ DAY #75 ✦

ON NAMES

Zsa Zsa Gabor once said, "I call everyone 'Darling' because I can't remember their names."

The first task given to Adam in the Garden of Eden was to name the animals. The animals were created to provide Adam with companionship. In naming them, Adam was able to assess if these creatures were indeed a match, a way to alleviate his loneliness, but he understood that none could serve as a true life partner.

"Then the Lord God said, 'It is not good for the man to live alone. I will make a suitable companion to help him.' . . . So the man named all the birds and all the animals; but not one of them was a suitable companion to help him."

We betray this primordial role each time we fail to use someone's name, don't remember someone's name or don't bother to take the time to learn someone's name. When we don't use people's names, they don't feel worthy of us.

Unless you have a medical condition where you cannot actually remember names or put names and faces together, don't give yourself a pass. Maybe you've convinced yourself that you are not good at remembering names, but in your leadership, surely you've faced harder challenges.

It is a basic courtesy, an act of decency and a spiritual nod to the divinity within us to use names. Often and accurately.

**Make a point of using the name of everyone
with whom you are in contact today.**

◆ DAY #76 ◆

ON PEACE

"Noninjury to all living beings is the only religion."

This is the first truth of Jainism, one of the world's oldest religions.

In the *Yogashastra*, a Jain scripture from about 500 BCE, we find the peaceful wisdom of not hurting others: "In happiness and suffering, in joy and grief, we should regard all creatures as we regard our own self, and should therefore refrain from inflicting upon others such injury as would appear undesirable to us if inflicted upon ourselves. . . . This is the quintessence of wisdom; not to kill anything. All breathing, existing, living sentient creatures should not be slain, nor treated with violence, nor abused, nor tormented, nor driven away. This is the pure unchangeable Law. Therefore, cease to injure living things."

Jainism is an ancient Indian religion started in the sixth century BCE by Jina Vardhamana Mahavira. It preaches a form of popular monasticism based on nonviolence and the importance of spiritual perfection. "All living things love their life, desire pleasure and do not like pain; they dislike any injury to themselves; everybody is desirous of life and to every being, his life is very dear."

If we truly believe in peace, then we believe that every life is precious and worthy.

**Do one thing to advance peace today to someone
who is not expecting your olive branch.**

ON ORDER

Flame-flower, Day-torch, Mauna Loa,
I saw a daring bee, today, pause, and soar,
Into your flaming heart;
Then did I hear crisp crinkled laughter
As the furies after tore him apart?

Thus wrote poet Anne Spencer (1882–1975) in "Lines to a Nasturtium: A Lover Muses." The nasturtium is indeed a flame-flower—a bright orange flower with a bright yellow center—that was likely found in Spencer's garden, a source of constant inspiration for her.

Spencer was an important Harlem Renaissance poet who regularly entertained other Harlem writers, artists and musicians in her beloved garden. Her home and garden in Lynchburg, Virginia, can be visited by the public today. Here visitors can see "A Lover Muses" painted and running vertically down a cabinet, right next to red leatherette padded doors that her grandfather salvaged from an old movie theater. Spencer wrote on her walls. And wrote out of sequence. She would sometimes finish a page of poetry and then continue on the preceding one.

The civil rights champion James Weldon Johnson was so taken by Spencer's writings that he sent her poems to scholar H. L. Mencken, who said: "Tell that woman to put beginnings and ends to her poems. I can't make heads or tails of them, but they're good."

In the end, she did not need Mencken's advice. Her lack of order was a creative gift.

As a leader, when does too much order
get in the way of your creativity?

ON FRIENDSHIP

"A friend is one that knows you as you are, understands where you have been, accepts what you have become, and still, gently allows you to grow." William Shakespeare understood that as we change, so do our relationships. Sometimes we grow apart from friends but sometimes, in that evolution of self, our friendships blossom.

Marcus Tullius Cicero (106–43 BCE) was a Roman philosopher and statesman whose works have had an enduring influence on Western civilization. The following excerpt is from his *De Amicitia* (On Friendship):

"Now the support and stay of that unswerving constancy which we look for in friendship, is loyalty; for nothing is constant that is disloyal. Moreover, the right course is to choose for a friend one who is frank, sociable, and sympathetic—that is, one who is likely to be influenced by the same motives as yourself—since all these qualities conduce to loyalty; for it is impossible for a man to be loyal whose nature is full of twists and twinings; . . . a friend must neither take pleasure in bringing charges against you nor believe them when made by others. And so, the truth of what I said in the beginning is established: 'Friendship cannot exist except among good men.'"

The better we become as people, the better we become as friends.

**Name one work relationship that developed
into a beautiful friendship and why. Reconnect
in some way with that friend today.**

ON CHAOS

In the summer of 1965, Nora Ephron and Susan Edmiston interviewed Bob Dylan. He had recently been booed at a New York concert. In the interview, he was described as "an underfed angel with a nose from the land of the Chosen People."

Q: Do you consider yourself primarily a poet?
A: No. We have our ideas about poets. The word doesn't mean any more than the word "house." There are people who write poems and people who write poems. . . . You don't necessarily have to write to be a poet. Some people work in gas stations and they're poets.

I don't call myself a poet because I don't like the word. I'm a trapeze artist.

Q: What I meant was, do you think your words stand without the music?
A: They would stand but I don't read them. I'd rather sing them. I write things that aren't songs.

In the interview, Dylan claimed that he'd never written anything hard to understand. But the interviewers pressed him about the fragmentary nature of some of his music. Was it full of curiosities?

Q: And contradictions?
A: Yeah, contradictions.

Q: And chaos?
A: Chaos, watermelon, clocks, everything.

Q: You wrote on the back of one album, "I accept chaos but does chaos accept me?"

A: Chaos is a friend of mine. It's like I accept him, does he accept me?

> Leaders love control. Name a chaotic
> time in your leadership that resulted
> in something extraordinary.

✦ DAY #80 ✦

ON LONELINESS

"I am lonely. Let me emphasize, however, that by stating 'I am lonely' I do not intend to convey to you the impression that I am alone. I, thank God, do enjoy the love and friendship of many. I meet people, talk, preach, argue, reason; I am surrounded by comrades and acquaintances. And yet, companionship and friendship do not alleviate the passional experience of loneliness which trails me constantly."

Rabbi Joseph Soloveitchik (1903–1993), Talmud scholar and philosopher, wrote *The Lonely Man of Faith* after a succession of family deaths that left him bereft of his chief anchors. His observations on the human condition took on a deeper, more personal sense of vulnerability and urgency. An existentialist, the Rav, as he was affectionately called by his disciples, wrote often about the religious personality being inherently alone.

Leadership, at times, can be so lonely. We feel abandoned by those who were once loyal or alienated by a polarizing and difficult decision. We feel ultimate accountability like no others with whom we work. There are days when there is no one to talk to, no one to relieve the ache of individuality.

And, at some moments, we are aware that the heartache of loneliness is not really because we are leaders. It is because we are human.

> Describe a lonely leadership moment
> and how you emerged from it.

ON TENDERNESS

"Tenderness and kindness are not signs of weakness and despair, but manifestations of strength and resolution." These words of Khalil Gibran push against our deeply held convictions about the relationship between success and aggression. Leadership seems hard, resilient, determined. When we think of tenderness, we think of something soft, blurry, fragile, delicate.

The toughness of any leader is always measured against his or her capacity to express and exhibit a range of emotions. In his song "Leave a Tender Moment Alone," Billy Joel asked us to let the tenderness stand. Don't work hard to cover it up. Learn to expose it.

Khalil Gibran's most famous work, *The Prophet*, was published in 1923. Gibran was born to a poor Catholic family and raised in Lebanon. His sister, brother and mother died of illness. Gibran himself died of tuberculosis when he was forty-eight.

The sense of otherness Gibran wrote about often in his poetry and prose emerged from an understanding that there are boundaries that we dare not cross in the search for self and other. Tenderness emerges not from the collapsing of these boundaries but from respecting them and reading the space between people.

"The reality of the other person lies not in what he reveals to you, but what he cannot reveal to you. Therefore, if you would understand him, listen not to what he says, but rather to what he does not say."

What leadership situation brings out your tenderness?

ON PRAISE

There are leaders—often of a certain generation—who don't believe in praising their employees. "Why should I praise her? I pay her!" Excellence isn't a bonus. It's a baseline. There are leaders—of a different generation—who praise all of the time, sometimes even when the work is not worthy.

Which approach works best in terms of outcome—underpraising or overpraising?

In *Mindset*, psychologist Carol Dweck shared research on the outcome of a nonverbal IQ test given to hundreds of students. The researchers praised some of the students, telling them "Wow, you got eight right. That's a really good score. You must be smart at this." Others were given different praise: "Wow, you got eight right. That's a really good score. You must have worked really hard."

The groups began to behave differently. Praising someone's ability rather than their effort led to what Dweck called a "fixed mindset." When given the choice to face new challenges, these students "didn't want to do anything that could expose their flaws and call into question their talent." When students were praised for their effort, "90 percent of them wanted the challenging new task they could learn from."

Students praised for effort enjoyed challenges more than those who were praised for being special. "In the fixed mindset, imperfections are shameful—especially if you're talented—so they lied them away." When we label people as special we "rob them of their zest for challenge."

Praise people today for effort.

✦ DAY #83 ✦

ON LISTENING

Ann Thomas and Jill Applegate in *Pay Attention!* wrote powerfully about the importance of listening in business. Those who are "service masters" treat customers with almost obsessive attention:

"They listen to them, study them, and learn from them. They are constantly trying to crawl inside their heads to find out what makes them tick. However, these masters do not simply take orders from their customers. Rather, they synthesize their sense of customers' wants, needs, and expectations into unique, clever, and sometimes highly innovative personal solutions."

Sadly, we understand why employees sometimes fail their customers or colleagues: They may not feel their company has any loyalty to them or that their job is merely transactional. This is exacerbated when the people to whom they should be paying attention are not paying any attention to them. Paying attention and giving great service may never get a thank-you or a notice from a CEO or a customer. "She only speaks to me when I'm not doing something right." We are not going to invest the best of ourselves under any of these conditions.

We get people to pay more attention and listen carefully when we model it and catch people doing good.

Stephen R. Covey wrote: "Most people do not listen with the intent to understand; they listen with the intent to reply."

Spend today listening to understand.

✦ DAY #84 ✦

ON SIMPLICITY

"Our life is frittered away by detail. Simplify, simplify."

Henry David Thoreau (1817–1862) shared this powerful advice in *Walden*, one of the most famous experiments in simplicity. His conclusion: "All good things are wild and free."

Thoreau wrote extensively about the environment and its relationship to human freedom. His observations are so well-known that aphorisms from *Walden* look like a string of yearbook quotes today. But they didn't at the time they were written. Who was this strange poet-philosopher who left "civilized" life to live in a wooden hut in a forest by a lake?

"I went to the woods because I wished to live deliberately, to front only the essential facts of life, and see if I could not learn what it had to teach, and not, when I came to die, discover that I had not lived. I did not wish to live what was not life, living is so dear; nor did I wish to practice resignation, unless it was quite necessary. I wanted to live deep and suck out all the marrow of life, to live so sturdily and Spartan-like as to put to rout all that was not life, to cut a broad swath and shave close, to drive life into a corner, and reduce it to its lowest terms."

In the end "I learned this, at least, by my experiment: that if one advances confidently in the direction of his dreams, and endeavors to live the life which he has imagined, he will meet with a success unexpected in common hours."

In fact, Thoreau went into the woods upon the recommendation of a friend and fellow writer to increase his focus and live without distraction for enough time to write a book. Little did he realize at the time that the book would be about living simply in a wooden hut in the woods for two years. This taught him that the pursuit of luxury is a hindrance to self-knowledge and the acquisition of meaning and purpose. Taking a break from the forward propulsion to achieve, acquire and impress allowed him to discover and celebrate the moment.

"You must live in the present, launch yourself on every wave, find your eternity in each moment. Fools stand on their island of opportunities and look toward another land. There is no other land; there is no other life but this." Not far from Walden Pond in Massachusetts today is a reconstruction of Thoreau's simple dwelling and a bronze statue of him outside of it. It invites us to experiment with living life more simply.

Name one area of your leadership that needs to be simplified right now. Take your first step into the woods.

+ DAY #85 +

ON COMPASSION

"I have walked that long road to freedom. I have tried not to falter . . . I have taken a moment here to rest. . . . But I can only rest for a moment, for with freedom comes responsibilities, and I dare not linger, for my long walk is not ended."

When Nelson Mandela (1918–2013) died, his long walk to freedom left enormous footprints to fill for those who came after him. Instead of anger and revenge, Mandela preached compassion and forgiveness.

In his autobiography, he outlined his essential philosophy of political reform: "No one is born hating another person because of the color of his skin, or his background, or his religion. People must learn to hate, and if they can learn to hate, they can be taught to love, for love comes more naturally to the human heart than its opposite." This love comes from the capacity to see the other person the way they really are—with their frailties and failures—and see beyond the biases and prejudices that obstruct that view. "Our human compassion binds us the one to the other—not in pity or patronizingly, but as human beings who have learnt how to turn our common suffering into hope for the future."

The ultimate compassion is persistence, to believe in human kindness even when you cannot experience it. That depth of hope creates real and lasting change.

"It always seems impossible until it's done."

Who needs more of your compassion right now?

◆ DAY #86 ◆

ON TECHNOLOGY

We often bemoan the way that technology has hurt human relationships, as Albert Einstein quipped: "It has become appallingly obvious that our technology has exceeded our humanity." Let's also bless technology because:

Old high school friends who lost touch can reconnect with ease.
A hospitalized churchgoer can live-stream a service and not feel alone.

We know about global disasters and can marshal resources, financial and human, to the area, often within hours.

When we make mistakes we can correct them instantly.

We can share good news quickly and simultaneously, enhancing our joy.

We have reduced the amount of paper use significantly. The world has more trees.

We can track how many steps we take, our food intake and how much we tossed while sleeping—allowing us to monitor our health more accurately.

We can share pictures of our children, pets and major milestones with those we love, across the world or across the street.

We can save gas and precious time by ordering the things we need online and use our time to study, spend with family or help out at a soup kitchen.

Search engines get us quick access to critical information, from an academic article with footnotes to a great recipe for brownies.

Thank you, technology, for making us smarter, more informed and more connected to the people and information that matters to us most.

**What tech innovation has most helped
you become a better person?**

✦ DAY #87 ✦

ON COMPROMISE

Avishai Margalit, in *On Compromise and Rotten Compromises,* wrote that no one wants to compromise. It feels like losing, and who wants to lose? Not most leaders we know.

"We very rarely attain what is first on our list of priorities, either as individuals or as collectives. We are forced by circumstances to settle for much less than what we aspire to. We should," Margalit concluded, "be judged by our compromises more than by our ideals and norms. Ideals may tell us something about what we would like to be. But compromises tell us who we are."

Compromise involves finding the acceptable ground between "opposing evaluative forces." You think we should do it one way. I think we should pursue something else. We set it up as a zero-sum game, and then it becomes one.

Many people believe that when we compromise we betray ourselves and chisel off our integrity little by little. Don't give up an inch. Never falter or waver. Yet, if as a society we developed a stronger moral language around compromise and ceased to view it as a pejorative word, we would not see it as giving up on our principles so much as acknowledging the presence of others. How would life and leadership look different if we were judged not by our ideals but by the dignity of our compromises?

**Name the most important compromise you've
made that you learned to live with.**

✦ DAY #88 ✦

ON WORTHINESS

Maria Shriver opened up *Just Who Will You Be?* by complaining to her daughter: "I don't know what I want to be." Her daughter replied, "I hate to break it to you, Mom, but this is *it* for you. You *are* all grown-up! You're cooked!" Shriver jumped up and retorted: "Not so. You may think I'm over, but I'm not done yet! I'm still a work in progress, and I'm writing my next act now."

In her next act, she offered a graduation speech in which she cited research that young people today value fame above everything. Some people become famous just for being famous. "Before you can say 'Andy Warhol' they're famous!"

"Famous people always seem to look happy. They always look rich. They always look thin. If they happen to be fat, they'll be thin next week. Famous people seem to have it all."

Fame can get you a good table at a restaurant, get you a good date and even get you invited to be a graduation speaker. Fame, however, cannot make you feel worthy or give you a life of meaning. That, Shriver said, is "strictly an inside job."

"I think now more than ever we need famous people with integrity, character and vision—people who want to lead, who want to change the world and make it a more peaceful, hopeful and compassionate place, a place where more people feel accepted and valued for who they are."

How are you using your fame for good?

✦ DAY #89 ✦

ON JOY

"'Who am I to be brilliant, gorgeous, talented, fabulous?' Actually, who are you not to be? You are a child of God. Your playing small does not serve the world."

These famous words belong to the writer and activist Marianne Williamson. Williamson wrote that our greatest fear is achieving our potential. Shining. We are afraid to shine. We worry that when we make ourselves bigger, others will become smaller. But, she, wrote:

"There is nothing enlightened about shrinking so that other people won't feel insecure around you. We are all meant to shine, as children do. We were born to make manifest the glory of God that is within us. It's not just in some of us; it's in everyone. And as we let our own light shine, we unconsciously give other people permission to do the same. As we are liberated from our own fear, our presence automatically liberates others."

With these words, Williamson offered an unusual permission: permission to experience real joy, the joy that comes from expressing and becoming the best of ourselves.

Elsewhere—in lesser-known words—Williamson offered another hint for making our own joy: "Children are happy because they don't have a file in their minds called 'All the Things That Could Go Wrong.'"

Close the file cabinet. Throw away the manila folder. You'll get to the real problems when they are real. Don't let the worries rob you of your joy.

Shine.

What would you label your ugliest file?

ON CRITICISM

Criticism is not the same as feedback. We criticize, but we *give* feedback, as if it is a present. It is an act of giving to invest ourselves in the improvement of others. It is a way we direct positive energy to growing another human being and mentoring someone else to achieve his or her personal best. Aristotle wisely captured the relationship between feedback and personal growth: "To avoid criticism say nothing, do nothing, be nothing."

Criticism is an act of taking. We take away another's self-esteem. We rob them of the strength to change because our words incapacitate them. In their smallness in our presence, they cannot stretch and become taller. We make them small.

Sometimes we make ourselves small through self-criticism. Listen to this inner monologue by C. JoyBell C., author of *The Sun Is Snowing*: "I am my own biggest critic. Before anyone else has criticized me, I have already criticized myself. But for the rest of my life, I am going to be with me and I don't want to spend my life with someone who is always critical. So I am going to stop being my own critic. It's high time that I accept all the great things about me."

People want your approval. They want to know what you think of them. Your criticism defeats those you want to change and paralyzes them, preventing them from improving.

Minimize your criticism.

Inspire with your feedback.

Change a criticism you have of someone into feedback.

ON ASSOCIATIONS

What a relief to know that Sigmund Freud used to forget things. Remembering and forgetting is selective, individual and not arbitrary, as he described it in *The Psychopathology of Everyday Life*. No one remembers the same way or the same things.

Freud shared that he himself had an exceptional memory. As a schoolboy he could repeat, he wrote, a page of a textbook that he had read. In university he could "write down practically verbatim the popular lectures" he heard. He described taking exams and reproducing his textbooks exactly after skimming them.

Those days ended as he aged. A patient would state that he had seen him before, yet Freud could not recall "the fact or the time." Freud was not afraid to use his own lapses of memory to study the subject. He distinguished between forgetting impressions and experiences—in other words, knowledge—and "forgetting of resolution," or omissions. Freud believed we forget things because of the displeasure they cause us. We block out certain information, making it, at times, virtually impossible to retrieve. Freud shared an occasion when he was very angry at his wife because of an interaction at a restaurant. He could recall the anger but not a single detail of the episode.

We revisit the world through emotional associations, connections that may be tenuous but can have a strong hold over our minds and hearts that far exceeds facts.

**What traces of negative emotional residue
does your leadership have?**

ON ACCEPTANCE

What if you knew you'd be the last
to touch someone?
If you were taking tickets, for example,
at the theater, tearing them,
giving back the ragged stubs,
you might take care to touch that palm
brush your fingertips
along the lifeline's crease.

When a man pulls his wheeled suitcase
too slowly through the airport, when
the car in front of me doesn't signal,
when the clerk at the pharmacy
won't say thank you, I don't remember
they're going to die . . .

How close does the dragon's spume
have to come? How wide does the crack
in heaven have to split?
What would people look like
if we could see them as they are,
soaked in honey, stung and swollen,
reckless, pinned against time?

This is an excerpt from Ellen Bass's "If You Knew," quoted from her collection *The Human Line*. At what point do we reach acceptance and have the capacity to accept others as they are, not as we want them to be? Did you ever hear someone who has lost a wife, a child, a friend, say, "If only we had one more day together . . ." It still would not be enough. But we tell ourselves that in that one day, we would have fixed all of the problems, displayed our full range of affection, accepted the cracks and fault lines and even loved the warts.

The good news: We don't have to wait.

Whom would you accept as they are if you knew you were going to lose them?

✦ DAY #93 ✦

ON SUPPORT

A woman recently widowed and struggling for support was speaking to a friend who encouraged her to get out of the house.

"So someone asked me today, 'How are you?' with that look of pity, and I made a mistake."

"What?"

"I told her that I feel lousy. I hate to be alone. I don't want to be a widow, and I never expected life to turn out this way."

"Why was that a mistake?"

"She needed me to say I was fine. She asked me a question she didn't want the answer to."

Bertrand Russell (1872–1970) instructed us to listen with our full humanity:

"The life of Man is a long march through the night, surrounded by invisible foes, tortured by weariness and pain, towards a goal that few can hope to reach, and where none may tarry long . . . [O]ur comrades vanish from our sight, seized by the silent orders of omnipotent Death. Very brief is the time in which we can help them, in which their happiness or misery is decided. Be it ours to shed sunshine on their path, to lighten their sorrows by the balm of sympathy, to give them the pure joy of a never-tiring affection, to strengthen failing courage, to instill faith in times of despair."

Be it ours to shed sunshine on the path. Ask someone who is hurting how they are doing and really listen this time.

ON DISCOVERY

Biologist E. O. Wilson discovered God as he discovered nature. In *Naturalist*, he wrote that when his parents' marriage fell apart he was placed in a foster home where he was exposed to religion and nature. "I was seven years old, and every species, large and small, was a wonder to be examined, thought about, and, if possible, captured and examined again."

Mother Raub, as Wilson called his caregiver, had a friend who saw a light in the corner of her room she believed was Jesus. "So I prayed long and hard, many evenings after that, glancing around occasionally to see if the light had arrived. . . . Nothing happened. I decided I just wasn't up to bringing God into my life, at least not yet."

A time did come for God.

Wilson went with Mother Raub to hear a recital of gospel hymns. Wilson was so moved he "wept freely in response to the tragic evocation" of Jesus being crucified. He asked to be baptized. But the baptism did not move him as he thought it would: "And something small somewhere cracked. I had been holding an exquisite, perfect spherical jewel in my hand, and now, turning it over in a certain light, I discovered a ruinous fracture."

He concluded: "In essence, I still longed for grace, but rooted solidly on Earth."

Childhood is a time of discovery, of the world within and the world outside. Sometimes the outside world becomes one's inner world.

Share an important discovery that shaped your childhood.

ON FAITH

I want to write about faith
about the way the moon rises
over cold snow, night after night

faithful even as it fades from fullness
slowly becoming that last curving and impossible
sliver of light before the final darkness
but I have no faith myself
I refuse to give it the smallest entry

Let this then, my small poem,
Like a new moon, slender and barely open,
Be the first prayer that opens me to faith.

—David Whyte

Faith requires complete trust and confidence. But it is not something we're born with. Whyte describes faith as waxing and waning like the moon. Faith isn't fluid. It changes and grows. It cycles out of favor and then back. It can be a sliver of light before final darkness or the slender opening of a new adventure.

It's hard to discuss faith because people treat it as something you have or you don't, something you're born with or you're not, like money or good health or intelligence. If we never speak of faith because it is only for someone else—believers—then we deny ourselves the possibility of that sliver ever appearing.

"It is Moses in the desert fallen to his knees before the lit bush. It is the man throwing away his shoes, as if to enter heaven and finding himself astonished, opened at last, fallen in love with solid ground."

Open your eyes to faith just a little
today—as a sliver of possibility.

ON GENEROSITY

Howard Behar, former president of Starbucks, was the son of a grocer. His father saw when money was tight with families. He would put a bunch of bananas in a bag. It was a small gesture, but it signaled a quiet generosity of spirit.

In *It's Not About the Coffee: Lessons on Putting People First from a Life at Starbucks*, Behar connected this memory with a Starbucks policy. Stores actually open ten minutes early "as a way to say yes to customers even before they placed their order." It's a small gesture that says rules can be bent just a little in the direction of generosity.

Even when you fire people, Behar recommended generosity: "The people who remain will be observing how you treat those who are leaving."

This was Behar's human bottom line: "At Starbucks, we are in the human service business, not the customer service business. . . . The vision has to be inspiring and meaningful to our partners, the communities we're a part of, and all the people we serve."

He called this approach compassionate emptiness, which "involves listening *with* compassion but *without* preconceived notions. Compassionate emptiness asks us to be caring but empty of opinions." Listening this way is also an act of generosity.

**Describe a moment you were particularly generous
with employees and share their reactions.**

ON CREATIVITY

"If you only do what you know and do it very, very well, chances are that you won't fail. You'll just stagnate . . . and that's failure by erosion." The dancer and choreographer Twyla Tharp made the case for change in *The Creative Habit: Learn It and Use It for Life*. For Tharp, creativity is "an act of defiance."

"Creativity is more about taking the facts, fictions, and feelings we store away and finding new ways to connect them. . . . It's not only how we express what we remember, it's how we interpret it—for ourselves and others."

And while we're on the subject of limitations, don't limit your definition of creativity to dance, music or the plastic arts. Many leaders are creative problem solvers or creative strategists.

Tharp instructed us to not be hard on ourselves when it comes to creativity because "there is no ideal condition for creativity. What works for one person is useless for another. The only criterion is this: Make it easy on yourself. Find a working environment where the prospect of wrestling with your muse doesn't scare you, doesn't shut you down. It should make you want to be there, and once you find it, stick with it. To get the creative habit, you need a working environment that's habit-forming. All preferred working states, no matter how eccentric, have one thing in common: When you enter into them, they compel you to get started."

What inspires you to be creative?

✦ DAY #98 ✦

ON INTEGRITY

"If it is not right do not do it; if it is not true do not say it."

Marcus Aurelius (121–180 CE) was a Stoic philosopher and Roman emperor with much wisdom to share: "Waste no more time arguing about what a good man should be. Be one." And yet, in leadership it is not always clear what is right and true, what a good man or woman is. Competing truths and values fight with each other daily.

How, then, do we retain our integrity? To answer that question, we turn very far away from ancient Rome, to nineteenth-century Eastern Europe.

Rabbi Nachman, a Hasidic rebbe, used to see the imprint of God's name across the face of each person. The divine was the lens and filter through which he saw the divine in others.

Rabbi Nachman had to leave the rabbinate for financial reasons and went into business. Business blurred the clarity of his truths. He no longer saw God's name on every face, so he hired a personal assistant. He had one job: to remind Rabbi Nachman of his holy filter in every encounter, helping him reclaim the dignity of others when he was about to compromise his own integrity and core values.

It is not enough to identify our core values. We have to put constant reminders in place so that we can retain our integrity in all leadership challenges.

**What reminder do you have in place
to keep your integrity intact?**

✦ DAY #99 ✦

ON FLEXIBILITY

"I can accept anything, except what seems to be the easiest for most people: the half-way, the almost, the just-about, the in-between."

Ayn Rand (1905–1982) created characters who were towering and inflexible.

"The man who refuses to judge, who neither agrees nor disagrees, who declares that there are no absolutes and believes that he escapes responsibility, is the man responsible for all the blood that is now spilled in the world. Reality is an absolute, existence is an absolute, a speck of dust is an absolute and so is a human life. Whether you live or die is an absolute." *Atlas Shrugged* told us that the world is one of absolutes and ultimatums.

"There are two sides to every issue: one side is right and the other is wrong, but the middle is always evil. The man who is wrong still retains some respect for truth, if only by accepting the responsibility of choice. But the man in the middle is the knave who blanks

out the truth in order to pretend that no choice or values exist. . . .
In any compromise between food and poison, it is only death that
can win." Rand painted a picture in which flexibility looks wishy-
washy and ambivalent. The choice of fools is a choice that always
ends in misery or death.

In *The Fountainhead*, she repeated this theme: "To sell your soul
is the easiest thing in the world. That's what everybody does every
hour of his life."

What softens your inflexibility?

◆ DAY #100 ◆

ON EXECUTION

"Execution is the greatest unaddressed issue in the business world
today," claims Larry Bossidy and Ram Charan in *Execution: The Discipline of Getting Things Done*. They realized that many leaders focus
and spend a lot of time on high-level strategy, on "intellectualizing
and philosophizing," but much less time than they need to on imple-
mentation.

Strategy and vision get all of the attention, while the tactical
side of leadership is often minimized and delegated. The perception
of being in the weeds gets in the way of getting things done.

"Execution is not just tactics—it is a discipline and a system.
It has to be built into a company's strategy, its goals and its culture.
And the leader of the organization must be deeply immersed in it.
He cannot delegate its substance." Those who leave the details to
someone else are, in their words, "building a house without a foun-
dation."

You may think there is nothing spiritual about details, but in
many ways being engaged in the substance of a vision, without
micromanaging, shows a deep level of concern and investment in
the lives of those you lead, who make good on your dreams with
you. Bossidy and Charan wrote that to execute well, leaders need

to invest at least 40 percent of "their time and emotional energy" in "selecting, appraising and developing people."

**Estimate the time and emotional energy
you spend developing people.**

✦ DAY #101 ✦

ON RESISTANCE

"Free societies are societies in which the right of dissent is protected."

Natan Sharansky was a prisoner of Zion, a Soviet dissident. In *Fear No Evil*, Sharansky took his title from the book of Psalms. "Though I walk through the valley of the shadow of death, I will *fear no evil*, for You are with me." He walked through that valley dozens of times. "When a man is afraid and accedes to fear, he will always find arguments to justify his own surrender."

Sharansky married his wife, Avital. They were forcibly separated a day after their wedding. She was permitted to emigrate to Israel but Natan was not. After three years as a public dissident, Sharansky was arrested by the KGB and sentenced to thirteen years in prison for "spying." Days before his arrest a tourist delivered a small and complete book of Psalms from Avital. He took it to prison for strength and to help him master Hebrew. He read until his eyes hurt. Sharansky committed to writing and translating all the psalms. It took forty days and left him "almost no time for sad thoughts and painful recollections. . . . My feelings of grief and loss were gradually replaced by sweet sorrow and fond hopes."

His psalmbook was snatched on more than one occasion. When he was finally released, the guard told him to walk straight. He swerved. He had his book of Psalms with him.

**Name a personal act of resistance—great or
small—that helped you manage your fears.**

ON GOODNESS

"People want to be happy, and all the other things they want are typically meant to be a means to that end." Daniel Gilbert, a Harvard psychologist, questions the relationship between goodness and happiness in *Stumbling on Happiness*.

In classic philosophical literature, goodness or virtue is associated with happiness. If we do good, we will feel good, and feeling good will make us feel happy. Many contemporary studies have shown that when we feel good—often as recipients of unexpected generosity—we spill it over to someone else.

Happiness can be prompted by goodness but not limited to it. Gilbert cites Willa Cather: "One cannot forecast the conditions that will make happiness; one only stumbles upon them by chance, in a lucky hour, at the world's end somewhere, and holds fast to the days, as to fortune or fame."

We are just not rational enough to know what triggers happiness in every instance, and even if we knew, we probably would not activate those triggers anyway. "Research suggests that people are typically unaware of the reasons why they are doing what they are doing, but when asked for a reason, they readily supply one." Gilbert added: "If you are like most people, then like most people, you don't know you're like most people."

Friends matter and mattering matters—which is a good reason for goodness.

"Impact is rewarding. Mattering makes us happy."

Use your leadership to make someone matter today.

ON VITALITY

One of the most famous stories of the Buddha emerged when he had to explain himself. After his enlightenment, he was traversing India and encountered a group of men who knew they had stumbled upon the presence of someone extraordinary: "Are you a god?" they wanted to know.

"No," he replied.

"Are you a reincarnation of god?"

"No," he said

"Are you a wizard, then?"

"No."

"Well, are you a man?"

"No."

Confused, they asked one more question: "So then what are you?"

"I am awake."

Vitality in leadership is the quality of full engagement. It is the sense of being fully awake or alive. The psychologist and writer William James wrote: "Seek out that particular mental attribute which makes you feel most deeply and vitally alive, along with which comes the inner voice which says, 'This is the real me,' and when you have found that attitude, follow it."

Identify in your leadership that which makes you most fully alive. The Buddha answered honestly. Who he was was not a function of an identity but of a feeling. The state of enlightenment was for him the experience of being awake.

Sometimes we coast through our leadership with eyes half-closed. We think no one notices. But we are not fooling anyone, least of all ourselves. You can always tell when someone is fully awake.

**Do something today that expresses the
vitality of your leadership.**

ON GRATITUDE

Sometimes our thanks are so casual or expected that they don't sound grateful at all. Maurice Sendak, author of so many magical children's books, learned this from an unusual correspondence with one of his young writers.

"Once a little boy sent me a charming card with a little drawing on it. I loved it. I answer all my children's letters—sometimes very hastily—but this one I lingered over. I sent him a card and I drew a picture of a Wild Thing on it. I wrote, 'Dear Jim: I loved your card.' Then I got a letter back from his mother and she said, 'Jim loved your card so much he ate it.' That to me was one of the highest compliments I've ever received. He didn't care that it was an original Maurice Sendak drawing or anything. He saw it, he loved it, he ate it."

In the words of a friend who first shared this story with me, there is only one conclusion to draw from it: Gratitude is delicious.

There is little that makes us more aware of the wonder in our lives than a sincere and heartfelt thank-you. There is little that can make you a more appreciated leader than showing gratitude to those who rarely get thanked.

**Write a distinctive and personal thank-
you note to someone that could only come
from you and could only go to them.**

ON ORIGINALITY

Experience and observation walk. Imagination sings. William Faulkner once said: "A writer needs three things, experience, observation, and imagination, any two of which, at times any one of which, can supply the lack of the others." You can keep using experience and observation, but if imagination never enters the equation, your universe will be flat.

Faulkner famously observed: "In writing, you must kill all your darlings." There are sentences and words you fall in love with because you believe they have the power to impress, to make you look smart or tall or important. But you have to kill those little darlings so that something truer and more authentic can emerge, something original.

Faulkner was not afraid to admit that he could have improved: "If I could write all my work again, I'm convinced I could do it better. This is the healthiest condition for an artist. That's why he keeps working, trying again: He believes each time that this time he will do it, bring it off. Of course he won't." We may not always find a refreshing new idea or a wellspring of innovation, but if we try hard enough, we might just realize that originality matters because it makes us more interesting to ourselves, not only to others. "I write when the spirit moves me," Faulkner said. "And the spirit moves me every day."

What can you do to set your imagination free today?

✦ DAY #106 ✦

ON INSIGNIFICANCE

The American writer Meg Wolitzer described being at a social gathering and encountering a guest who found out she was a writer. Unthinkingly, he asked her, "Would I have heard of you?"

Something makes us laugh and then squirm uncomfortably at this anecdote. Wolitzer mentioned her name, saw there was no recognition in the blank stare that looked back at her and humbly went on to explain the kind of novels she wrote.

Leaders are so often guilty of this same kind of casual arrogance: Do I need to know who you are? Are you someone?

We cannot afford to be friends or good colleagues with everyone. We need filters. We cannot respond to every call or e-mail or letter, and it's not because we think we are better than other people. It's because we answer to a watch, and the watch does not lie.

It is impossible for a leader to feel both insignificant and powerful simultaneously. You may submit yourself to the decisions of others, believe in the wisdom of teams and give others credit for the work, all the while believing in your own self-importance. If you don't believe in yourself, why should anyone else believe in you? But, to lead well, your humanity must be visible. You have to care more, not less.

**As a leader, what techniques do you use
to turn strangers into friends?**

✦ DAY #107 ✦

ON SILENCE

"I need to be alone. I need to ponder my shame and my despair in seclusion; I need the sunshine and the paving stones of the streets without companions, without conversation, face to face with myself, with only the music of my heart for company."

How many times have we felt like Henry Miller's character in *Tropic of Cancer*? Give us a pair of noise-canceling headphones and block out the cacophony of voices inside: the voices of anger, self-doubt, longing, frustration. And then there's the outside voices making their demands. We want to be free of all the sounds so that we can be truly alone with ourselves in whispers of darkness, like the hours before the dawn when the mind dreams in the embrace of quiet. We want to walk alone without companions or conversation and luxuriate in the silence. Leaders are rarely given such moments unless they create them.

And then there is the silence of being with many strangers and feeling alone because, despite the throngs, there is no one to talk to, not a friend. Maybe the boardroom feels lonely or the office is painfully silent because we've made a decision whose consequences we need to face alone.

Created silence.
Forced silence.
Shared silence.
You cannot always choose.

Share the time of day when silence is loudest.

✦ DAY #108 ✦

ON CAPACITY BUILDING

The leadership writer Warren Bennis was awarded a Purple Heart and a Bronze Star for his military service. He was one of the youngest men to ever earn both decorations. Bennis had earned his stripes, so when he began to work in the discipline of leadership, he had a lot of street credibility. He was the president of several universities and advised four United States presidents. Bennis wrote that leadership is a combination of personal ethics and experience that is shaped by one's core self-awareness.

"Too many companies believe people are interchangeable. Truly gifted people never are. They have unique talents," Bennis observed in *Organizing Genius: The Secrets of Creative Collaboration*. "Such people cannot be forced into roles they are not suited for, nor should they be. Effective leaders allow great people to do the work they were born to do."

In organizations, most people supervise to accommodate company needs, not employee needs. But when individual capacity building does not take place, many of those talented people we'd love to retain seek their fortune elsewhere, fearing that no one is really growing them. In the failure to grow individuals, we also fail our companies because people need to do the work they were born to do.

We often try to fit in because we do not think standing out will serve our long-term interests. Ironically, it's the only thing that ever will.

Take one step into growing someone else's capacity today.

ON CLOSURE

We all want endings. We want to know when something is over, when we can let go, when we can call a thing done. In Genesis, God declared the world complete: "And when the work of the heavens and the earth is over . . ." But it seems that a leader's work is never done. There is never a time when we can declare with divine confidence, "This is officially finished."

And perhaps there is an authenticity in acknowledging that we may never be done. Richard Rohr, a Franciscan friar and the founder of the Center for Action and Contemplation, wrote: "The theological virtue of hope is the patient and trustful willingness to live without closure, without resolution, and still be content and even happy because our satisfaction is now at another level, and our source is beyond ourselves." The hope and need for closure may be illusory. There is no such thing.

As leaders, we have to prepare ourselves and others to live without the neatness of closure. Genesis tells us that a finish line is critical. It helps us pause and reflect on what we have created and can open us up to celebration or relief or loss. But there are rarely hard stops, and the blurriness and ambiguity of not closing everything can help us trust others and live without resolution and still be content.

What do you seek closure for that refuses to close?

ON BUSY-NESS

One afternoon, an eight-year-old boy asked his father how much money he made an hour. "None of your business, son." The boy kept at it, and the father caved in: "I make fifty dollars an hour." The son then had the audacity to ask his dad for twenty-five dollars. Dad said no, and he meant it. Later, the father thought about the unusual request. His son had never asked him for that kind of money. Maybe there was something he really needed. He went up to his son's bedroom and said, "Maybe I spoke too soon. Here is twenty-five dollars." The son already had money rumpled under his pillow. Why did he need more? The son thanked his father, put all the bills together and said, "Dad, here is fifty dollars. Can I please have an hour of your time?"

No one who needs you should have to buy your time. As a leader, we have to step out of the busy-ness competition, where being constantly preoccupied is regarded as a status symbol.

We try to impress someone with how demanding our life is, how many people need us, how special it is that we have made time in our hectic swirl for them. What we are saying is often "I am more important than you."

What we should say is this: "You are the most important thing in my life right now. I am fully present here with you."

The next time you feel crazy busy, keep it to yourself.

◆ DAY #111 ◆

ON DEFENSIVENESS

In military terms, a defense is the way we fortify, resist or respond to attack; we shrink and block. We become smaller and then puff ourselves up in protection. The need to defend oneself is deep and primal.

Imagine that each act of defense is a brick. Soon enough, there are so many bricks in your wall—it is so high—that you cannot see the person on the other side.

It is very hard to listen when you become defensive. When most people are criticized, they rush to save themselves. They build that fortress. If you are leader, you may feel criticized all of the time, and you rely on defensiveness as your default posture. The writer and critic Christopher Hitchens observed: "It's often a bad sign when people defend themselves against charges which haven't been made."

It is time to take down that wall. When someone criticizes you, wait until they are done, and ask them if they have any other issues. Let them get it all out. Just listen. Act counterintuitively and watch the result. It will surprise you. You will surprise yourself.

No one wants to speak to a defensive leader more than once. Because if no one can hear you, it is not worth talking. Be the leader people want to approach.

What can you do to lower your defensive wall right now?

✦ DAY #112 ✦

ON ENLIGHTENMENT

Thousands of years ago, a famous Jewish sage, Rabbi Yossi, was walking down the road, when he encountered a blind man carrying a torch.

Rabbi Yossi thought his behavior was foolish.

What use can a torch have for a man who all his life walks in darkness? He asked the blind man why he carried a torch.

"Rabbi, this torch is not so that I can see you. It is so that you can see me. When you can see me in the darkness, you will also be able to see the dangers in the road. That is why I carry this torch."

At that moment, the blind man became the sage while the sage was in the dark.

Leading is about carrying the torch: aiding, assisting, supporting and creating the conditions for others to achieve their dreams.

All human beings can carry this torch. It is the small light we carry for others. It is the opportunity we offer others when we recognize their potential and see light in them when they see only darkness.

When we think of enlightenment in historical terms, we think of a period of time when science and reason often eclipsed religion. When we think of enlightenment in mystical or spiritual terms, we

think of what it means to burn brightly, to ignite others, to be illuminated by ideas.

Be the light.

**Who is in the dark right now who needs
the torch and light you hold?**

✦ DAY #113 ✦

ON MEDITATION

"Thought reveals itself only through contemplating a little without content, contemplating sheer spirit. The contemplation is imperfect: you understand—then you lose what you understood. Like
pondering a thought: the light of that thought suddenly darkens,
vanishes; then it returns and shines—and vanishes again." These
are the words of the thirteenth-century mystic Moses de León, as
translated by Daniel C. Matt in *The Essential Kabbalah.*

In meditation, you often begin with a mantra or the repetition
of a counting pattern, and then you allow your thinking to transcend
letters and numbers to achieve a mental blank space. If a thought or
a distraction approaches, you think of it as a cloud that passes and
leaves. All the static dissipates.

It is very hard to clear the mind, to achieve what the mystics
call empty mental space. Jonathan Haidt, in *The Happiness Hypoth-
esis*, contends that meditation is like a free and effective "pill" and
one of the very few things we can do to enhance our personal happiness. "Sit still and focus awareness only on your breathing, or on a
word, or on an image, and let no other words, ideas or images arise
in consciousness."

Meditation teaches us to let go of attachments. It is easier than
we think. We have to try. We have to start. Create inner calm. You
can do it. To lead well, you should.

**Schedule five minutes on your calendar to meditate
every day at the same time for a week.**

ON SUFFERING

There are anguished decisions we have to make in leadership. We fire people. We are shouldered with blame and sometimes criticized mercilessly. When people tell us that the only way to lead is by developing a thick skin and an iron stomach, we know that leading from within precludes that. We will always feel some things deeply. Pain is one of them.

In her book *Loving-kindness*, the spiritual teacher and practicing Buddhist Sharon Salzberg offers us insight into the importance of connecting with others when we are suffering

"The unrelenting flux of life's changing conditions is inevitable, yet we labor to hold on to pleasure, and we labor equally hard to avoid pain. So many images from our world tell us that it is wrong to suffer; advertising, social mores and cultural assumptions suggest that feeling pain or sadness is blameworthy, shameful, humiliating. Underlying these images is an expectation that somehow we should be able to control pain or loss. When we experience mental or physical pain, we often feel a sense of isolation, a disconnection from humanity and life. Our shame sets us apart in our suffering at the very times when we need most to connect."

**Who can you connect to professionally
when you feel you are suffering?**

ON SHOULDERING
A LOAD

Lou Holtz (1937–) is a retired football coach and current sportscaster. Football coaches are in the motivation business, trying to get athletes to play their best and keep their egos in check to work as a team. Holtz was known for his ability to move players. He made it sound easy: "Motivation is simple. You eliminate those who are not motivated."

But Holtz also understood that sometimes you can't find the strength. "It's not the load that breaks you down; it's the way you carry it," Holtz wrote. We don't always wear our circumstances lightly. When you're a leader, everyone is looking at the way you shoulder your load to gauge if they can shoulder theirs.

This coach believed in keeping burdens to oneself: "Don't tell your problems to people: eighty percent don't care; and the other twenty percent are glad you have them." This may be true, but a burden shared is often a burden halved.

"It's not the load that breaks you down; it's the way you carry it."

**What load are you shouldering right
now, and can everyone tell?**

✦ DAY #116 ✦

ON CHARITY

Ignatius of Loyola (1491–1556) was a Spanish knight turned priest turned religious leader. His spiritual life took a turn when he was wounded in battle and sought out a life transformation, forming the basis of a classic work of religious depth, *The Spiritual Exercises of St. Ignatius*. There he shared his views on charity:

"I should place before my mind a person whom I have never seen or known, and whom I wish to be wholly perfect in the office and state of life which he occupies. Now the same standard of action that I would like him to follow in his way of distributing alms for the greater glory of God and the perfection of his soul I myself will observe, and do neither more nor less. The same rule I would like him to follow, and the norm I judge would be for the glory of God I shall abide by myself."

In order for me to give charity more perfectly, I have to contemplate what I believe the ideal is for someone else.

In charitable giving, we often judge others rather than take the view of Ignatius.

Sadly, research shows that those who have more give less percentagewise than those who have less. They are often too far removed geographically and mentally from needs, so they don't see them. The needs are too far away from the corner office.

How can you become a more charitable leader?

ON KINDNESS

Small acts of kindness are a currency of affirmation. When we share them we are saying: "It is good to be alive. This world is a good place. It is a place where kindness matters, where I matter." No one owes you a kindness. It is a gift without need for recompense.

A young man of eighteen went to Calcutta to work with Mother Teresa. In the chapel he saw a handwritten note on the wall: "When I was homeless you opened your doors. When I was naked you gave me your coat. When I was in prison you came to my cell. When I was lonely you gave me your love. When I was searching for kindness you held out your hand. When I was happy you shared in my joy."

A leader who bestows a small kindness on someone who is sad or depleted helps return and renew that individual's sense of self-worth and belief in humanity. In an office where a leader can have a thousand employees, the fact that a leader sent you a note, picked up flowers for you, gave charity in your name, makes all the difference. People follow those who are kind. They will do more because they have been given more.

It does not matter if no one else can see your act of kindness. You've inspired yourself.

**In your leadership, do one small act of kindness
today for someone who is not expecting it.**

ON EXCESS

Mae West went to prison for eight days in the heat over a racy Broadway show she wrote and staged in 1926. City officials claimed she was corrupting the morals of youth. Mae West made her mint on bad behavior. "I wrote the story myself. It's about a girl who lost her reputation and never missed it." The moment one of her plays was condemned, it packed the house. Her saucy mouth brought in the crowds. She allegedly said: "I believe in censorship. I made a fortune out of it."

West, a sex symbol for decades, said of excess: "Too much of a good thing can be wonderful." And she lived that way. "Those who are easily shocked should be shocked more often." And shock she did.

Her relationships also tended toward excess. Failure in love only spiked her tongue, "Marriage is a great institution. I'm not ready for an institution yet."

Many leaders become fat off the perks and the bonuses, the gifts and the flattery. They buy things because they can. They exploit people because they can. They act unreasonably because they can.

Too many followers feel powerless to stop the excesses of their leaders because they fear the repercussions, a change of relationship or the possibility of unemployment. They don't want to tarnish the star, so they go down with it.

As a leader, you can model restraint or excess.

What excessive behavior do you need to keep in check?

ON REVENGE

Revenge is a subtle monster, a breathing, heartless beast that lurks in corporate offices behind desks, in cubicles and personal electronic devices. It takes on the form of saying no when you could have said yes or blocking a deserved promotion because of a petty insult or firing an employee for challenging the norm.

"Do not seek revenge," cries Leviticus. The Talmud does not look at the obvious and bold manifestations of revenge, like murder or stealing, but at the small and innocent transactions of an individual borrowing something from another. Because you didn't lend something to me, I won't lend something to you. I can. I just don't want to.

For novelist Mary Higgins Clark, revenge is a way to get back: "When someone is mean to me, I just make them a victim in my next book." For boxer Muhammad Ali, it's a form of self-respect: "I got no respect for a man who won't hit back. You kill my dog, you better hide your cat." For Anne Lamott, it's poison: "Not forgiving is like drinking rat poison and then waiting for the rat to die." Revenge is poison. Stop drinking it.

Think of one act of revenge that you wish upon someone. How can you let go?

✦ DAY #120 ✦

ON ANGER

"Never go to bed mad. Stay up and fight," said Phyllis Diller.

"Anger never went to bed with me," according to a Talmudic sage.

Who got the better sleep?

We find this observation on anger from another sage of the Talmud (*Ethics of the Fathers* 5:14):

"There are four types of temperaments. One who is easily angered and easily appeased—his virtue cancels his flaw. One whom it is difficult to anger and difficult to appease—his flaw cancels his virtue. One whom it is difficult to anger and is easily appeased is pious. One who is easily angered and is difficult to appease is wicked."

Anger is easy to muster. The best spiritual temperament, according to this text, is to be slow to anger and quick to be appeased.

That is harder when, as a leader, you hold the balance of power in many relationships. Another ancient spiritual master, Lao-tzu, wrote: "The best fighter is never angry." Fight your leadership battles with your wits. When we fight them with anger, the anger only gets in the way of our intelligence, cloaking our best intentions and outcomes, paralyzing us.

Out of the four temperaments mentioned above, which is yours?

✦ DAY #121 ✦

ON LEAVING

"The search for the exotic, the strange, the unusual, the uncommon has often taken the form of pilgrimages, of turning away from the world, the 'Journey to the East,' to another country or another religion," wrote Abraham Maslow in the preface to *Religions, Values, and Peak-Experiences.*

In order to capture holiness, we believed for too long that we had to leave where we were and become external seekers. Maslow, perhaps the most articulate spokesman for the Third Force movement in psychology, challenged this notion.

"The great lesson from the true mystics . . . that the sacred is *in* the ordinary, that it is to be found in one's daily life, in one's neighbors, friends, and family, in one's backyard, and that travel may be a *flight* from confronting the sacred—this lesson can easily be lost."

The confrontation with the sacred, the numinous, the ineffable mystery and enigma of all life, is most likely available right at home, right in front of us. We just think it lives somewhere else because it excuses us from seeking it where we are.

"To be looking elsewhere for miracles is . . . a sure sign of ignorance that *everything* is miraculous."

What holiness would you encounter right now if you believed you didn't have to go anywhere else to find it?

ON CALLOUSNESS

General George Smith Patton (1885–1945) was one of the world's most successful military leaders. He was also one of the meanest, known for saying "You name them. I'll shoot them." He believed that profanity was essential to military life and believed that the longer you experienced war, the less death meant to you: "It is rather interesting how you get used to death."

Like a callus, where the skin toughens under continued abrasion, the callous leader gets results through hard-hearted, singularly focused direction that usually lacks empathy, understanding or kindness. He or she believes that toughness is a hallmark of leadership. And it is here where Patton's voice on leadership may ring loudest: "We herd sheep. We drive cattle. We lead people. Lead me, follow me, or get out of my way."

In *Bad Leadership*, Barbara Kellerman identified why we let leaders like this get away with the abuse. We believe that such leaders will drive desired results. When they do, we justify their behavior, minimizing the tyranny of the process for the gains, usually short-term. Callous leaders not only instill fear in followers, they leverage that fear to keep their positions. We tolerate callous leadership at an extreme price: the long-term health of our organizations, the dignity of employees, the integrity of a board.

Some of history's most influential leaders lacked human compassion, sensitivity and kindness. They are remembered that way.

**How can you make amends for a callous
moment in your leadership right now?**

ON INDIFFERENCE

Mewlana Jalaluddin Rumi, better known as Rumi (1207–1273), was a medieval Persian poet mystic whose words—translated into virtually every spoken language—shake us with their piercing understanding of the human condition. Listen to these thoughts in "Be with Those Who Help Your Being":

"Be with those who help your being. Don't sit with indifferent people, whose breath comes cold out of their mouths. Not these visible forms, your work is deeper. A chunk of dirt thrown in the air breaks to pieces. If you don't try to fly, and so break yourself apart, you will be broken open by death, when it's too late for all you could become. Leaves get yellow. The tree puts out fresh roots and makes them green. Why are you so content with a love that turns you yellow?"

Why would you settle for a love that turns you yellow? Rumi continued the theme in "Confused and Distraught":

"Again I am raging, I am in such a state by your soul that every bond you bind, I break, by your soul. I am like heaven, like the moon, like a candle by your glow. . . . My joy is of your doing, my hangover of your thorn; whatever side you turn your face, I turn mine, by your soul."

Our joy is often "of your doing," determined by someone else. So is our pain. You don't have time or energy to waste. Don't invest in those who are indifferent to you.

Who are you indifferent to as a leader?

ON SUCCESS

"If a society has no moral foundations, then success is a threat. Every successful person thinks everyone else is a failure, and this is the proof of failure. Conquering the world and dying empty-handed on foreign shores is a paradox of such success."

Sufi master and poet Wasif Ali Wasif (1929–1993) wrote this teaching in one of his most famous collections of spiritual wisdom, *Dil Darya Samundar*. Wasif gathered people twice a week to lecture with no set topic; he just responded to questions.

The Sufi tradition that birthed and nourished Wasif's intellect is very ancient. Some date it before organized religion itself, but most regard it as the mystic or esoteric stream of Islam that focuses on perfection of worship and faith.

Wasif observed this about work: "In order to spend out our time (life) we sell some of this time. We work for someone, we labor. In freedom, we do slavery." In freedom, we do slavery. We define success in limited ways, not realizing perhaps that personal success is all too often on the altar of someone else's definition or standard.

Wasif understood that humans were often slow to acknowledge the reach of the inner life: "This life is but a dream. A state of sleep but how unfortunate that man's eyes open only when they are about to be closed (forever)." If we open our eyes early enough, we may redefine success.

What's your personal definition of success?

+ DAY #125 +

ON HOLINESS

No spiritual challenge is greater or harder to understand than the command in Leviticus 19:2, "You shall be holy." This is written in a didactic style that assumes the reader would naturally be acquainted with the notion of holiness and understand its demands. You cannot ask someone to do something unambiguously if the demand itself is laden with uncertainty.

Holiness in Hebrew—*kedusha*—is from a verb, *l'kadesh*, which implies separation. To become holy is to engage in a subtle process of separation. Ways of being, acts of morality, emotional reactions, are all choices we make to separate ourselves from others and from former ways of acting in the universe. As we separate ourselves on a path to individuation, we discover challenges of excellence that separate the ordinary from the extraordinary. Holiness is a state of being extraordinarily good, generous, loving, expansive.

Choices are placed before leaders all of the time, every day, every hour. These choices potentially separate leaders from others. Striving for excellence through continuous improvement both for the company and for the self makes life a ladder of challenge. Push yourself a little harder and get one step closer to transcendence.

Imagine a ladder of holiness. What rung are you on and where would you like to be on that ladder?

✦ DAY #126 ✦

ON NEGOTIATION

The page of an in-flight magazine is stark white with a close-up of a large fortune cookie in the right-hand corner whose inside note reads as follows:

"You don't get what you deserve. You get what you negotiate."

Who determines what we deserve? Destiny is not what you open up at random like a message in a crisp, golden casing. It is what you create through determination, will and compromise.

Some leaders think of negotiation as a rotten compromise, a betrayal of ideology or mission. No one's needs are served. Some leaders enjoy negotiations for the thrill of seeing how much they can get without having to give. Such negotiations are not spiritual but adversarial, a win-lose proposition.

Spiritual negotiations are collaborative rather than competitive, building bridges to reduce the abyss between two people or two partners. The span tells us that there is a way to get to the other side. A bridge is not only instrumental in getting us to another side. Most bridges are not only functional but also objects of beauty.

Imagine negotiation as a beautiful bridge that carries us closer to where the other side lives.

With whom can you create a bridge right now to better negotiations?

✦ DAY #127 ✦

ON FEEDBACK

How well do you respond to feedback?

We all would like to believe that we respond well to feedback. We learn and change when we hear it because we are always striving to be better. But leaders are just like everybody else. Feedback makes us defensive. Our first impulse is self-protection and then deflection. We shield ourselves and then throw the feedback to the sender— maybe that's why it's called "feed back."

Actually, that is why it's called *feedback*. The word probably originated in the 1920s but became accepted usage in the 1950s as the return of an electronic circuit or mechanical device to its input, modifying its original characteristics. In negative feedback, elevated energy output reduces the input of energy, and the opposite occurs in positive feedback. There is a relationship between input and output.

The biblical book of Proverbs helps us understand that feedback is about both the receiver and the giver. "Do not criticize a scoffer, for he will hate you. Rebuke a wise person and he will love you. Instruct a wise person and he will grow wiser" (Proverbs 9:8–9).

Before you give feedback, consider whether the person you are critiquing can handle it. If not, the relationship will be compromised. But there is another dimension to this equation: If you are a wise person receiving feedback, you will love the person giving you the feedback.

**What is the most important piece of feedback
you have ever been given as a leader?**

ON MEETINGS

"If you had to identify, in one word, the reason why the human race has not achieved, and never will achieve, its full potential, that word would be 'meetings.'"

Dave Barry echoes what all of us feel.

In a *Reader's Digest* column, Barry wrote that there are two major kinds of work in modern organizations. You can either go to meetings or take messages for people who are already in meetings. He suggests that, for status reasons, you aim for going to meetings.

"Sometimes you go to meetings where the purpose is to get your 'input' on something. This is very serious, because what it means is, they want to make sure that in case whatever it is turns out to be stupid or fatal, you'll get some of the blame. So you have to somehow escape from the meeting before they get around to asking you anything. One way is to set fire to your tie."

**Before you set your tie on fire, how can you
give your next meeting real meaning?**

ON RENEWAL

In *Self-Renewal*, John W. Gardner bemoaned the way that adult development is often arrested at too young an age. We get stuck voluntarily. We settle into routines, select a relatively small pool of people to befriend and keep relying on the way we have always done things: "As we mature we progressively narrow the scope and variety of our lives."

For leaders, this lack of self-renewal gets in the way of personal and professional growth and organizational innovation. Gardner writes that renewal often comes with travel or major life changes, like moving, marriage, job changes or national emergencies that shake us and wake us up existentially. "Unlike the jailbird," he pointed out, "we don't know that we've been imprisoned until after we've broken out."

Gardner notes that there are some people more prone to self-discovery than others. One manifestation of the tendency to self-renewal is for a person to be aware of the "full range of his own potentialities" and the systematic development of them. "He looks forward to an endless and unpredictable dialogue between his potentialities and the claims of his life." These include the capacity for "sensing, wondering, learning, understanding, loving and aspiring."

Self-discovery awaits us. As a leader, you can invite renewal or keep it at bay because you fear its unpredictability.

**What can you do to renew your
spirit and energy right now?**

✦ DAY #130 ✦

ON IMMORTALITY

It's hard to face death without thinking of Woody Allen: "I don't want to achieve immortality through my work.... I want to achieve it through not dying." Him and everybody else. But Allen was onto something. We don't want to die, and we do want our work to live past us. If we cannot live forever, we hope that what we create can live beyond us in some skin of eternity. As Allen remarked, "Why are our days numbered and not, say, lettered?"

Research on mortality tells us that high achievers generally have a greater fear of death than others. Leaders, take note. This correlation makes sense. People who are highly driven and highly successful hate the fact that we are running out of time. Leaders may be used to controlling their environments, and they rail against the possibility that, when it comes to our mortality, we have very little control. And here we turn to Allen once again: "If it turns out that there is a God, I don't think that he's evil. But the worst that you can say about him is that basically he's an underachiever."

We'll give the last words to our existentialist comedian: "Death doesn't really worry me that much, I'm not frightened about it. . . . I just don't want to be there when it happens."

What would you like your leadership legacy to be?

✦ DAY #131 ✦

ON MOODINESS

Remember mood rings? They changed color based on body temperature. When you're a leader, your moodiness temperature is often the subject of office talk. In "How to Manage a Moody Boss," *Forbes* writer Jacquelyn Smith asked, "Does your boss experience mood swings on a regular basis? Does he or she suddenly become irritable, negative, or isolated for no apparent reason? This isn't uncommon, especially in a demanding, high-stress environment—but moody bosses can be extremely difficult to work with."

Lynn Taylor, author of *Tame Your Terrible Office Tyrant*, offered us the ten recommendations for dealing with a moody boss:

1. Watch for patterns.
2. Limit interactions if it is impacting your productivity or mood.
3. Keep your cool.
4. Make sure it's not you.

5. Don't take it personally—unless, of course, it is personal.
6. Protect yourself by documenting behavior.
7. Don't trigger it through your actions.
8. Set meetings at times of the day when moodiness seems to be in check.
9. Don't confront your boss during a mood swing.
10. If the problem cannot be kept in check, find a good time to speak to your boss.

But what happens when *you* are the moody boss? Manage yourself the same way you might manage someone else. Protect your best self from your worst self.

What does your mood ring say about you right now?

✦ DAY #132 ✦

ON CONFLICT

"I move towards the man who contradicts me: he is instructing me," Michel de Montaigne (1533–1592) wrote in his essay "The Art of Conversation." "The cause of truth ought to be common to us both."

Montaigne was an intellectual giant of the French Renaissance who was not afraid of conflict; indeed, he embraced and absorbed it as a way to grow and evolve.

"I welcome truth, I find it in whomsoever's hand I find it; I surrender to it cheerfully, welcoming it with my vanquished arms as soon as I see it approaching from afar." Our own point of view is strengthened when held up to challenge. If it isn't, then it's best to be rid of it early.

We should be strong enough to depersonalize conflict and learn from it. Instead we often opt for the highly manicured politeness that changes nothing and no one.

"So contradictory judgments neither offend me nor irritate me:

they merely wake me up and provide me with exercise. We avoid being corrected: we ought to come forward and accept it. . . . Whenever we meet opposition, we do not look to see if it is just but how we can get out of it, rightly or wrongly. Instead of welcoming arms, we stretch out our claws."

Invite Montaigne into your day and have a healthy and rigorous debate for the sake of truth and growth.

+ DAY #133 +

ON WORRY

Scott Stossel has abandoned dates, walked out of exams and had breakdowns during job interviews, on flights and just walking down the street. He is terrified of public speaking, vomiting, heights, germs, fainting, flying, cheese and enclosed spaces. He has tried therapy, medication, meditation, alcohol, hypnosis, prayer, massage, yoga and acupuncture.

"Here's what's worked: nothing."

In *My Age of Anxiety*, Stossel described how worry eats away at the fabric of normalcy, inhibiting travel and work performance, corroding personal relationships and undermining confidence.

"The truth is that anxiety is at once a function of biology and philosophy, body and mind, instinct and reason, personality and culture. Even as anxiety is experienced at a spiritual and psychological level, it is scientifically measureable at the molecular and physiological level. It is produced by nature and it is produced by nurture. . . . The origins of a temperament are many-faceted; emotional dispositions that seem to have a simple, single source—a bad gene, say, or a childhood trauma—may not."

But that's not the whole story:

"In weakness and in shamefulness is also the potential for transcendence, heroism, or redemption." His anxiety "remains an unhealed wound that, at times," he confesses, holds him back and fills him with shame, "but it may also be, at the same time, a source of strength and a bestower of certain blessings."

Name a healthy worry that keeps you on your toes as a leader and one unhealthy worry that has become an emotional obstruction in your work.

ON INNOCENCE

In 1789, William Blake wrote and illustrated *Songs of Innocence and Experience*.

How can the bird that is born for joy
Sit in a cage and sing?
How can a child, when fears annoy,
But droop his tender wing,
And forget his youthful spring?

Freedom was central to innocence for Blake (1757–1827)—the youthful spring of childhood when cages and fears do not limit us. Innocence represents a time before guilt, blame, sin and awareness of sin, before corruptibility has jaded us. Innocence appears to us as a wholesome flight of fancy and whimsy that returns us to the wonder of childhood.

In every cry of every Man,
In every Infant's cry of fear,
In every voice, in every ban,
The mind-forg'd manacles I hear.

We hear sounds that cut away at innocence—cries of fear and trauma, abuse and disappointment. But the fears that Blake most emphasizes are those that are self-created: the mind-forg'd manacles.

Reading Blake, we are reminded of a painting that has received much attention recently, *The Goldfinch*. It is an arresting image, a small oil painting of a finch with an ankle chain locked to a wooden perch with two brass rings. It is literally a forged manacle. The bird stares at us as if we, the onlookers, can free it. But instead we do nothing. It is everything that we imagine innocence isn't. A bird is born for joy, Blake tells us, but can have no joy without true flight.

Carel Fabritius (1622–1654), its painter, did not live a long life. He painted the goldfinch in the last year of his life, the year he died in an accidental gunpowder explosion, his wings clipped too early.

The bird is innocent. The shackle is not. The bird's instinct is to fly. Human instinct is to stay grounded, often trapped in cages of our own design. We let go too easily of the playfulness of youth.

Think of a time of innocence in your own life and create a metaphor for it. Innocence is like . . .

✦ DAY #135 ✦

ON SACRIFICE

"What is it about sacrifice that is so essential to human expression and life?"

This is the question that contemporary philosopher Moshe Halbertal asked in *On Sacrifice*. Sacrifice is a primal human need that took its expression in the ancient world of religion as the literal sacrifice of animal and vegetable offerings. The Talmud calls the impulse to sacrifice one of the greatest desires of human life, greater in its passion, expression and ambition than the need to eat, have sex and own things.

Halbertal made a distinction between the act of giving and sacrificing. When you give a gift among equals, you enter a giving cycle in which reciprocity, while not always articulated, is generally expected. I acknowledge an occasion or act of goodness with generosity, and it is repaid with a gift. And the gift-giving cycle continues.

We don't worship on altars anymore. At least, most of the Western world doesn't. But leaders make sacrifices all of the time, placing their time, ideas and passions on the altar of work—giving but not always receiving, struggling to gain acceptance and avoid rejection. We do this not out of guilt but out of nobility. We are pleased, indeed blessed, to have the capacity to give. "Sacrifice is a part of life. It's supposed to be. It's not something to regret. It's something to aspire to," wrote Mitch Albom.

**Name the single biggest sacrifice you
have made in your leadership.**

✦ DAY #136 ✦

ON SELF-DECEPTION

"When I betray myself, others' faults become immediately inflated in my heart and mind. I begin to 'horribilize' others. That is, I begin to make them out to be worse than they really are. And I do this because the worse they are, the more justified I feel."

This simple idea forms the core of *Leadership and Self-Deception*, produced by the Arbinger Institute, founded by C. Terry Warner. When we betray our best selves, we engage in self-justifying behaviors that also prompt us to find fault and blame others precisely because we are really disappointed in ourselves. When we make narcissistic choices, we justify them by making everyone else look selfish and self-serving.

If I can make my problem your fault, I can salvage myself but at your expense. "Self-deception obscures the truth about ourselves, corrupts our view of others and our circumstances, and inhibits our ability to make wise and helpful decisions."

The price of self-deception is very high.

We can act on our primary impulses of goodness, generosity and selflessness or descend into our secondary impulse of selfishness, defensiveness and self-protection. Just know that when you go there, you are taking everyone else down with you.

Act quickly on your primary impulse of giving today.

ON EXPECTATIONS

"If you expect nothing from anybody, you're never disappointed."

These words from Sylvia Plath (1932–1963) in her semiautobiographical novel, *The Bell Jar,* echo the earlier wisdom of Alexander Pope: "Blessed is he who expects nothing, for he shall never be disappointed." It seems a fair enough route to satisfaction.

A bell jar is a glass cover used to enclose fragile or delicate objects, usually in a laboratory. It is also a metaphor for that which protects and separates something from the outside world while still keeping it visible. "To the person in the bell jar, blank and stopped as a dead baby, the world itself is a bad dream." That is one way of viewing the world. Alternatively, a beautiful world unfolds, waiting to be experienced.

"At this rate, I'd be lucky if I wrote a page a day. Then I knew what the problem was. I needed experience. How could I write about life when I'd never had a love affair or a baby or even seen anybody die? A girl I knew had just won a prize for a short story about her adventures among the pygmies in Africa. How could I compete with that sort of thing?"

In the end, Plath chose not to compete. The experiences she could have had, she was never to have. She left too many beautiful words in the shadows.

As a leader, when has a change in your expectations helped you better negotiate reality?

ON AGING

"A doctor to whom I occasionally talk suggests that I have made an inadequate adjustment to aging.

"*Wrong*, I want to say.

"In fact I have made no adjustment whatsoever to aging.

"In fact I had lived my entire life to date without seriously believing that I would age."

We might recognize ourselves in Joan Didion's words. We're still young, vibrant and relevant. Never mind that we pass a mirror and wonder who is staring back at us. When did we lose that hair, get those love handles, shrink?

In her tender book *Blue Nights*, Didion shared her intimate struggles with aging, recognizing the primal fear of losing her balance or not being able to stand up. "I find myself increasingly focused on this issue of frailty. . . . I feel unsteady, unbalanced, as if my nerves are misfiring, which may or may not be an exact description of what my nerves are in fact doing."

Many leaders age with the fear of slipping into obsolescence. The corporate titan cannot be too young, but he or she cannot be too old either. We cannot hide the internal anxieties of aging when it often has its external telltale signs.

Didion can help us be honest because of her honesty: "I write entirely to find out what I'm thinking, what I'm looking at, what I see and what it means. What I want and what I fear."

**Take a moment to write your deepest fears
about aging and your leadership.**

ON DISADVANTAGE

"Power can come . . . in breaking rules, in substituting speed and surprise for strength." Disadvantage can become a source of remarkable advantage with a bit of reframing.

This is the central thesis of Malcolm Gladwell's book *David and Goliath: Underdogs, Misfits, and the Art of Battling Giants*.

"The David and Goliath story is famous for its satisfying underdog victory. David, the youngest of many sons all prized for their soldiering strength and military prowess, was ignored when it came to military service. David was shepherding the family sheep at a time of war, taking care of the animals as his older, stronger brothers took on the enemies. His father sent him to deliver care packages to the battle-field, and David stepped into a challenge that would change his life forever."

David did not engage in hand-to-hand combat but used his powerful slingshot, surprising his enemy with an unexpected form of attack.

"Why," Gladwell asked, "do we automatically assume that someone who is smaller or poorer or less skilled is necessarily at a disadvantage?" He called this capitalization learning. "We get good at something by building on the strengths we are naturally given. . . . What is learned out of necessity is inevitably more powerful than learning that comes easily."

You may be weaker but smarter, smaller but more powerful. Sometimes, compensation is our greatest strength.

**Name your own capitalization learning, the
way that you turned a disadvantage into
an advantage in your leadership.**

ON POVERTY

Poverty is viewed by some as a divine punishment: People create their own misery, and, therefore, they must create their own success. It is a compelling argument but not one that favors humanity.

We might view poverty as a divine opportunity that affirms the love we have for others, particularly strangers, particularly those upon whom fate has smiled less. A Jewish mystical tradition contends that "the poor man is closer to God than anyone else . . . for God abides in these broken vessels, as it is written, 'I dwell on high, amid holiness, but also with the contrite and humble in spirit' (Isaiah 57:15). . . . Therefore, we have been taught that he who reviles the indigent scoffs at the Divinity. . . . Happy is he who encounters a poor man, for this poor man is a gift sent to him by God."

Every chance to give charity is an opportunity to encounter the divine spirit within others and ourselves. Instead of making a judgment about someone's poverty, make a commitment to ameliorating it. Goodness knows how hurt we have been by unfair judgment. As John Green wrote: "There is no Them. There are only facets of Us."

Don't allow the fog of determinism to cloud the open hand of generosity. Walk in the world with grace.

Make a point of combating homelessness today with a generosity of pocket and a generosity of spirit.

ON IRRITATION

We can feel it coming on in meetings, at airports and at lunches that drag on: that slight annoyance, slight impatience, slight anger, slight vexation that we call irritation. It's not full-blown to the point of exasperation. Exasperation would be too dramatic. Anger has outlets. Irritation stews and festers.

British journalist and novelist John Lanchester offered us this wonderful description of irritation in families in his novel *Capital*, about the postfinancial bust in modern-day London: "All the Kamals were fluent in irritation. They loved each other but were almost always annoyed by each other, in ways that were both generalized and existential (why is he like that?) and also highly specific (how hard is it to remember to put the top back on the yogurt?)."

The Kamals are a Pakistani family who own the corner store that sells newspapers, cigarettes and Cadbury bars. Here, irritation is a language, constantly spoken and felt.

"That was the main thing wrong with Mrs. Kamal. She spent such an extraordinary amount of mental energy feeling irritated that it was impossible not to feel irritated in turn. It was oxygen to her, this low-grade dissatisfaction, shading into anger; this sense that things weren't being done correctly."

Sometimes irritation becomes our oxygen, taking up lots of unnecessary space in our emotional landscape.

Give yourself an IQ (irritation quotient) test right now. How irritated are you generally and how could you better manage your irritation at work?

◆ DAY #142 ◆

ON DECISION MAKING

Are you a good decision maker? For some people, good decision making is about speed. If you've made a decision quickly, you can often get out of it quickly without being dragged down into ambivalence and torment.

For others, a good decision is made thoroughly and slowly, weighing the pros and cons carefully so that the consequences are laid out. Taking a lot of time, getting a lot of advice, considering all the possible contingencies, creates greater confidence and mental preparedness.

Barry Schwartz, in *The Paradox of Choice: Why More Is Less*, reminds us how many hundreds of types of shampoo or denim jeans or toothpaste we can purchase today. As consumers, we are exposed to decision overload:

"When people have no choice, life is almost unbearable. As the number of available choices increases, as it has in our consumer culture, the autonomy, control, and liberation this variety brings are powerful and positive. But as the number of choices keeps growing, negative aspects of having a multitude of options begin to appear. As the number of choices grows further, the negatives escalate until we become overloaded. At this point, choice no longer liberates, but debilitates. It might even be said to tyrannize."

Schwartz advises that we narrow our choices to three and pick one. It hurts to close an opportunity, but it may hurt more to keep every opportunity open.

Reduce a complex choice you have in front of you today to one of three choices.

✦ DAY #143 ✦

ON MANAGING UP

In *The Little Prince*, Antoine de Saint-Exupéry (1900–1944) created a planet ruled by a king with no subjects. When the Little Prince yawns, the king commands him to yawn. When he wants to ask a question, the king commands him to ask a question: "What the king fundamentally insisted upon was that his authority should be respected. He tolerated no disobedience. He was an absolute monarch. But, because he was a very good man, he made his orders reasonable."

Managing up requires an understanding of authority. Reasonable leaders want to use their authority to achieve the best for everyone. By managing up thoughtfully, you are making your boss better at his or her job. In *Managing Your Boss*, John Gabarro and John Kotter make the case that managing up and not only down and sideways is critical to leadership success: "Some people behave as if their bosses were not very dependent on them. They fail to see how much the boss needs their help and cooperation to do their job effectively. These people refuse to acknowledge that the boss can be severely hurt by their actions and needs cooperation, dependability, and honesty from them."

When the Little Prince took leave of the king, he observed that the king had "a magnificent air of authority." But he did have another thought as he continued his journey: "The grown-ups are very strange."

How can you invite those you manage to manage you?

✦ DAY #144 ✦

ON PHILANTHROPY

In August of 2012, *The Chronicle of Philanthropy* presented its most recent findings on charity related to state zip codes. Their starkest conclusion was reflected in the title of the article: "Wealthiest Don't Rate High on Giving Measure." Here are three of their findings:

"The rich aren't the most generous. Low-income earners give a far bigger share of their discretionary income to charities. People who make $50,000 to $75,000 give an average of 7.6 percent of their discretionary income to charity, compared with an average of 4.2 percent for people who make $100,000 or more."

"The 1 percent really are different. Rich people who live in neighborhoods with many other wealthy people give a smaller share of their incomes to charity than rich people who live in more economically diverse communities."

"Religion has a big influence on giving patterns. Regions of the country that are deeply religious are more generous than those that are not. Two of the top nine states—Utah and Idaho—have high numbers of Mormon residents, who have a tradition of tithing at least 10 percent of their income to the church. The remaining states in the top nine are all in the Bible Belt."

Arthur C. Brooks, author of *Who Really Cares*, concluded that religious people even give more to nonreligious charities, like the arts, medically based nonprofits and environmental causes.

Where is everyone else?

What's your zip code?

◆ DAY #145 ◆

ON MEMORY

"I have been forgetting things for years. . . . In my early days of forgetting things, words would slip away, and names. . . . I always knew that whatever I'd forgotten was going to come back to me sooner or later. Once I went to the store to buy a book about Alzheimer's disease and forgot the name of it. I thought it was funny. And it was, at the time."

These are the words of journalist and screenwriter Nora Ephron (1941–2012), in her essay in her book of the same title, "I Remember Nothing."

Sometimes, we believe that it is only a matter of retrieval, a process that may take time but will happen with patience. As we age or life gets more complex, we might come to terms with a different reality: that the idea, name or event we can't quite remember with clarity is never coming back.

"But here's the point: I have been forgetting things for years, but now I forget in a new way. I used to believe I could eventually retrieve whatever was lost and then commit it to memory. Now I know I can't possibly. Whatever is gone is hopelessly gone. And what's new doesn't stick."

In leadership, we are guilty. We forget a name, a significant event, the exact number on an account, the name of a colleague's wife. In each act of forgetting, we hurt someone. Forgetting is human. But it's still a problem.

What strategies do you use to strengthen your memory?

ON BEING SILLY

Leadership is serious business, so serious that we forget to have fun, to make jokes, to feel joy, to be silly. Horace gave us a good cocktail recipe: "Mix a little foolishness with your serious plans. It is lovely to be silly at the right moment."

Quintus Horatio Flaccus (65–8 BC)—Horace—was not exactly a comedian. He was an elegant poet of the ancient Roman world with friends among Rome's elite. He studied in Plato's Academy, and his elegant lines of poetry entertained the aristocrats of his day. With such a platform, it is hard to imagine the poet loosening up, and yet he believed in the loveliness of silliness.

To be silly is to be playful and creative, foolish or mindless. . . . It can be an adjective or a noun. You can be silly or you can be, silly.

Silliness is fun. Leadership can be too serious for fun. But fun reminds us how truly lucky we are, and it offers it own magnetism. When we take ourselves too seriously, we may also give others the impression we are superhuman and above having a good laugh or taking a pause for fresh air.

When was the last time you were silly?
Do something silly today.

ON SATISFICING

We hate making do, just getting by, finishing under the wire, stumbling ahead. We want excellence. But we can't always have it 24/7. Something's got to give.

In the 1950s, Herbert Simon, a professor of organizational psychology and political science, came up with the idea of *satisficing*, morphing the words *suffice* and *satisfy* into one verb that means almost its opposite, choosing an option that is not optimal but that seems best given the alternatives.

It is not hard to divide the world of leaders into two basic categories: maximizers and satisficers.

Debora L. Spar, president of Barnard College, wrote all about satisficing in *Wonder Women: Sex, Power and the Quest for Perfection*. She looked at the students in Barnard and across the life spectrum and observed that today "women are straining to reach impossible standards." In a newspaper interview, Spar said: "Satisficing is this concept in economics that jumped out at me as I was finishing the book. To satisfice is to settle for something that's second best. I use the term warily. You don't want to go out there and say that women should settle for second best. But sometimes second best is really good, and second best is much better than fourth best or worse. Women in particular feel if I didn't become the top CEO or perfect mother, I've somehow blown it."

Where can you satisfice more in your life right now?

◆ DAY #148 ◆

ON DELIBERATIVE PRACTICE

Geoff Colvin, author of *Talent Is Overrated*, warns that it's not enough to do something again and again. "Many people not only fail to become outstandingly good at what they do, no matter how many years they spend doing it, they frequently don't even get any better than they were when they started."

Colvin argues for deliberative practice, knowing how to do something correctly and then repeating it sufficiently for it to become an ingrained behavior. Top athletes, musicians and chess players practice for hours but they usually do so under the guidance of a coach or mentor, often working most on what they like to do least. Top performers also practice alone, seeing practice not as a social opportunity but as a time for intensified focus.

Colvin describes deliberative practice in terms of working on an activity with a defined and desired outcome that is difficult or personally challenging. The outcome needs to be something you can repeat again and again on the road to mastery. And the practitioner needs the benefit of an outside observer to determine if there is a notable improvement. If it's all about changing outcomes, the process itself has to be highly critiqued by someone who is invested in the individual's success.

"Being good at whatever we want to do is among the deepest sources of fulfillment we will ever know."

As a leader, determine one deliberative practice that would make you more effective. How are you going to get there?

✦ DAY #149 ✦

ON PUBLIC SPEAKING

If, when you get up to speak in public, your knees go weak, you breathe rapidly, the butterflies in your stomach are about to burst out of their respective cocoons and you begin to perspire, read on.

If you never suffer nervousness when you speak, if you find words easily and everyone high-fives you when you step down from a podium, read on.

Because public speaking is an art, it gets better with experience. If you're already a ten every time, make it an eleven. Work harder on dramatic beginnings. Explain your points more simply. Streamline your language so that every word feels necessary. Deliver a punch. Make it shorter. Show a broader emotional range. Refine the message. Close on a higher note. Develop a better charge.

As Cicero instructed, "A good orator is pointed and impassioned."

If you are a three or a four on the ten range, you know your job as a leader is compromised. It is nearly impossible to inspire followers if your talks are tepid, low on content and free of elegance. If you are nervous, your audience becomes nervous. No one wants to watch someone fail in public. Your audience wants to cheer. Give them a reason.

Dionysius of Halicarnassus warned: "Let thy speech be better than silence, or be silent."

Ralph Waldo Emerson wrote: "Speech is power: speech is to persuade, to convert, to compel." What will you do today to become a better public speaker?

✦ DAY #150 ✦

ON CLICHÉS

Nothing hurts more than a well-placed cliché. Ouch.

You had an opportunity to say something original, to move people to someplace new and fresh, and you decided instead to fall back on what's already been said and done a million times before. According to comedian Stephen Fry, "It is a cliché that most clichés are true, but then like most clichés, that cliché is untrue." So why did you reach for the cliché?

Were you lazy? Or were you hiding?

People often hide the complexity of an issue behind a cliché. When seeking an answer or a solid response to a difficult challenge, the cliché always offers itself up as a benign alternative.

Smoke screens dissipate. It does not take long.

In thinking about literary characters, the Portuguese Nobel Prize winner José Saramago shared his approach: "I never appreciated 'positive heroes' in literature. They are almost always clichés, copies of copies, until the model is exhausted. I prefer perplexity, doubt, uncertainty, not just because it provides more 'productive' literary raw material, but because that is the way we humans really are."

Saramago identified why clichés fail to move us: They do not acknowledge the complexity of being human and the odd confluence of factors that contribute to the uniqueness of any given moment.

Following the advice of Samuel Goldwyn—"Let's have some new clichés"—check yourself today for overuse of an empty filler. Be the original you were created to be.

✦ DAY #151 ✦

ON REFRAINING

The American Buddhist nun Pema Chodron, in *Comfortable with Uncertainty*, wrote that the choice to refrain from an act is "the quality of not grabbing for entertainment the minute we feel a slight edge of boredom coming on." We all do it. We do it more than ever before. We have a few minutes of downtime but then we quickly fill them. We grab a cell phone, play a few minutes of a video game, check messages, text a friend. We can't stay in the pause for long.

"Refraining—not habitually acting out impulsively—has something to do with giving up the entertainment mentality. Through refraining, we see that there's something between the arising of the craving—or the aggression or the loneliness or whatever it might be—and whatever action we take as a result. There's something there in us that we don't want to experience, and we never do experience, because we're so quick to act."

Refraining means that we don't use up all the available space and time—we step back and away from it. We allow ourselves to stay in the moment between thought and action that could have been about impulse but instead became an act of patience.

What is it about human nature that fears quiet and equates it with boredom? For leaders, the impulse to act first and think later comes too naturally.

The next time you are about to say something you shouldn't, visualize a large red stop sign in front of you. Pause. You can do better.

ON FRIENDSHIP

Order of Cistercians
Ewell Monastery Water Lane
West Malling
Kent ME 19 6HH

This is the address of a former monastery where only the chapel and one monk remains. The Order of the Cistercians is a religious order of Catholic monks and nuns, based on the name of monastery in a small village in France, an experiment from 1966 to 2004 that never had more than five members. Father Aelred, the remaining monk today, took the name of another Aelred, a medieval Cistercian monk who wrote *Spiritual Friendship* between 1164 and 1167. The core of the texts was woven together from Cicero's *On Friendship*, Ambrose's *On the Duties of the Clergy* and Augustine's *Confessions*.

Aelred the ancient offered us the key components to spiritual friendship: "There are four qualities which characterize a friend: loyalty, right intention, discretion and patience."

Aelred described the joy: "How happy, how carefree, how joyful you are if you have a friend with whom you may talk as freely as with yourself, to whom you neither fear to confess any fault nor blush at revealing any spiritual progress, to whom you may entrust all the secrets of your heart and confide all your plans. And what is more delightful than to unite spirit to spirit and so to make one out of two?"

Think of one person who is a spiritual friend to
you. What makes yours a spiritual friendship?

ON SERENITY

"Be calm. God awaits you at the door."

This is an invitation to serenity.

Nobel Prize–winning South American novelist Gabriel García Márquez, in *Love in the Time of Cholera*, extended this invitation to a character in the novel, offering us this observation: "If I knew that today would be the last time I'd see you, I would hug you tight and pray the Lord be the keeper of your soul. If I knew that this would be the last time you pass through this door, I'd embrace you, kiss you, and call you back for one more. If I knew that this would be the last time I would hear your voice, I'd take hold of each word to be able to hear it over and over again. If I knew this is the last time I see you, I'd tell you I love you, and would not just assume foolishly you know it already."

It is impossible to read this without the impulse to reach out to someone we love with urgency.

Serenity enters our lives only when we allow it to find shelter within us, when we take responsibility for creating our own unhappinesses and invite ourselves to stand before a happier door.

> **Leadership can feel so turbulent and dramatic at times that we lose the portal into serenity. What can you do today to access your emotional oasis?**

ON INTROVERSION

Susan Cain has something to say about introverts. "There's zero correlation between being the best talker and having the best ideas," wrote Cain, author of the book *Quiet*. Introverts unite. Cain claimed that her introversion is her greatest strength: "I have such a strong inner life that I'm never bored and only occasionally lonely. No matter what mayhem is happening around me, I know I can always turn inward." Cain said she does not need others to entertain her.

"Don't think of introversion as something that needs to be cured."

Introverts, according to Cain, are neither timid nor afraid to talk. They just have different notions of what makes for good communication and relationships; they prefer to go deep. Cain made an important distinction between being shy and being introverted: "Shyness is the fear of social disapproval or humiliation, while introversion is a preference for environments that are not overstimulating. Shyness is inherently painful; introversion is not."

Leaders come in all kinds of packages, and Cain offered this word for leaders: "We don't need giant personalities to transform companies. We need leaders who build not their own egos but the institutions they run."

"Everyone shines given the right lighting," claims Cain. What lighting helps you shine if you're an introvert, and how can you let introverts you work with shine on their own terms?

✦ DAY #155 ✦

ON DELIGHT

Delight is a hard thing to contain. It's the kind of glee we feel when something we've worked on for a long time comes to a satisfying end. It's the laugh that escapes us when we create a team that works well together and whose members really enjoy each other's company. It's the smile of pride when we've supervised someone who has grown because of our advice.

Delight doesn't last long. It can get quickly eclipsed by worry or boredom. We must take delight in it when it happens, that momentary burst of pleasure that makes everything worthwhile.

The writer W. Somerset Maugham (1874–1965) made exactly

this point: "Nothing in the world is permanent, and we're foolish when we ask anything to last, but surely we're still more foolish not to take delight in it while we have it."

Maugham had a rough start in life. He lost both his parents before he was ten. He served in the First World War and found himself in an unhappy marriage. He once wrote of never feeling that those he loved ever properly reciprocated his feelings. Perhaps he understood the importance of holding on to a rare moment of enchantment, embracing a little magic before it slipped out of his fingers.

Pause on a moment of delight today at work. See how precious it is. Hold it tightly. Share it.

✦ DAY #156 ✦

ON MONEY

The Australian philosopher John Armstrong wrote a short book for the School of Life series on big questions we have in this lifetime. Armstrong's book is called *How to Worry Less About Money*, and it may be worth the money to buy the book if only for its cover.

Armstrong made the case that there are two kinds of anxieties: money troubles and money worries. Money troubles, he argued, have to do with actual financial difficulties.

Money worries have less to do with the reality of money in our lives and more to do with emotions and fantasies around money that we may never be able to satisfy. This inability causes immense anxiety: envy of others, perceived status that comes with money, the inability to make distinctions between what we need and what we desire.

"One's relationship with money is lifelong, it colors one's sense of identity, it shapes one's attitude to other people, it connects and splits generations; money is the arena in which greed and generosity are played out, in which wisdom is exercised and folly committed. Freedom, desire, power, status, work, possession: These huge ideas that rule life are enacted, almost always, in and around money."

Armstrong recommended that people list their worries about money and delve deeper to see if the problem is really money or the symptom of a larger fear of adult life.

**Name the worries you have about money
and what they really represent.**

✦ DAY #157 ✦

ON PERSUASION

Persuasion was the last novel by Jane Austen (1775–1817) before her untimely death. Austen did not even name the book, which was provisionally called *The Elliots* but was renamed by her family with a punchier title upon publication. If she intended it with a family-based story, then why go with a title suggesting that someone was convinced of something?

The novel centers around an initial act of persuasion that sets the plot in motion. Lady Russell persuades Anne not to marry Captain Wentworth; he would not be able, in Lady Russell's well-intentioned argument, to support her properly. "She was persuaded to believe the engagement a wrong thing—indiscreet, improper, hardly capable of success, not deserving it." The plot unravels; Anne is wistful and sad about how she allowed herself to be persuaded and how her future would have been different had she not subjected herself to Lady Russell's advice.

Leaders often achieve a position of prominence through the powers of persuasion. They can make the case coherently, articulately and thoughtfully. But it is a gift to be used lightly. Be careful that the advice you give is not about you. Persuasion, at *its* best, helps others achieve *their* best. Anything less is self-serving.

**Desmond Tutu once said, "Don't raise your voice,
improve your argument." Persuade someone
you know to do something that will improve
his or her life—even in some small way.**

ON ATTRACTION

In his book *Leaders Who Transform Society*, Micha Popper, a professor of organizational psychology, described this scene from a Japanese war movie. The soldiers are weighed down with battle fatigue. Yet when, in the distance, they suddenly notice their leader waving from a hilltop, they soon straighten and sparkle. Their energy returns. When the camera closes in on the leader, it becomes clear that he is not actually alive but being held up in order to inspire his soldiers.

Popper offered three explanations why leaders are so potently attractive that we make ourselves bigger and more attractive in their presence. This is the psychoanalytic approach to the law of attraction.

Then there is the cognitive psychological explanation. Since people generally ascribe more power and responsibility to people than to the complex dynamic of a situation, leaders are both more available and more representative in our minds than events. Leaders are more accessible to us for the purposes of explanation than "evaluating and judging informatively complex situations."

Popper then introduces the social psychological explanation. We are attracted to leaders because they model attitudes, decisions and behaviors that we need to help us sort out our own identities.

We are attracted to leaders. We can also become repelled by them. Be the kind of leader that attracts because people can see a better version of themselves in you.

What is your most attractive character trait, and how can you make it more visible today?

ON BLISS

"If I look upon my whole life, I cannot think of another time when I felt more comfortable: when I had no worries, fears, or desires, when my life seemed as soft and lovely as lying inside a cocoon of rose silk." Amy Tan used this description of bliss in her first novel and runaway best-seller, *The Joy Luck Club*. With its story of the difficulties of living in two worlds, unhappy in both—overlaid by the tensions of a mother and daughter caught in a widening generational and cultural gap—the novel seems an unlikely place to discover bliss.

We think of bliss as an anxiety-free state in which we experience no aches and pains, where we are cosseted and loved.

If you're a leader, you are paid to manage tension—and not only your own—and not to supply bliss. Bliss—with its inviting, hanging *hiss* at the end—seems a faraway fantasy, the purview of those whose lives are easier than yours.

In the *Dhammapada*, a collection of sayings attributed to the Buddha that reflect a special occasion or situation in Buddha's life and community, we find this blessing of bliss: "Now may every living thing, young or old, weak or strong, living near or far, known or unknown, living or departed or yet unborn, may every living thing be full of bliss."

**Create the conditions of bliss today—if possible—and
stay in those moments a little longer than usual.**

ON CONTROVERSY

John Newton (1725–1807) was an Anglican minister who wrote "Amazing Grace." He was once asked by a fellow minister if he should write an article criticizing the theological beliefs of a colleague. Newton wrote back:

"As you are likely to be engaged in controversy, and your love of truth is joined with a natural warmth of temper, my friendship makes me solicitous on your behalf. You are of the strongest side; for truth is great, and must prevail; so that a person of abilities inferior to yours might take the field with a confidence of victory. I am not therefore anxious for the event of the battle; but I would have you more than a conqueror, and to triumph, not only over your adversary, but over yourself. . . .

"And yet we find but very few writers of controversy who have not been manifestly hurt by it. . . . What will it profit a man if he gains his cause and silences his adversary, if at the same time he loses that humble, tender frame of spirit in which the Lord delights, and to which the promise of his presence is made?

"Your aim, I doubt not, is good; but you have need to watch and pray for you will find Satan at your right hand to resist you."

Some people love controversy. Proving someone else wrong can be satisfying—and cruel.

**Think of a good fight you were going
to pick right now, and hold off.**

✦ DAY #161 ✦

ON BEGINNINGS

Dunamis is an ancient Greek word used in schools of philosophy to describe the move from potentiality to actuality, the power that animates us to go from one to the other. It all begins with a beginning.

Dunamis is also the title of a book by Israelmore Ayivor, a spiritual writer from Ghana who ponders human motivation and religion. Ayivor shares his own fear of beginnings.

"What should be standing in the shoes of passion, and be walking on the plans of action is sitting in the ink on the paper. Why? Because of the fear to start."

Ayivor wrote of his belief that "God does not give a forward movement to someone who is already on the wrong path as an answer to his/her prayer. He tells you to GO BACK and begin well!"

Walk back to the beginning. Start again. Take strength from the first step in the *right* direction. It's not enough to start. We have to start well.

If we can't begin because we lack faith in ourselves, Ayivor pushes us again. "Self-esteem is the switch in the circuit of your life that dims the brightness of your future. Bring it low and you don't shine your light; raise it up and you brighten the corner where you are."

Begin and shine.

**What do you need to begin today that you
have been putting off? Begin well.**

✦ DAY #162 ✦

ON SACRED SPACES

One of the names of God in Hebrew is *Makom*, or "place." It is a great spiritual paradox to call an intangible God a place, but it speaks to the human need to locate ourselves within time *and* space. When praying or studying, traditional Jews often pick a *makom kavua*, or regular and routine space in order to have an established place where they can carry out their daily rituals and locate themselves spiritually.

This same recommendation is present in many other faiths.

For as long as space exists
And sentient beings endure,
May I, too, remain,
To dispel the misery of the world.

In this Buddhist prayer of the bodhisattva, the individual assumes that as long as space exists and that the person praying exists, there is the possibility of redeeming pain and suffering.

We all need to identify and seek out places from which blessings emanate, especially when we are not feeling very blessed and need a sacred space to nourish us. We create all kinds of cathedrals in our lives, spaces where we make offerings, be they real or only imagined. What we don't always realize is that while we are giving, we are also taking, because we need the space to fill in a void, to hold out joy, thanksgiving, guilt, pain and forgiveness.

**Create—if you do not already have one—a
sacred space where you can anchor and center
yourself and receive and give blessings.**

✦ DAY #163 ✦

ON PUNCTUALITY

"I've been on a calendar, but I have never been on time," said Marilyn Monroe.

Those of us who work hard at being on time have trouble understanding lateness. It seems selfish and self-important.

Journalist Alexandra Petri tried to explain her chronic lateness in her article "In Defense of the Habitually Late." Here are the lies she tells about time.

"I am coming downstairs: I will respond to an e-mail, eight minutes will pass, then I will come downstairs.

"I am a block away: I am two blocks away.

"I am five minutes away: I am ten minutes away.

"I am seventeen minutes away: I am giving you an oddly specific number to disguise the fact that I am probably something like half an hour away.

"Twenty minutes away! I am lost somewhere miles away, but optimistic.

"I'm en route! I am still in my apartment."

Petri wrote: "The curse of the habitually late person is to be surrounded by early people. Early people do not think of themselves as Early People. They think of themselves as Right."

She concluded that lateness is great, but that's only for those who are late. It stinks for the rest of us.

Please don't use the fact that you are busy to excuse the fact that you are late. We're all busy. Try an apology, a dose of honesty and a new watch.

**Name an event that you would never
be late for and explain why.**

◆ DAY #164 ◆

ON READING

Many leaders claim they don't have a minute to read. But reading helps us escape, relax, enter another world, critique, argue and think.

Will Schwalbe discovered another reason to read when he created an informal book club with his mother during her diagnosis and losing battle with cancer. He wrote in *The End of Your Life Book Club*: "Books had always been a way for my mother and me to introduce and explore topics that concerned us but made us uneasy, and they had also always given us something to talk about when we were stressed or anxious. Like all book clubs, conversation jumped between text and life.

"She never wavered in her conviction that books are the most powerful tool in the human arsenal, that reading all kinds of books . . . is the grandest entertainment and is also how you take part in the human conversation. . . . Books really do matter: They're how we know what to do in life, and how we tell others . . . books can be how we get closer to each other, and stay close, even in the case of a mother and son who were very close to each other to begin with, and even after one of them has died."

**Explain, in one hundred words or less, why you read.
How can it bring you closer to those you lead?**

ON CONFORMITY

New York Times columnist David Brooks believes that we are extremely confused today about one question: When should you care about what other people think and when should you not? Should we care about religious or political views that make us unpopular, or the fact that we've fallen in love with someone no one likes? In "Other People's Views" (February 6, 2014), he wrote:

"Officially, we tell each other we don't care. We are heirs to a 19th-century rugged individualism that says the individual should stand strong and self-reliant, not conform to the crowd. We are also heirs to a 20th-century ethic of authenticity that holds that each of us is called to be true to our sincere inner self, and that if we bend to please others we are failing in some fundamental way." We want to be admired and that often means locking ourselves into the conventions expected by those in our communities and limiting our individualism.

That's not always a bad thing. We need others, if only to help us figure ourselves out and determine the boundaries of what is conventional, acceptable or out there. We may be fine with bucking the trend, we may even revel in it. Or in the immortal words of John Lennon: "It's weird not to be weird." We determine who we are by acting and reacting to something and to someone.

Name one thing you do that others would consider weird.

ON MORAL RESPONSIBILITY

"You shall surely admonish your neighbor" (Leviticus 19:17).

As more politicians, athletes and celebrities get mired in

scandal, leadership loses its noble edge, its sense that we give authority to those who are moral exemplars. The more senior that leaders become, the more feedback they need, but the less feedback they receive. As the relationship between leadership and ethics has thinned, colleagues have become increasingly wary of giving leaders feedback. They are afraid that if they see something and say something that they may change the relationship or compromise their jobs. This has punctured the fabric of the moral responsibility that we should feel toward each other.

Maimonides (1135–1204), the Spanish philosopher and physician, interpreted the Leviticus directive above as a moral obligation to improve others. In his *Laws of Character* (6:7), he codified the commandment to rebuke another in this very light. "It is a commandment for a person who sees that his fellow . . . has sinned or is following an improper path [to attempt] to correct his behavior and to inform him that he is causing himself a loss by his evil deeds. . . . Whoever can chastise a wrongdoer and fails to do so is considered responsible for that error for he had the opportunity to rebuke the [wrongdoer]."

**Identify a moral lapse that
requires your involvement.**

✦ DAY #167 ✦

ON ENERGY

We get energy from many different sources. In *The Celestine Prophecy*, a spiritual metaphor of a journey to discover truth, energy comes from putting oneself in a place that gives a good vibe. "The human perception of this energy first begins with a heightened sensitivity to beauty." Beautiful places increase our energy. We know that putting ourselves in certain places heightens our energy, while other locations deplete it.

James Redfield quit his job to write *The Celestine Prophecy* and then self-published it to reflect many of the spiritual truths he studied from philosophy and Far Eastern religions. He probably never expected it to sell more than 20 million copies and spend weeks and weeks on the *New York Times* best-seller list. Redfield hit a powerful nerve. People were seeking, and one of the things they were seeking was stronger, more positive energy sources—and a means of actually becoming moved and inspired by that energy.

The problem, Redfield contended, is how we usually get our energy: "We humans have always sought to increase our personal energy in the only manner we have known, by seeking to psychologically steal it from the others—an unconscious competition that underlies all human conflict in the world."

We don't need to steal energy. We just need to make it.

Identify places, people and activities that could give you a positive energy surge now.

✦ DAY #168 ✦

ON DETACHMENT

The lotus is a symbol of detachment and appears in virtually all Hindu sacred writings. The goddess Lakshmi holds one in her hand, as does Lord Vishnu. The Buddha is often depicted sitting on a lotus. A disciple of Confucius said he loved the stunning flower "because while growing from the mud, it is unstained." The lotus also flowers petal by petal, representing the expansion of the soul and the unfolding of wisdom. The dome of the Taj Mahal is fashioned after an upside-down lotus flower.

The lotus stands alone, separate and distinct from the muddy waters in which it grows.

In the Buddhist tradition, detachment is not about seclusion, isolation or aloofness but a conscious and intentional choice to be able to relinquish objects, thoughts, drives and sometimes even relationships. There are three types of withdrawal: physical detachment, mental detachment and detachment from suffering. Water drips off the lotus petals.

The Buddha warned that detachment could come with a spiritual price tag. When we withdraw from conventional life, we may develop feelings of superiority, pride, arrogance, judgment and hypocrisy. The lotus is in danger of lording its beauty over that which is more simple and less ornate. Free of pain, of lust, of suffering, of compassionless existence, we too can flower. Detachment allows wisdom to expand us, petal by petal.

Name one area of your leadership that would benefit from detachment right now.

✦ DAY #169 ✦

ON FIXING OTHERS

Ah, the leadership temptation to fix others.

Judith Martin, best known as Miss Manners, warned us to be wary of fixers:

"Miss Manners has been accosted by a variety of people who do missionary work under the pretense of friendship, generously spreading their newly acquired insights in the hope of making others as attractive as themselves. . . . The zeal of such people is so great that they will spare nothing, not even the feelings of those they want to save, in the quest to make others feel good. If you are skeptical about their solutions working for you, then affect a patronizing smile and say, 'That's the way I felt once.'"

You may wonder at an advice columnist who is not filled with zeal for fixing others. But Miss Manners has revealed to us her secret: "Miss Manners corrects only upon request. Then she does it from a distance, with no names attached, and no personal relationship, however distant, between the corrector and the correctee. She does not search out errors like a policeman leaping out of a speed trap."

Keep your fix-it instinct in check all day, no matter how much patience and lip-biting are involved.

ON ILLNESS

Even leaders get sick. The crack in their armor of invincibility begins to show, but they often feel pressure to dismiss it: "I don't have time to get sick," as if saying it were enough to take an illness off the schedule. Leaders used to pushing themselves believe that ignoring illness is another way to show leadership, toughing it out for sniffles and sore throats. But every once in a while illness stops us in our tracks because we cannot push the limits any longer.

"Why do some people find hope despite facing severe illness, while others do not?"

This question opens Jerome Groopman's book *The Anatomy of Hope: How People Prevail in the Face of Illness*. Hope, Groopman wrote, is not the same as optimism; hope is "rooted in unalloyed reality." He set out to understand how and why hope worked and when it didn't. He met patients who hoped they would get better even when confronting difficult but not impossible medical odds. He met doctors who gave patients false hope and spoke to those who gave up hope on their bodies but still hoped for their souls. "To hope under the most extreme circumstances is an act of defiance that permits a person to live his life on his own terms. It is part of the human spirit to endure and give a miracle a chance to happen."

When was the last time you *let* yourself be sick?

ON MATURITY

I don't know what I want to be when I grow up, you joke. But in your mind, you know two things to be true: (1) You are still restless and unsure of who you are, and (2) you are grown up.

In his short story "White Nights," Fyodor Dostoyevsky

(1821–1881) wrote: "You do grow up, you do outgrow your ideals, which turn to dust and ashes, which are shattered into fragments; and if you have no other life, you just have to build one up out of these fragments. And all the time your soul is craving and longing for something else."

We love the spirit of childhood, as Jesus remarked in Luke: "Let the little children come to me, and do not hinder them, for the kingdom of God belongs to such as these. I tell you the truth, anyone who will not receive the kingdom of God like a little child will never enter it" (18:16–17).

Yet at some point we all need a mature and professional persona. The apostle Paul understood that there comes a time to mature. We cannot hold on to childhood forever, nor should we:

"When I was a child, I spoke as a child, I understood as a child, I thought as a child: but when I became a man, I put away childish things (I Corinthians 13:11).

**Describe an interaction in which you were
proud of your mature leadership.**

✦ DAY #172 ✦

ON COGNITIVE
DISSONANCE

In the 1950s, the psychologist Leon Festinger infiltrated a group who believed the world was coming to an end on December 21, 1954. It didn't. Did this group have the capacity to realize the error of its beliefs?

This famous psychological research appears in Carol Tavris and Elliot Aronson's book on the justification of foolish beliefs, *Mistakes Were Made (But Not by Me)*. The authors are both psychologists themselves who are interested in "the engine that drives self-justification" and "the energy that produces the need to justify our decisions and actions."

On December 20, a group leader, Marian Keech, promised that a spaceship would be coming to take her people to safety. Some of her followers sold their homes and quit their jobs. Keech gathered them together. Festinger made a prediction: Those who had sold their things or made commitments to this prediction would justify the mistake. Those who had not would lose their faith in Keech. (Her own husband went to bed that night.) That morning, when the spaceship did not show, Keech came up with a new prophecy: "The world had been spared, she said, because of the impressive faith of her little band." The group's mood "shifted from despair to exhilaration." Those who had not proselytized before had new zeal.

Leon Festinger came up with an expression to describe this behavior: cognitive dissonance.

What decision have you spent too much time defending?

✦ DAY #173 ✦

ON COMMUNICATION

"Why is there such an epidemic of 'poor communications' within organizations?" asked Margaret J. Wheatley in *Leadership and the New Science: Discovering Order in a Chaotic World*. In every organization with which she has ever been involved, she said, this has been the number one complaint of employees. She became numb to the problem, assuming it was a simple cover for deeper issues, masking the real problems at the heart of organizational failure.

"Now I know I was wrong. . . . They were right. They were suffering from problems related to information. Asking them to identify smaller, more specific issues was pushing them in exactly the wrong direction, because the real problems were big—bigger than anything I imagined."

Communication problems center around how we regard and treat information: as a tangible commodity. We expect and need information to be "controllable, stable and obedient" and, therefore, manageable. Instead, information is fluid and in a continual process of reorganizing itself, as if it is literally "in-formation."

When there is not enough transparency, misinformation, gossip and rumors have lots of room to grow. The office is like a petri dish, blooming all kinds of untruths in the absence of solid and open communication.

Not telling people what is going on does not help them function better in their jobs but creates a rumor mill. Who started it? You did. You didn't say enough, early enough and with enough direction. Trust yourself more. Trust the people you lead more.

**Make an intentional effort at transparency
and "overcommunication" today.**

✦ DAY #174 ✦

ON THE BODY

"I like to think I treat my body like a temple. A Temple of Doom, but a temple nonetheless."

Are you taking care of yourself? Comedian Jim Gaffigan isn't. In fact, he has made laziness into an art form: "I'm a fan of relaxing, and when I get tired of relaxing, I like to do nothing." This attitude has spilled over into his ideas about nutrition and exercise, as he writes in *Food: A Love Story*: "Has peeling an orange ever really been worth it?"

Taking care of the body, for some leaders, seems a luxury or a waste of time. Yet if the body housing the heart and soul is not cared for, then the heart and soul may one day have to find somewhere else to live.

There's an old Weight Watchers saying: "Nothing tastes as good as thin feels." (I for one can think of a thousand things that taste better than thin feels.)

Taking care of yourself also means getting enough sleep. Gaffigan has a few words on that in his book, *Dad Is Fat*: "I love sleep. I need sleep. We all do, of course. There are those people that don't need sleep. I think they're called 'successful.'"

Take a few minutes to schedule a checkup, exam, test or meeting with a nutritionist. Get a good night's sleep. Do something to show you love and will nurture your body today.

✦ DAY #175 ✦

ON ACCOMPLISHMENT

"I've always had a healthy sense of myself and my abilities. I tend to say what I'm thinking and what I believe. I don't have much patience for incompetence," said a successful scientist.

"These are traits that have mostly served me well. But there are times, believe it or not, when I've come across as arrogant and tactless." (In university, he made a friend who described him as so confident he was "universally acclaimed as the person quickest to offend someone he just met.")

Accomplishment is the currency in professional relationships: the need to impress, the desire to imprint, the need to be seen and heard above others.

One day, a colleague and mentor of this successful scientist took him for a walk, put his arm around his shoulder and said, "It's such a shame that people perceive you as being so arrogant, because it's going to limit what you're going to be able to accomplish in life."

Randy Pausch (1960–2008) accomplished a great deal in his life before pancreatic cancer robbed him of a future. He was a professor of computer science, an award-winning teacher, a devoted husband and father. When he gave his famous last lecture, he told his audience it was for his kids, and he showed a photo of himself holding all three of his children.

Sometimes, if we are really lucky, someone will put an arm around us and remind us how unimportant we are.

Name a moment of profound humility.

✦ DAY #176 ✦

ON WHAT-IFS

"What if choosing to read this page at this moment is also a choice *not* to stand on your head, go to France or do a million other things?"

"What-if" questions can torment us. What if I had picked a better career? Married a different person? Bought that stock when it was at a low? We imagine, with just one stroke of a what-if question, we could have been smarter, more sensitive, more risk taking or more patient. But we're not.

Miggs Burroughs is a graphic artist who has designed flags and postage stamps and wrote a whole book of what-if questions.

"What if you were to write an ad for the story of your life? Would it be full of hype or hope?"

"What if hurting, leaving and ending are just mirror images of healing, arriving and starting?"

"What if your thoughts and values suddenly appeared as pictures all over your body? Would you stay inside or go to the beach?"

You cannot be a leader and not ask what-if questions. They often form the core of personal and organizational vision and offer strategic possibilities. They can unfold the future.

**Think of one what-if question about the past that
it is time to throw away and entertain one what-if
question about the present that it is time to answer.**

ON PROCRASTINATION

You'll often hear people say that they wait until the last minute because they work best that way. The adrenaline pump pushes them forward into a vortex of creativity and productivity. But waiting until the very edge of a deadline means that it becomes harder to review and check your work or that of others, deal with late, unexpected problems and minimize the sense of creeping anxiety that others may feel who are depending on you.

Addicted to the rush, you languish while they panic.

If you're a leader, others are watching you procrastinate, observing how you keep pushing away responsibilities until they simply fall off your desk. Your last-minute approach so often becomes their next problem. Gee, thanks.

Motivational speaker and writer Denis Waitley wrote: "Time is an equal opportunity employer. Each human being has exactly the same number of hours and minutes every day. Rich people can't buy more hours. Scientists can't invent new minutes. And you can't save time to spend it on another day. Even so, time is amazingly fair and forgiving. No matter how much time you've wasted in the past, you still have an entire tomorrow."

Think of a *New Yorker* cartoon of a man standing behind a corporate desk, scheduling a meeting on the phone: "No, Thursday's out. How is never—is never good for you?"

**Get something done today—big or small—
that you've been putting off for too long.**

ON REGRET

We all carry big regrets—failed important relationships, bad career decisions, hurt people we love; and small regrets—things we didn't buy or affection we didn't share, things we did or said that we wish we could vacuum back into nonexistence.

In the biblical story of Joseph, our hero was thrown into a pit and hated by his brothers for being overly sure of himself; he was sold into slavery but then worked his way up.

Then came the gob-smacking moment when Joseph became a vizier of Egypt and confronted his brothers who came to Egypt begging for food. When he finally revealed his identity, they staggered in shock. "Then Joseph said to his brothers, 'Come close to me.' When they had done so, he said, 'I am your brother Joseph, the one you sold into Egypt! And now, do not be distressed and do not be angry with yourselves for selling me here, because it was to save lives that God sent me ahead of you. . . . God sent me ahead of you to preserve for you a remnant on earth and to save your lives by a great deliverance'" (Genesis 45:4–17).

The brothers' criminal mistake led to fortuitous consequences, as do many bad decisions. Arthur Miller once said: "Maybe all one can do is hope to end up with the right regrets."

> **You regret bad decisions less when you can shape them into good outcomes. Identify a regret that you can turn into a win.**

ON DISTRUST

"If you haven't got anything nice to say about anybody come sit next to me," said Alice Roosevelt Longworth.

Researchers are trying to convince us that gossip is good. It minimizes bullying. "Groups that allow their members to gossip sustain cooperation and deter selfishness better than those who don't. And groups do even better if they can gossip and ostracize unworthy members," concluded a researcher at Stanford University. Often a selfish or exploitative person will be left out of a group intentionally and may have to adjust his or her behaviors to be accepted. We may adjust ourselves to be more kind and generous to create a better impression and reputation.

But wait a second before you head out to the watercooler. What about the distrust and toxicity that pervade office cultures where gossip is the norm? As a leader, your distrust can be the most dangerous and enervating of all.

The satisfaction from gossip is only temporary, like that piece of rich cake that you probably should have refused. When it comes to gossip, a moment on the lips and our relationships slip.

And don't forget: If you leave the watercooler too early, then *you* become the topic of conversation.

Elevate your leadership today by *not* saying something.

＋ DAY #180 ＋

ON HATE

Václav Havel (1936–2011) had a thing or two to say about hate: "The person who hates is never able to see the cause of his metaphysical failure in himself and the way he so completely overestimates his own worth. In his eyes, it is the surrounding world that is to blame." The hater, Havel claimed, must hang his strong enmity on something.

"It has to be personified, because hatred—as a very particular kind of tumescence of the soul—requires a particular object. And so the person who hates seeks out a particular offender. Of course this offender is merely a stand-in, arbitrarily chosen and therefore easily replaceable. I have observed that, for the hater, hatred is more important than its object."

Havel was painfully aware of how hard he fought against a regime and the dangers of sudden power when he led the same country.

"It is said that those who hate suffer from an inferiority complex. This may not be the most precise way to put it. I would, rather, say that they are people with a complex based on the fatal perception that the world does not appreciate their true worth." The hateful person feels himself unloved, worthy of praise that eludes him.

Leaders sometimes have to lead people who hate them. It pays, therefore, to understand them.

**Think of a hater. How can you engage that
individual differently based on Havel's insights?**

✦ DAY #181 ✦

ON RESIGNATION

We accept fate as if we have no choices, as if what happens to us is inevitable, and we are merely passive recipients. Leaders want to manipulate their circumstances, control what happens, shape an exciting future. When we think of what it means to resign professionally, it means taking ourselves out of the competition, leaving a job because we simply cannot change the conditions and create our own successes.

Irish poet W. B. Yeats (1865–1939) captured resignation as a falcon in the falconer's view.

Turning and turning in the widening gyre
The falcon cannot hear the falconer;
Things fall apart; the center cannot hold;
Mere anarchy is loosed upon the world,

The blood-dimmed tide is loosed, and everywhere
The ceremony of innocence is drowned;
The best lack all conviction, while the worst
Are full of passionate intensity.

Turning and turning, the circle in the sky widens. Things fall apart because "the center cannot hold." Conviction wanes or, worse, mediocrity assumes its own intensity. We relinquish our privilege or our position because our center cannot hold anymore; it becomes a signal for us that it is time to leave. It is not always easy to know when it is time to go. Leaders can stay where they are not wanted or well-served because they think they can fix "it" when it may be broken beyond repair or out of their control.

Think of a time when you should have accepted a situation but spent too much time fighting it. Why?

✦ DAY #182 ✦

ON FAILURE

"My life has been nothing but a failure.

"I'm not performing miracles, I'm using up and wasting a lot of paint . . ."

Reading this confession makes us feel the dejection of this artist. There was only one thing he lauded: his work as a gardener.

Every day I discover
more and more
beautiful things.
It's enough to drive one mad.
I have such a desire
to do everything,
my head is bursting with it.

He was surrounded by beauty, even if he felt he could not replicate it well on canvas. His head was bursting with saturated color from nature's palette: "Color is my day-long obsession, joy and torment." He kept at painting because it enabled him to spend time outdoors—in *plein air*—in his beloved garden. "I am following Nature without being able to grasp her; I perhaps owe having become a painter to flowers." The pictures Claude Monet (1840–1926) made were meant to put his garden on canvas.

The *New Yorker* once ran a cartoon of two people in Monet T-shirts, carrying Monet water-lily umbrellas standing on the bridge at Giverny, looking out on Monet's water lilies. Despite his popularity today, Monet saw himself as a failure during his own lifetime, an artist who lacked talent and wasted paint.

It was enough to wash the canvas in this love to make others love what he loved. That much love can never result in failure.

**Name something you love so much
that it can never fail you.**

✦ DAY #183 ✦

ON ENDURANCE

When Christopher Huh was thirteen years old and learning about the Holocaust in his Maryland middle school, he could not believe it had ever happened. As a Korean-American, this was not part of his own cultural heritage. It seemed to defy any understanding he had of the safe world in which he lived. He went home and began his own research. It was all true and worse than he imagined.

To organize all the information he had collected, he started a graphic novel called *Keeping My Hope*. It was a way to remember and integrate the many facts and details of World War II that he was learning in school. It took him thousands of hours of research, writing and drawing, approximately a year and a half. He sorted and organized all of these facts into a compelling story of a grandfather named Ari who shares his survivor memories of the Holocaust with his granddaughter Sarah by reliving them with the reader.

On the last page of the book, Ari takes a photo with his living children and grandchildren. Moments before, he looks at a photo of the first family he had that he lost during the war. 'Through those years, I never thought I would have another family."

Suddenly joy arrives. A new life unfolds because of survival. And the story of survival endures because a thirteen-year-old decided he was not afraid to face its sadness and redeem it.

What trauma has taught you endurance?

◆ DAY #184 ◆

ON PROSPERITY

"Jabez cried out to the God of Israel, saying, 'Oh that you would bless me and enlarge my territory! Let your hand be with me, and keep me from the evil one.' And God granted his request" (I Chronicles 4:9–10).

We know virtually nothing about Jabez, an obscure biblical character. And yet his simple prayer is rich in meaning. He asked God for blessings, for intimacy, for protection, an expansion of his borders. "And God granted his request."

It's rare for a biblical blessing to achieve best-seller status, but *The Prayer of Jabez*—Bruce Wilkinson's small book that popularized the prayer—did just that. Suddenly our obscure Jabez had millions of new friends following a gospel of prosperity.

The prosperity or wealth gospel gained traction several decades ago, rising in popularity with the growth of many evangelical church movements. It posits that gifts to the church and positive thinking can change one's financial destiny, along with the notion that faith is a portal to success. Human beings are empowered with the strength to change their financial situations through charity, hard work, belief and an attitude of constant improvement.

Jabez felt empowered. Jabez was not afraid to ask for material abundance—"Bless me and enlarge my territory"—as a deserving petitioner. We should not be afraid to ask for sustenance when we use wealth wisely and generously.

**Don't be shy. Take a lesson from the Jabez playbook.
State a bold request for your life and leadership.**

✦ DAY #185 ✦

ON DOMINANCE

"Engage people with what they expect; it is what they are able to discern and confirms their projections. It settles them into predictable patterns of response, occupying their minds while you wait for the extraordinary moment—that which they cannot anticipate."

This military advice is over two thousand years ago. We find it in *The Art of War*, by Sun-tzu, an important Chinese general.

Sun-tzu believed in the element of surprise. "All warfare is based on deception." Waiting for the extraordinary moment throws off the enemy, locking him into the predictable while searching for the time when he is off his game. It gives fighters the edge. "Let your plans be dark and impenetrable as night, and when you move, fall like a thunderbolt."

Deception for Sun-tzu went beyond positioning soldiers to fight at unexpected times through a difficult mental battle. "Appear weak when you are strong, and strong when you are weak." Do not let the enemy know where your strength lies or you will be acutely vulnerable.

Dominance lies in breaking the resistance of the enemy so that one never goes to war. "The supreme art of war is to subdue the enemy without fighting." This posture Sun-tzu considered one of "supreme excellence."

Leading can feel like going out to war every day. It wears us down and eats away at our energy and optimism. Put the armor and the shield down.

When does leading feel like war to you?

✦ D A Y #186 ✦

ON LAZY DAYS

Plum Village is a mindfulness practice center in France started by Vietnamese Zen monk Thich Nhat Hanh. He wrote: "It is possible that the next Buddha will not take the form of an individual. The next Buddha may take the form of a community—a community practicing understanding and loving kindness, a community practicing mindful living." Jean-Pierre and Rachel Cartier described Plum Village in *Thich Nhat Hanh: The Joy of Full Consciousness*.

When Nhat Hanh visited the West, he noticed the speed at which people worked and communicated with each other, afraid of empty time. Nhat Hanh responded to this phenomenon:

"In the West, we are completely driven by our goals. We want to know where we are going, and we mobilize all our energy to get there. Buddhism places importance on achieving the absence of a goal, a state in which it is meaningless to go after objects of desire because everything is already in oneself." He said, "Often we tell ourselves, 'Don't just sit there—do something!' Perhaps we should tell ourselves: 'Don't just do something—sit there!'"

Every Monday at Plum Village is Lazy Day. There is no work or structure. You can rise whenever you like and do whatever you like. Many younger nuns find Mondays a challenge. It is not as easy to be lazy as we might imagine, especially with full consciousness.

Think of the last lazy day you experienced—that was laziness with full consciousness. Schedule one today.

ON SEEKING

"Seek and you shall find," the apostle Matthew tells us (7:7).

If you don't seek, you shall never find. If you don't open yourself up to possibility, it will not open up to you. The act of seeking itself offers a sliver of holiness. Matthew reminds us: "First seek his kingdom and his righteousness, and all these things will be given to you as well" (6:33). When you seek, you may not only find what you are looking for, you may open all kinds of other doors as well. Knock.

In Song of Songs, seeking and finding are not linear. "My lover put his hand to the door, and I was thrilled that he was near. I was ready to let him come in. My hands were covered with myrrh, my fingers with liquid myrrh, as I grasped the handle of the door. I opened the door for my lover, but he had already gone. How I wanted to hear his voice! I looked for him, but couldn't find him; I called to him, but heard no answer" (5:4–6).

We seek different things at different times. We might seek happiness, status, money, fame, wisdom or God. Just because we are ready to seek does not mean that we will find. Seeking requires tenacity, patience and good timing. But we can't forget to knock loudly on the door of opportunity.

What is one thing you are seeking right now?

ON PURPOSE

"In the beginning, God created the earth, and He looked upon it in His cosmic loneliness.

"And God said, 'Let Us make living creatures out of mud, so the mud can see what We have done.' And God created every living creature that now moves, and one was man. Mud as man alone could speak. God leaned close to mud as man sat up, looked around, and spoke. Man blinked. 'What is the purpose of all this?' he asked politely.

"'Everything must have a purpose?' asked God.

"'Certainly,' said man.

"'Then I leave it to you to think of one for all this,' said God. "And He went away."

These poignant lines from Kurt Vonnegut's *Cat's Cradle* push us to understand the centrality and urgency of discovering human purpose. The God who placed Adam in a mythic Garden of Eden, in this Vonnegut scene, could not determine human purpose. That is a job for humans; even a Creator cannot create that for us. We must be self-determining when it comes to meaning.

Vonnegut (1922–2007) fought in World War II, served time as a prisoner of war and witnessed the firebombing of Dresden, Germany. "How complicated and unpredictable the machinery of life really is." Uncovering human purpose inspires productivity. It takes work. "Live by the harmless untruths that make you brave and kind and healthy and happy."

**What truths and "untruths" give you
a sense of purpose as a leader?**

✦ DAY #189 ✦

ON CONTRITION

We often feel alone, bereft of intimacy and closeness. Even when we experience it, we dread the reality that it may one day—and at random—all be taken away from us. Indian writer R. K. Narayan (1906–2001), in *The English Teacher*, absorbed us in one of these moments in one of his fictional characters in his fictional southern India town, Malgudi:

"I returned from the village. The house seemed unbearably dull. But I bore it. 'There is no escape from loneliness and separation . . .' I told myself often. 'Wife, child, brothers, parents, friends . . . We come together only to go apart again. It is one continuous movement. They move away from us as we move away from them. The law of life can't be avoided. . . . A profound unmitigated loneliness is the only truth of life. . . . No sense in battling against it.'"

We separate ourselves from others. One of the few ways we can ever restore intimacy is through contrition, acknowledging the abyss between us and others and expressing remorse about the distance.

Contrition is from a Latin word meaning "to be ground to pieces"—the breaking apart of our insecurities and inadequacies. These can be put together, not totally, but little by little. Tenderly.

**Today, mind the gap and reach out
to someone in contrition.**

✦ DAY #190 ✦

ON SPIRITUAL EATING

Most faith traditions create rituals around food—blessing, fasting or breaking bread with strangers—because eating is a constant feature of daily living. Michael Pollan wrote: "The wonderful thing about food is you get three votes a day. Every one of them has the potential to change the world." Pollan was referring not only to the act of eating itself but to the entire context of food: the problems with agribusiness today, how we support growers and farmers and how we end hunger. Food has the potential to engage us in an act of gratitude, a moment of grace, a stab at social justice.

Too often, we eat because we can, not because we need to. We eat out of boredom, restlessness, a desire to please the cook or shut up the food pushers around us. We eat to fill a gaping emotional hole, for comfort or solace. We barely look at what we eat or experience its texture or the depth of its flavor.

Spiritual eating involves intention and a change of speed. Turn the dial to slow. Close your eyes before a meal and contemplate who must be thanked for giving you this repast. Cut up your food in small pieces. Chew it so that you engage with its complexity, the nuance of flavor, its slipperiness or its burst of spices.

Today make each meal a movable feast. Slow down. Taste each bite. Fill your mouth and heart with blessing.

✦ DAY #191 ✦

ON PAIN

The word *pain* appears in the Koran in close to eighty places. Most uses of the term involve the pain that we bring upon ourselves through lack of belief, lack of remorse or lack of trust in God and others. We make our own misery. Pain is twinned with torment in these sacred verses.

"In their hearts is a disease, and Allah has increased their disease. A *pain*ful torment is theirs because they used to tell lies" (*Al-Baqara* 2:10).

"And for the disbelievers there is a *pain*ful torment" (*Al-Baqara* 2:104).

"Verily, those who purchase disbelief at the price of faith, not the least harm will they do to Allah. For them, there is a *pain*ful torment" (*Aal-e-Imran* 3:177).

"And of no effect is the repentance of those who continue to do evil deeds until death faces one of them and he says: 'Now I repent,' nor of those who die while they are disbelievers. For them we have prepared a *pain*ful torment" (*An-Nisa* 4:18).

Pain is usually used to describe a momentary physical or emotional wound. We experience the pain of a sprain, a fall, a rupture, a heartache, a disappointment, a rejection. Torment describes the aftermath of pain, the slow, percolating sense of loss and grief.

Leading can be painful.

Think of a painful moment of leadership that became, over time, a torment. How can you stop making your own misery *now*?

ON LOVE

Chief Dan George (1899–1981) led the Squamish Band of the Salish Indian Tribe of Burrard Inlet in British Columbia. He worked in construction, drove a bus and served as the chief of his nation before his life took an odd turn. He became an actor in a number of famous films and was even nominated for an Academy Award as best supporting actor. His beautiful face was captured in a postage stamp for a collection called "Canadians in Hollywood."

Chief Dan George wrote two books of poetry, *My Heart Soars* and *My Spirit Soars*, that capture in simple phrases the Native American connection with nature. His 1981 *New York Times* obituary shared that he was "impressed by the progress that Indians made in his lifetime, noting that he himself, as an old man, had become 'more forward and bold.'" He taught himself to soar because he wanted to "do something that would give a name to the Indian people."

"Love is something you and I must have. We must have it because without it we become weak and faint. . . . With it we are creative. With it we march tirelessly. With it, and with it alone, we are able to sacrifice for others." On his tombstone it is written: "His heart soared like the eagle."

When in your leadership has your heart soared?

ON WALKING AWAY

Julia Child (1912–2004) loved her years in France. "They marked a crucial period of transformation in which I found my true calling, experienced an awakening of the senses, and had such fun that I hardly stopped moving long enough to catch my breath."

In 1963, she bought a home, La Pitchoune, "the Little One."

Many years later, when a close friend died, she decided to pack up with her niece Phila.

"People seemed surprised when I told them that it wasn't an especially difficult or emotional decision. But I have never been very sentimental."

She was feeling upbeat during the packing, but at one point Phila began to cry. It was the last time they would be in the house.

"That's true," Child replied. "But I will always have such wonderful memories."

"But aren't you going to miss it?"

She shrugged and said: "I've always felt that when I'm done with something I just walk away from it—*fin!*"

Walking away from something you love—a place, a role, a job, a relationship—does not mean erasing it from your consciousness. "I tried to hold on to my impression," Child wrote of France, "but it was hopeless. As if I were trying to hold on to a dream."

**Think of something you once walked away from
and write down three lessons or memories you
still carry with you from the experience.**

+ DAY #194 +

ON RECEIVING

"I have a saying: Receive everything . . ."

Amanda Owen wrote two books on the subject, *The Power of Receiving* and *Born to Receive*, because she realized how few of her clients were experiencing reciprocity in their relationships.

"I became overly dependent on others' approval. . . . I also created relationships in which I gave much more than I got back and that left me feeling exhausted, resentful, and distressed. . . . The more I thought about receiving, the more I wondered why we are taught to denigrate 50 percent of every transaction."

When we are always giving, we also minimize the capacity of

others to give back. "Create a pathway for those you help to give back," she advised. And if you want something, don't wait for others to guess what that is. Initiate. Don't be afraid to make a request of others. "Once you get used to people giving to you as much as you give to them and receive all of the benefits of a less stressful life, you will not consider putting yourself last."

Leaders often give too much of themselves, crashing when the relationship is not reciprocal. Giving is also a way we control others and our experiences. Receiving involves relinquishing control, waiting and allowing others to serve us. It means accepting our vulnerability and dependence on others.

Make a point of asking and *graciously* receiving help today from someone who is usually on the receiving end of your help.

* DAY #195 *

ON LYING

Dan Ariely is a behavioral economist and a professor at Duke University. He runs the Center for Advanced Hindsight and wrote *Predictably Irrational: The Hidden Forces That Shape Our Decisions*, about the myth that we behave rationally when we virtually never do. Not about food. Not about money. Not about relationships. He followed that up with another swing at human nature: *The (Honest) Truth about Dishonesty: How We Lie to Everyone—Especially Ourselves.*

The take-home message: We naturally lie, even if we are usually good, so don't make it easy for us, and we won't do it. Ariely advises us to put deterrents in place to prevent us from lying to ourselves: "As long as we are doing something that is somewhat connected to our self-image, it can fuel our motivation and get us to work much harder."

As a teenager, Ariely was in a terrible fire, suffering third-degree burns on most of his body—a story he shared in his first book—which led him to think about how to deliver better care to patients when pain is unavoidable. And, in the spirit of irrationality, he got an Ig Nobel award for research on how patients who buy high-cost placebos will heal more quickly than those who purchase low-cost placebos. We really are nuts.

> **As a leader, can you share an exaggerated story about yourself that you tell because it propels a myth you cling to about your own self-image?**

✦ DAY #196 ✦

ON GRIEF

When Charlotte Brozek lost her husband to cancer, she wrote an op-ed piece for the *New York Times*, "No Husband, No Friends," to describe the irrationality of her grief. She left her home, moved into a small apartment down the road and auctioned off or threw away most of her possessions. She then had to repurchase things, since she realized that basic amenities were still basic.

"I went from depression to panic attacks back to depression to migraines, to abdominal migraines, to not sleeping, to sleeping too much, to never leaving the bunker, to not wanting to go back to the bunker. To deal with my mood swings, I have seen a grief counselor and a psychiatrist and attend a support group. My counselor advised me I wasn't acting irrationally—it was all just coping mechanisms. She suggested I make friends. My psychiatrist prescribed antidepressants so I would stop acting irrationally. How can I go wrong?"

But she could not make it right. She lost her hair and felt like she was losing her mind. "Someone once said that being a widow is like living in a country where nobody speaks your language."

When you are a leader and you have lost someone you love, you live in another country, but you still need to lead those dependent on you. Give them a passport by speaking about your pain.

> **Name a significant loss you had to grieve when your leadership could not take a hiatus.**

ON THINKING

Philosopher John Locke (1632–1704) did a lot of thinking. He also did a lot of thinking about thinking. In *An Essay Concerning Human Understanding* (book II, chapter 1), he wrote that thinking about thinking is pleasant and useful. "An inquiry into the understanding, pleasant and useful. Since it is the understanding that sets man above the rest of sensible beings, and gives him all the advantage and dominion which he has over them. . . .

"All ideas come from sensation or reflection. Let us then suppose the mind to be, as we say, white paper, void of all characters, without any ideas: How comes it to be furnished? Whence comes it by that vast store which the busy and boundless fancy of man has painted on it with an almost endless variety? Whence has it all the materials of reason and knowledge? To this I answer, in one word, from experience."

No idea forms in your mind that the mind never knew, according to Locke. You got the idea from somewhere and you may take it somewhere else. There is no such thing as pure thought without mental origins: "The mind is of all truths it ever shall know."

Leaders need to generate ideas. All the time.

In your quiet hours, what occupies your mind?

ON SHEPHERDING

In the Bible, the MBA of leadership is shepherding. Abraham, Isaac, Rebecca, Rachel, Jacob, Joseph and his brothers, Moses, Saul, David—all of them were shepherds before they were leaders.

The shepherd is the perfect metaphor for leadership. A shepherd leads from behind, watching the movement of his flock, paying attention to the strays and the predators. The shepherd is vigilant about finding new terrain and is prepared to move continuously and adapt to changing conditions. The shepherd is at one with God and nature and watches the weather; even the slightest change can impact the flock. The shepherd can work alone, unable to communicate fully with those he leads.

Make no mistake: It is really, really hard to move sheep. Ever try it?

When Moses was told that he would no longer lead the Israelites in the Promised Land, he petitioned God to grant him a competent successor. His flock needed a shepherd: And God heard him and told Moses to appoint Joshua—"a man in whom is the spirit, and lay your hand on him." They got a new shepherd. God in Psalm 23 is described as the ultimate shepherd.

**What aspects of shepherding are you good
at and what skills need fine-tuning?**

✦ DAY #199 ✦

ON PERSEVERANCE

In 1973, Stephen King was in his fifth year of teaching English at a Maine prep school when he heard his name over the school intercom system: "Stephen King, are you there? Stephen King? Please come to the office." His wife, Tabby, was on the phone. People joked that King had married Tabby for her typewriter. They were two struggling writers with a pile of rejections and a pile of bills. She worked the second shift at Dunkin' Donuts. They lived in a double trailer. He drove a rusty Buick.

He wrote a few pages of *Carrie*, then tossed them in the garbage can. Tabby took the crumpled balls out, unwrinkled them and told her husband that she thought he was onto something. Thirty publishers rejected the manuscript.

Tabby read a telegram to King over the phone:

CONGRATULATIONS. *CARRIE* OFFICIALLY A DOUBLEDAY
BOOK. IS $2500 ADVANCE OKAY? THE FUTURE LIES AHEAD.
LOVE, BILL.

Finally, they had enough money for a telephone.

Carrie sold 13,000 copies until Signet Books bought the paper-back rights for $400,000. Half was coming to King. No one else was home when the call came. There was no one to tell. King went to downtown Bangor to buy Tabby a special present for Mother's Day: a hair dryer.

To date, King has sold more than 350 million copies of his books.

When you persevere, as King says, "the future lies ahead."

Name one area where your perseverance paid off.

✦ DAY #200 ✦

ON HEALING

"What happens when people open their hearts?" . . .

"They get better."

This conversation in Haruki Murakami's *Norwegian Wood* gets to the heart of the heart. Healing happens when you puncture yourself just a little bit.

A similar sentiment is the key to love and healing in the thirtieth chapter of Deuteronomy:

"I have now given you a choice between a blessing and a curse. When all these things have happened to you, and you are living among the nations where the Lord your God has scattered you, you will remember the choice I gave you. If you and your descendants will turn back to the Lord and with all your heart obey his commands that I am giving you today, then the Lord your God will have mercy on you. . . . And he will make you more prosperous and more numerous than your ancestors ever were. *The Lord your God will circumcise your heart* and that of your children so that you will love him with all your heart, and you will continue to live in that land."

Circumcise your heart. Open a wound just a little to let the light in.

**How can you crack open just a bit
more to let the healing begin?**

◆ DAY #201 ◆

ON BEING A MULTIPLIER

We open others up when we say yes. We generate possibilities. We help people take pride in themselves and their work. We multiply them or build professional, spiritual and emotional capacity in others when we give them our trust, our good energy and our inner sunshine.

In the spirit of expansion, Liz Wiseman and Greg McKeown wrote an article that became a full-length book: *Multipliers: How the Best Leaders Make Everyone Smarter*. In it, they tried to capture and distill the ingredients of expansive leadership.

They identified common multiplier behaviors to describe their thesis. A multiplier:

Attracts talented people and uses them at their highest point of
   contribution;
Creates an intense environment that requires people's best
   thinking and work;
Defines an opportunity that causes people to stretch;
Drives sound decisions through rigorous debate; and
Gives other people the ownership for results and invests in their
   success.

Contrast these behaviors with those of diminishers. A diminisher:

Hoards resources and underutilizes talent;

Creates a tense environment that suppresses people's thinking and capability;

Gives directives that showcase how much they know;

Makes centralized, abrupt decisions that confuse the organization; and

Drives results through their personal involvement.

Diminishers often get immediate results but fail to cultivate long-term relationships because people do not grow and flourish under their leadership.

We all want to believe we are multipliers.

As a leader, are you a multiplier or a diminisher? Prove it.

✦ DAY #202 ✦

ON GOOD MANNERS

"Manners are the lubricating oil of an organization. It is a law of nature that two bodies in contact with each other create friction. This is as true for human beings as it is for inanimate objects. Manners—simple things like saying 'please' and 'thank you' and knowing a person's name or asking after her family—enable two people to work together whether they like each other or not. Bright people, especially bright young people, often do not understand this. If analysis shows that someone's brilliant work fails again and again as soon as cooperation from others is required, it probably indicates a lack of courtesy—that is, a lack of manners."

This wisdom does not hail from Emily Post, the queen of manners and civility, but from Peter Drucker, the king of management and leadership, in his classic workbook *Managing Oneself*.

Give yourself a courtesy quiz. Are you a role model of manners or do you lack civility?

There is no good excuse for a lack of manners, in oneself or in the work culture that a leader creates. You create and enforce the culture.

Take a step into organizational civility. What is one policy, memo or conversation that would enhance organizational good manners?

✦ DAY #203 ✦

ON TEMPTATION

"A silly idea is current that good people do not know what temptation means. This is an obvious lie. Only those who try to resist temptation know how strong it is. . . . A man who gives in to temptation after five minutes simply does not know what it would have been like an hour later. That is why bad people, in one sense, know very little about badness. They have lived a sheltered life by always giving in."

C. S. Lewis (1898–1963) reframed the way that we think of temptation. We tend to regard temptation as telling ourselves "yes" when it should be "no."

No, said Lewis. Resisting temptation is meaningful because it involves a struggle, a personal bout with what we know to be right in a head-on collision with what we know will have negative consequences. And right and wrong may be more nuanced than the black-and-white varieties that are often thought of when using the word *temptation*.

Lewis is known to many of us as the writer of *The Chronicles of Narnia*, but his works on theology overwhelm his explorations into fantasy.

As a religious thinker, Lewis struggled with the meaning of temptation. If you have no moral barometer, then you are not tempted. You are, in Lewis's words, sheltered because you know only "badness." You can only know temptation if it is a genuine confrontation.

Share one temptation you have as a leader
and describe the wrestling match.

✦ DAY #204 ✦

ON ASKING QUESTIONS

The Lord God called out to the man and said to him, *"Where are you?"*

The question "Where are you?" seems easier to answer than "Who are you?" But it becomes more difficult when we're hiding. Adam had a lot of explaining to do.

"'I heard the sound of You in the garden, and I was afraid because I was naked, so I hid.' Then He asked, *'Who told you that you were naked? Did you eat of the tree from which I had forbidden you to eat?'* The man said, 'The woman You put at my side—she gave me of the tree, and I ate.'"

More questions. More excuses.

"And the Lord God said to the woman, *'What is this you have done?'* The woman replied, 'The serpent duped me, and I ate'" (Genesis 3:9–13)

More questions. More blame.

We can't always run away from the questions that haunt us most. Giving excuses is just another way in which we run.

As a leader, ask yourself a difficult question today.

ON INTERRUPTIONS

Leadership is one long interruption. We expect interruptions and then barely question them.

Socio-linguist and academic Deborah Tannen wrote that, instead of viewing interruptions as rude, we could see them as "high-involvement cooperative overlapping." Tannen has argued that certain cultures and ethnicities tolerate a surplus level of interruption. These also include "a fast rate of speech, the avoidance of inter-turn pauses and faster turn-taking among speakers."

Those with an interruptive style believe that jumping in and stopping someone else's thought midway shows curiosity and concern. Those unaccustomed to this style may be intimidated or feel unheard and frustrated. They see interruptions as rude, thoughtless and selfish. *Why can't anyone let me finish a thought?*

The speed of leadership thinking can inadvertently translate into a message of arrogance: My ideas are better than yours, and that is why I cannot let you finish your thought. I cannot award you the dignity to listen to you, to probe your mind, to mine your thought processes, to achieve deeper understanding, to show you respect, to accord your views dignity.

Interrupt enough and you'll find that soon you are left talking to yourself. Because that's what you were doing anyway.

**Restrain the impulse to interrupt by letting everyone
you speak to today complete a sentence.**

ON WORSHIP

When Henri Nouwen wrote *Can You Drink the Cup?* he was just shy of having been a priest for forty years. He recalled his ordination and the golden chalice that his uncle gave him to drink from when celebrating his first Mass. He was overwhelmed by the grace of the moment, the mystical quality of the worship and the presence of Jesus in his life as close as any friend had ever been.

Every day from then until his death—barring few exceptions—he celebrated the Eucharist.

"I have looked at many cups," Nouwen wrote, "golden, silver, bronze and glass cups, splendidly decorated, and very simple cups, elegantly shaped, and very plain cups." People drink to stay alive or drink themselves to death. Cups serve as trophies and they have served as the harbingers of doom: the silver cup Joseph placed in Benjamin's sack or those of Isaiah and Jeremiah, "the cups of God's wrath and destruction" or Socrates's poisonous cup of hemlock. We celebrate life's great occasions with a drink. When we say that someone drinks too much, we are referring to alcoholism.

Be aware of what's in your cup. Nouwen reminds us that the word *entertainment* comes from the Latin for two words that, together, mean "to keep someone in between." Entertainment keeps us "distracted, excited or in suspense." It can be useful but it can also take us away from the silence and beauty of a worshipful moment.

**Today, drink as if every cup you hold
spills over with abundance.**

✦ DAY #207 ✦

ON OPPORTUNITY

When philosopher Alain de Botton studied entrepreneurship for his book *The Pleasures and Sorrows of Work*, he visited the British Inventors Society. At one gathering, an inventor unveiled his plan for a deodorant-dispensing machine to be installed at train stations. This was to be a public service to travelers, especially—it would seem—during the unfortunate intimacy of rush hour.

Opportunity is seeing what others don't see and creating the future.

There are times when we fall back on the doom of Ecclesiastes—there is nothing new under the sun: "Is there anything of which one can say, 'Look! This is something new?' It was here already, long ago; it was here before our time." Anything we create has already been created.

But hold on a minute . . .

"It is a mere eighty years since deodorant was introduced, the remote-control garage door opener has been in existence for barely thirty-five and only in the last five years have surgeons discovered how safely to remove tumors from our adrenal glands and insert aortic keyhole valves into our hearts. We are still waiting for computers to help us identify whom we might confidently marry, for scanners to locate our lost keys, for a reliable method of eradicating household moths and for medicines which will guarantee us eternal life. Untold numbers of new businesses lie latent in our present inefficiencies and wishes."

**Name something new that you contributed
through your leadership.**

✦ DAY #208 ✦

ON PERCEPTION

"There are things known and there are things unknown, and in between are the doors of perception." Perception, in other words—or in Aldous Huxley's words—is the mental space between the known and the unknown where intuition and mystery live.

The word for *perception* in Hebrew is *bina*, from the root word *bein*, or "in between." There is the form, and the negative space around the form, something in between which cannot easily be described. There is a line of text and the words unspoken between the text, and somewhere in between lies personal meaning. Perception is an impression or an imprint, taken from the Latin word for *understanding*, not for *seeing*.

Aldous Huxley (1894–1963) was born in England but died in

the United States. He gave us *Brave New World* as his most famous literary offering, but he also wrote a collection of essays titled *The Doors of Perception* when later in his career he explored spirituality, mysticism and psychedelic drugs.

Perception may have been particularly important to Huxley because he was nearly blind for most of his life. He tried various and, at times, controversial means to regain his sight, claiming that he was able to see again in his book *The Art of Seeing*.

Influential leadership involves reading in between what is spoken and written.

**Name an event, conversation or negotiation
where your perception was at its height.**

✦ DAY #209 ✦

ON INDUSTRY

John Singer Sargent (1856–1925) painted wonderful watercolors of women, lush gardens and Venetian bridges. Although he offered us these magnificent postcards of the world—from the Galilee to Carrara to Boston—he was not on vacation. He was working.

A friend described Sargent's travels well: "A holiday meant simply a change from the work of the moment to work of another description."

Sargent was born in Florence to expats who frequently moved around Europe. The artist spoke four languages and had a cosmopolitan education. As Richard Ormond wrote in his biographical sketch of the artist, Sargent immersed himself in his art, sacrificing what many would deem a normal social life for the joy of work. "He did not relish intimacy, and he avoided emotional entanglements likely to complicate his life and compromise his independence."

His eyes were always working: "You can't do sketches enough. Sketch everything and keep your curiosity fresh. Cultivate an ever continuous power of observation. Wherever you are, be always ready to make slight notes of postures, groups and incidents. Store up in the mind . . . a continuous stream of observations from which to make selections later. Above all things get abroad, see the sunlight and everything that is to be seen."

Sargent's blockbuster exhibits today take us through room after room of his industry and help us understand the sacred nature of his ambition.

"To work is to pray."

Describe the pleasures of your career that keep you progressing and working.

✦ DAY #210 ✦

ON UNANSWERED QUESTIONS

In life we often cycle through the same questions, hoping for better answers. Sometimes we can only hope to ask a better version of the same question.

Every question we ask will not have an answer—or a good answer, an answer that satisfies. Over time, we must learn to live with the questions, maybe even love them.

"Have patience with everything that remains unsolved in your heart," advised Rainer Maria Rilke in *Letters to a Young Poet*. "Try to love the questions themselves, like locked rooms and like books written in a foreign language. Do not now look for the answers. They cannot now be given to you because you could not live them. It is a question of experiencing everything. At present you need to live the question. Perhaps you will gradually, without even noticing it, find yourself experiencing the answer, some distant day."

If you live with the questions without wrestling them but abiding with them gently and tenderly, answers sometimes emerge that are not anticipated, that are lateral.

Every locked door does not have to be open. The door can be silent and present and a reminder that being human is living in mystery. Living in mystery means living with unanswered questions and asking them anyway because curiosity is the thin membrane covering the soul.

**Name one unanswered question you have
been carrying with you for a long time.**

✦ DAY #211 ✦

ON HABIT

"The Golden Rule of Habit Change: You can't extinguish a bad habit, you can only change it."

Charles Duhigg wrote this in *The Power of Habit: Why We Do What We Do in Life and Business*. Finally, someone to explain those bad—and good—habits and give us some hope that we can indeed change bad habits. Here's what Duhigg had to say about habits at work:

"Companies aren't big happy families where everyone plays together nicely. Rather, most workplaces are made up of fiefdoms where executives compete for power and credit, often in hidden skirmishes that make their own performances appear superior and their rivals' seem worse. Divisions compete for resources and sabotage each other to steal glory. Bosses pit their subordinates against one another so that no one can mount a coup.

"Companies aren't families. They're battlefields in a civil war.

"Yet despite this capacity for internecine warfare, most companies roll along relatively peacefully, year after year, because they have routines—habits—that create truces that allow everyone to set aside their rivalries long enough to get a day's work done."

Habits save us from ourselves.

It is a matter of choice and work. "This is the real power of habit: the insight that your habits are what you choose them to be."

**Name one bad habit of the organization you
lead that needs to change. What will you do to
create a small win on the way to bigger wins?**

ON WRITING

"I believe that art is the highest expression of the human spirit.

"I believe that we yearn to transcend the merely finite and ephemeral; to participate in something mysterious and communal called 'culture.'"

Joyce Carol Oates wrote this in *The Faith of a Writer*.

"Writing, for me, is primarily remembering . . . [I]t's as likely to be cinematic, dramatic, emotional, auditory, and shimmeringly unformed before it becomes actual language, transformed into words on a page."

For Oates, the writing comes only later, as part of a process in which she swallows and digests the world.

"Often I surprise myself, I exasperate and frustrate myself, by entirely rewriting chapters of novels that had seemed quite acceptable the previous day. . . . For always I feel that I have new ideas, always there seems to me more felicitous ways of expressing what I want to say."

She concluded: "I spend much of my time away from the study, in fact. I spend much of my time in motion."

Leaders spend so much time in motion. Writing is merely the last part of expression that helps us articulate experience, and that is why it helps us process and remember experience. Too many leaders are poor writers. They undervalue the role of sharp, clear, crisp and creative expression that comes with good writing.

Oates described inspiration as being "filled suddenly and often helplessly with renewed life and energy, a sense of excitement that can barely be contained."

Write something today that inspires you and others.

ON RISK

Imagine, for a moment, that you are a beauty pageant queen, used to being adored and envied for your good looks and your ability to turn heads. You win.

One day a family member contacts you and tells you that you need to risk it all on an important lifesaving mission. Would you do it?

When we turn to the book of Esther in the Bible, we meet such a queen. Originally an orphan, unseduced by the wiles and attractions of the king, she gains his favor through grace. But her people are in mortal danger. She must reveal her identity that, up until then, had been concealed and leverage her position to save her people. Beauty school did not prepare her for this.

When Mordecai received Esther's refusal, he sent her this message, "Who knows—maybe it was for a time like this that you were made queen?"

Her life up to then had been determined by influential men. She initially refused Mordecai's request. Connie Glaser and Barbara Smalley, in *What Queen Esther Knew: Business Strategies from a Biblical Sage*, distilled the leadership lessons in Esther's narrative for clever business strategies, including this one: Take the risks worth taking. Not fighting is not always the noble option.

What leadership risk made you hesitate
but was morally worth it in the end?

ON SHARING

These are sixteen things that Robert Fulghum learned in kindergarten that have served him for life and formed the basis of his best-selling book, *All I Really Need to Know I Learned in Kinder-garten:*

1. Share everything.
2. Play fair.
3. Don't hit people.
4. Put things back where you found them.
5. Clean up your own mess.
6. Don't take things that aren't yours.
7. Say you're sorry when you hurt somebody.
8. Wash your hands before you eat.
9. Flush.
10. Warm cookies and cold milk are good for you.
11. Live a balanced life—learn some and drink some and draw some and paint some and sing and dance and play and work every day some.
12. Take a nap every afternoon.
13. When you go out into the world, watch out for traffic, hold hands, and stick together.
14. Be aware of wonder. Remember the little seed in the Styrofoam cup: The roots go down and the plant goes up and nobody really knows how or why, but we are all like that.
15. Goldfish and hamsters and white mice and even the little seed in the Styrofoam cup—they all die. So do we.
16. And then remember the Dick-and-Jane books and the first word you learned—the biggest word of all—LOOK.

Sharing is first. As we move up the ladder of success, we find fewer people willing to share their contacts, their vulnerabilities, their resources, their secrets, their pain, their happiness.

How could you spend today sharing more generously of your wisdom, laughter and pain?

ON WELCOMING

Doors are important. They are the threshold to experience. They are neither here nor there, but the in-between place where we imagine some new and exciting adventure can begin—or end. The retailer John Nordstrom understood that if a door is a place of such great anticipation and anxiety, then the welcome people get or do not get at the door can make all the difference when it comes to joining or belonging.

"When customers first come into the store, we've got about 15 seconds to get them excited about it." Robert Spector and Patrick D. McCarthy, in *The Nordstrom Way: The Inside Story of America's #1 Customer Service Company*, described how people need to feel they are in a different atmosphere from virtually the moment they step inside.

Now think of the door to your office. What does a stranger, colleague, client or customer experience when walking through your door? You may be sitting behind a desk and barely look up. You may walk around your desk and offer a hearty greeting.

Glass walls. Cubicle walls. Partitions. Heavy doors with names on them. Work has lots of walls. Don't forget that your office is not only a corporate space. It is *your* space. People tread lightly on the space of others. The invitation to make yourself at home in an office is a way we share professional space and make room for others.

What can you do to make the first fifteen seconds after entry to your office or building more welcoming?

ON RIVALRY

Rivalry can help us even as it hurts us. It can make us fiercer, stronger, more articulate, more driven. Rivalry usually begins for us, however, as a disease of childhood. Aging can make sibling rivalry worse. The childhood arguments and casual punches give way to deeper tensions. A brother's success can highlight our failures. A sister's achievements or talents can make ours look thin and insignificant. A parent's uneven division of an inheritance can make even a good relationship sour. And if you are a successful leader, you may be the subject of sibling envy.

"Take two kids in competition for their parents' love and attention. Add to that the envy that one child feels for the accomplishments of the other; the resentment that each child feels for the privileges of the other; the personal frustrations that they don't dare let out on anyone else but a brother or sister, and it's not hard to understand why in families across the land, the sibling relationship contains enough emotional dynamite to set off rounds of daily explosions." This is how Adele Faber and Elaine Mazlish explained the subject in *Siblings Without Rivalry*.

We may not love the adult decisions that a sibling has made or the mistakes. But it may be time to put judgment aside and let forgiveness prevail.

Has sibling rivalry fueled your leadership in any way? Call a sib today—the one you don't speak to as much.

✦ DAY #217 ✦

ON BLAME

When you blame someone, you assign responsibility for wrongdoing or error. If you are fair, you make that judgment carefully. No one likes to be blamed for what he or she has not done. It breaches our most primal sense of justice. In the ancient days of the Israelites, the Bible recorded the fate of the scapegoat, an animal that was destined to carry the sins of a community, a ritual loaded with mystery.

Aaron, the high priest, was to come to the Tabernacle's Tent of Meeting with two goats. According to later rabbinic literature, the goats had to be the same in height, weight and color. "He is to cast lots for the two goats—one lot for the Lord and the other for the scapegoat" (Leviticus 16:8).

Two goats looked exactly the same. One would be sacrificed to seek atonement. The other was to be sent into the wilderness to a fate unknown.

The scapegoat ritual places blame on something that did no crime and, as a result, symbolizes the harsh and unforgiving nature of blame. Blame is random; it looks exactly like what is not blame (the other goat) and goes off to wander in a solitary place. Where blame lives, no one else can live.

**Think of a time in your leadership when
you blamed someone unfairly, and consider
the emotional cost of that act.**

✦ DAY #218 ✦

ON CHALLENGE

"I always loved running . . . it was something you could do by yourself, and under your own power. You could go in any direction, fast or slow as you wanted, fighting the wind if you felt like it, seeking out new sights just on the strength of your feet and the courage of your lungs." For Jesse Owens (1913–1980), running was about freedom and self-control.

"In running, it doesn't matter whether you come in first, in the middle of the pack, or last. You can say, 'I have finished.' There is a lot of satisfaction in that."

For Fred Lebow (1932–1994), a cofounder of the New York City Marathon, running was about finishing a really significant enterprise.

"You also need to look back, not just at the people who are running behind you but especially at those who don't run and never will. . . . You're still here." Thus former editor of *Runner* magazine Joe Henderson explained that running is about observing those who cannot do what you do and realizing that success is about outlasting the others.

Canadian Olympic rower Silken Laumann said it's about the process: "It's important to know that at the end of the day it's not the medals you remember. What you remember is the process— what you learn about yourself by challenging yourself."

"Ask yourself: 'Can I give more?' The answer is usually: 'Yes'." For Kenyan marathoner and world record holder Paul Tergat, it's about the challenge.

How do you challenge yourself physically?

✦ DAY #219 ✦

ON COMMON SENSE

OBITUARY: THE SAD PASSING OF COMMON SENSE
"Three yards of black fabric enshroud my computer terminal. I am mourning the passing of an old friend by the name of Common Sense. His obituary reads as follows: Common Sense, aka C.S., lived a long life, but died from heart failure at the brink of the millennium. No one really knows how old he was, his birth records were long ago entangled in miles and miles of bureaucratic red tape."

These words were first written by Lori Borgman in the *Indianapolis Star* on March 15, 1998. The obituary ended tenderly:

"As the end neared, doctors say C.S. drifted in and out of logic but was kept informed of developments regarding regulations on low-flow toilets and mandatory air bags. Finally, upon hearing about a government plan to ban inhalers from 14 million asthmatics due to a trace of a pollutant that may be harmful to the environment, C.S. breathed his last."

This obit went viral before there was a viral and spurred other, related obits for common sense:

"Common Sense was preceded in death by his parents, Truth and Trust, his wife, Discretion, his daughter, Responsibility, and his son, Reason. He is survived by three stepbrothers: I Know My

Rights, Someone Else Is to Blame, and I'm a Victim. Not many attended his funeral because so few realized that he was gone."

How can you bring common sense "back from the dead"?

ON DIVERSITY

Are you an allophiliac?

Allophilia is from the Greek "to like or love another" and is a term used today to describe those who have strong affection for members outside of their group, ethnicity or inner circle. It's a term created by Professor Todd Pittinsky when he couldn't find one to describe some of his psychological findings that have been used in public policy and organization development.

Allophilia is measured in five statistical ways: affection, comfort, engagement, enthusiasm and kinship. Around whom do we feel most engaged, comfortable, enthusiastic? Discovering this may lead us to understand not only our own proclivities but our own prejudices as well.

Diversity work in the corporate sector tends to try to minimize racism, gender biases and negative feelings about sexual orientation. But tolerance is not the same as allophilia. When I tolerate something, I just barely stomach it or can endure it but have not learned to love it.

Curiosity about others breeds love.

Schedule an opportunity for those you lead to share their stories and create a little more allophilia in the workday.

ON CHOICES

The Jesuit theologian Bernard Lonergan (1904–1984), in *Understanding and Being*, wrote: "Choice is a determinant in personal development. . . . By my free acts I am making myself." Choice allows us to become self-determining. In cultures or regimes where choice is limited, our sense of self-control is severely undermined.

Moving from theology to philosophy, the Danish philosopher Søren Kierkegaard (1813–1855) understood that one of the most challenging aspects of being human is exercising choice. The philosopher tackled the difficult and almost indefinable nature of choosing in *Either/Or: A Fragment of Life*.

"The moment of choice is for me very serious, less on account of the rigorous pondering of the alternatives, and of the multitude of thoughts that attach to each separate link, than because there is a danger afoot that at the next moment it may not be in my power to make the same choice, that something has already been lived that must be lived over again. . . . One discovers that there is something that must be done over again, that must be retracted, and that is often very difficult."

The process of choosing does not take us on a straight path. We live and relive good and bad choices.

**Think of a poor choice you made in your leadership
that caused a lot of rethinking and retracting.**

ON DIFFICULT
CONVERSATIONS

When you have to have a difficult conversation, it's like holding a hand grenade, wrote Douglas Stone, Bruce Patton and Sheila Heen in *Difficult Conversations: How to Discuss What Matters Most*. A difficult conversation is potentially explosive, often lobbed at unexpected times, and it almost always leaves shrapnel, small splinters of pain and insult that can be impossible to dislodge.

It doesn't matter if this difficult conversation is taking place in the boardroom, the living room or the office; the gut-wrenching discomfort of it all can be paralyzing.

Here's the problem with our hand grenade. If you're holding one and you decide not to launch, but take out the pin, it's still going to go off.

"Coated with sugar, thrown hard or soft, a hand grenade is still going to do damage. Try as you may, there's no way to throw a hand grenade with tact or to outrun the consequences. And keeping it to yourself is no better. Choosing not to deliver a difficult message is like hanging on to a hand grenade once you've pulled the pin."

Difficult Conversations recommends that we institute a change of language. If we call a conversation difficult, then the very descriptive challenge of naming may make us pull away. If, instead, we use the term *learning conversation*, we may be more willing to enter its sometimes treacherous but often rewarding terrain.

Name a learning conversation you are avoiding.

ON HURT

The doctor asks you to judge your pain on a scale of one to ten. She pokes you. "Does it hurt?"

Someone insults you—or, worse, they offer a criticism with the expression "No offense," which instantly offends. Someone overhearing the conversation asks you later and in private, "Does it hurt?" For a moment, your forehead wrinkles in consternation but then you shrug and say you barely noticed. The hurt registered.

At some point, if we walk without defenses, we realize how much physical and emotional hurt one human being can carry: rejection, loss, grief, insult, abuse, damage, bruises, sprains, breaks, aches, distress, suffering. On the scale the doctor used to measure pain, she did not list them all.

Author Jonathan Safran Foer wrote in *Everything Is Illuminated*: "There are only so many times that you can utter 'It does not hurt' before it begins to hurt even more than the hurt. You become enlightened of the feeling of feeling hurt, which is worse, I am certain, than the existent hurt."

The hurt is layered; every hurt also includes the layer of metaphysical hurt that accompanies and outlives the pain itself.

Hurt serves a function. It is a warning. It is a reminder. It is also a glue that helps us bond with others, because only through what hurts us do we become truly empathic.

What kinds of wounds can only leaders administer?

ON SECURITY

"Security is mostly a superstition. It does not exist in nature, nor do the children of men as a whole experience it. Avoiding danger is no safer in the long run than outright exposure. Life is either a daring adventure, or nothing."

Helen Keller (1880–1968) was not born blind but she became deaf and blind as a toddler. Her disabilities closed many doors initially, but her heroic teacher Anne Sullivan drew her out and, as a result, Keller became an inspiration to the world. Living in darkness, Keller understood that there is no such thing as security.

"For, after all, everyone who wishes to gain true knowledge must climb the Hill Difficulty alone, and since there is no royal road to the summit, I must zigzag it in my own way."

Lest we think that Keller's path was linear, she told us how hard it was: "I slip back many times, I fall, I stand still, I run against the edge of hidden obstacles, I lose my temper and find it again and keep it better, I trudge on, I gain a little, I feel encouraged, I get more eager and climb higher and begin to see the widening horizon. Every struggle is a victory. One more effort and I reach the luminous cloud, the blue depths of the sky, the uplands of my desire."

We see her luminous cloud, even if she couldn't.

**What in your leadership feels secure right
now and what feels insecure?**

✦ DAY #225 ✦

ON RESPONSIBILITY

In *A Year by the Sea: Thoughts of an Unfinished Woman*, Joan Anderson recorded her thoughts on the painful transitions that midlife threw her when her sons had grown up and out of the family home and her husband took a new job out of state. Instead of joining him, she retreated to a family cottage on Cape Cod to recenter a life built on responsibility to others that made her forget her responsibility to herself. "I am simply a person who wanted to become a scholar of self and soul."

She walked along the beach and observed her surroundings. "A gentle wave suddenly rises and towers overhead. Impulsively, I dive

under, coming out on the other side. I haven't dared that for years. . . .
Why am I more cautious as I age instead of the other way around? I
wonder if it's all tied in to failure. I tend to forget my gains and remember only the losses. The failures have piled up, wreaking havoc with
my confidence until, as an adult, I've become afraid to take chances."

Then she took one big chance and stepped out of her life for a
long time before returning. "Destiny won, as it always does. I'm no
longer in control of my marriage, the children, or my future. Nothing is certain. . . . On occasion being dead wrong and human offers
some solace."

**Name a responsibility you have right now that
is clouding you from seeing your own needs.**

✦ DAY #226 ✦

ON CHANGE

"When people try to change things, they're usually tinkering with
behaviors that have become automatic. . . . The bigger the change
you're suggesting, the more it will sap people's self-control. . . . .In
other words, they're exhausting precisely the mental muscles needed
to make a big change."

This caution is offered by Dan and Chip Heath in *Switch: How
to Change Things When Change Is Hard.* If change is hard, then the
presiding question is how to make change easier. The Heath brothers recommend a "destination postcard," a picture of what an organization will look like after the change. People need to know what
you are aiming for if you want them to go there. Resistance in many
instances is simply a lack of clarity.

Perhaps the best advice in *Switch* is to shrink the change. Make
the change smaller than you need it to be so that people can do what
you ask. It's not such a big stretch that they keep coming up short.
Be wary of the fundamental attribution error: attributing behavior
to the way people are rather than to the situation they are in. If you
can change the situation, even slightly, then you are more likely

to change the outcome. Small successes then snowball into greater momentum: "Small targets lead to small victories, and small victories can often trigger a positive spiral of behavior."

**Think of one change you want to make
as a leader. Now shrink it.**

✦ D A Y # 2 2 7 ✦

ON TELLING YOUR STORY

"All of us tell stories about ourselves. Stories define us. To know someone well is to know her story—the experiences that have shaped her, the trials and turning points that have tested her."

So wrote Herminia Ibarra and Kent Lineback in their *Harvard Business Review* article "What's Your Story?" Leaders need stories to answer questions: Why are we doing this now? What do you need from us? Where are we going?

These experts aren't asking for tall tales: "We're talking about accounts that are deeply true and so engaging that listeners feel they have a stake in our success." People want to be part of a majestic story that is unfolding. "We oscillate between holding on to the past and embracing the future," because, according to the authors, "we have lost the narrative thread of our professional lives."

Ever look at your résumé and realize it reads like a Chinese puzzle, without one piece connected coherently to another, the transitions virtually absent? "Without a compelling story that lends meaning, unity and purpose to our lives, we feel lost and rudderless. We need a good story to reassure us that our plans make sense."

Listeners are "particularly sensitive to lapses of coherence in life stories," so don't fudge. Don't hold back the drama that will engage others, and do let people know a slice of your struggles, because overcoming conflict makes every story more credible and inspiring.

**Write five sentences of your professional
story that include one major conflict.**

ON GUILT

Some people believe guilt is a useless feeling. It mires you in a past you can do nothing about while failing to inspire you to do anything different in the future because you are so angry at yourself. Guilt is anger turned inward.

Ask Franz Kafka. In *The Trial*, Joseph K. is found guilty, put under arrest and put in prison—all for a crime that is never articulated. He never learns of his charge, nor do we as readers. Having committed no crime, Joseph should stand up for his innocence. Instead, he is wracked by guilt over a possible crime he cannot imagine. The court that serves up Joseph's invisible crime continuously tries to ambush his mind into accepting his guilt. He is finally executed, and although we still do not know why he deserved this punishment, we regard it as a relief.

He knows something is wrong without knowing why. There is no one to hear a whimper or a protest.

No one can make us feel guilty without our permission. If guilt is real, then it can hook our hearts and change the way we act in the future, as Voltaire wrote: "Every man is guilty of all the good he did not do." If guilt is imagined, however, and the "crime" is not one we committed, it is time to let it go.

Who is ambushing you with guilt, and why are you letting them?

ON ADMIRATION

Admiration is that infectious combination of approval, high regard and affection that forms the foundation of respect. We often admire people who have talents and qualities that we don't have. But admiration coupled with a smattering of envy can make for a complex relationship. True admiration is pure and unalloyed.

> You can't, if you can't feel it, if it never
> Rises from the soul, and sways
> The heart of every single hearer,
> With deepest power, in simple ways.
> You'll sit forever, gluing things together,
> Cooking up a stew from others' scraps,
> Blowing on a miserable fire,
> Made from your heap of dying ash.
> Let apes and children praise your art,
> If their admiration's to your taste,
> But you'll never speak from heart to heart,
> Unless it rises up from your heart's space.

Johann Wolfgang von Goethe (1749–1832), in *Faust*, wrote of the real admiration that must come from the heart's space. It's not something we can ever conjure or fake. And we only really appreciate those who admire us when we value their opinion.

At the same time, we often admire people most when we know little about them. Our innocence helps foster respect. The distance helps grow our affections while inuring us to the fault lines.

It's wonderful when people admire us because they know us and even better when the feeling is reciprocated.

Name one person who deeply knows you and still admires you. Name one person you deeply know and admire.

✦ DAY #230 ✦

ON MYSTERY

Ever hear at the end of a lecture: "He was brilliant. I had no idea what he said"? Incomprehension becomes a sign of genius, rather than a deficiency in the communicator.

Frederick William Robertson (1816–1853) appreciated this conundrum well.

"A silent man is easily reputed wise. A man who suffers none to see him in the common jostle and undress of life easily gathers round him a mysterious veil of unknown sanctity, and men honor him for a saint. The unknown is always wonderful."

The unknown, as Robertson understood, is not always wonderful. And this was articulated by a man who himself was an enigma.

At age twenty-four, Robertson was ordained and served as a minister but he had a nervous breakdown from his heightened monkish behaviors. He memorized the New Testament in Greek and Hebrew and worked so hard as a missionary that he needed a respite for a year. He moved into and out of spiritual work and gave us small nuggets of wisdom born of a sensitive heart.

Robertson's delicate nature inspired remarkable sermons that he left the public after his premature, mysterious death in 1853. The darkness that was a mystery to him is no mystery to us. His depression went undiagnosed and untreated at a time when mental illness was itself a mystery. Not every mystery is shrouded in wonder. Sometimes it is a cover for ignorance.

**What "mystery" trails you that you can
make more transparent for others?**

✦ DAY #231 ✦

ON HYPOCRISY

Not long after William Bennett was America's appointed secretary of education (1985–1988), he wrote a thick and popular book called *The Book of Virtue*. In his political and his religious life, he took a tough stance on drugs and addiction, sexual deviance and low education standards. He was regarded as a crusader against divorce, bankruptcy, abuse, welfare. He wrote *The Death of Outrage: Bill Clinton and the Assault on American Ideals* in protest, questioning why the country was not more upset about the presidential scandal.

Bennett did not fare well under his own moral microscope. He had a gambling problem; newspapers claimed he had lost more than $8 million in casinos. He didn't deny it. He fell in love with gambling as a child at church bingo. One casino source claimed that he had lost half a million over two days.

Ouch.

Hypocrisy hurts.

Maybe Bennett should have stuck with a smaller text, like H. Jackson Brown Jr.'s *New York Times* best-seller *Life's Little Instruction Book*. It contains wisdom like this: "Our character is what we do when we think no one is looking," and "Your religion is what you do when the sermon is over." And the sermon *is* over.

When you are a leader, you set yourself up as a moral exemplar, whether you bargained for that label or not. Live up to it, because people love a hypocrite. A hypocrite makes us all feel better.

**Do you feel that any part of your life
now smacks of hypocrisy?**

✦ DAY #232 ✦

ON CRISIS

Imagine you are the CEO of 1,779 employees, and 129 visitors are in your office. You look out the window and see a plane crash into one of two towers in your building. On floors 93 to 100 of One World Trade Center, there are 845 employees; 934 are on floors 48 to 54 in the other tower.

Would you have the presence of mind to gather a team of colleagues and craft a plan before the towers collapsed?

That's exactly what Jeffrey W. Greenberg did as the head of Marsh & McLennan Companies. He shared his firsthand account in his article "September 11, 2001: A CEO's Story," in the *Harvard Business Review*.

"I think I was the only person who left the windows. Everyone was glued to the scene, trying to phone colleagues in the two buildings. I needed to get to my office and start dealing with what this atrocity meant."

The word *crisis* has its roots in Greek for the turning point in a disease when it finally spreads beyond control. At the nexus where fear meets urgency, we need direction, guidance and reassurance. Greenberg wrote: "In a time of crisis, there is something reassuring about hearing the voice of a person in a position of authority, even if the information being provided is scant."

As a leader, you have to make sure your business doesn't fall apart. You have to manage crises so that normalcy slowly returns.

What is the biggest crisis you have ever handled as a leader? How did you do?

✦ DAY #233 ✦

ON LEANING IN

Sheryl Sandberg climbed to the very top of the corporate ladder. She had a supportive upbringing, had an Ivy League education, had been mentored by the best and brightest and was eventually voted one of the hundred most influential people in the world by *Time* in 2012. Gender, she predicted, will one day not be an issue in leadership: "In the future, there will be no female leaders. There will just be leaders." She wrote:

"Many people, but especially women, feel fraudulent when they are praised for their accomplishments. Instead of feeling worthy of recognition, they feel undeserving and guilty, as if a mistake has been made. . . . They really are impostors with limited skills or abilities."

Sandberg in *Lean In* emphasized that women often hold themselves back from success. "Women need to shift from thinking 'I'm not ready to do that' to thinking 'I want to do that—and I'll learn by doing it."

Learning, wrote Sandberg, is critical to stretching yourself, learning on the job rather than knowing everything before you apply for the job. "There is no perfect fit when you're looking for the next big thing to do. You have to take opportunities and make an opportunity fit you, rather than the other way around. The ability to learn is the most important quality a leader can have."

Think of your next leadership challenge.
Now lean in.

✦ DAY #234 ✦

ON PROMISES

Sometimes we break promises. Sometimes they break us.

Jephthah was a brave soldier in the biblical book of Judges who made a promise to God: *Let me win this war, and I will sacrifice the first thing that comes through my door.* Jephthah had only one thing he wanted in his life: triumph.

"When Jephthah went back home to Mizpah, there was his daughter coming out to meet him, dancing and playing the tambourine. She was his only child. When he saw her, he tore his clothes in sorrow and said, 'Oh, my daughter! You are breaking my heart! Why must it be you that causes me pain? I have made a solemn promise to the Lord, and I cannot take it back!'"

Instead of renegotiating the terms, Jephthah got trapped by his own words: "I cannot take it back."

The solution: Don't make promises.

Name a promise you did not keep or one
that you did that caused you pain.

✦ DAY #235 ✦

ON SETBACKS

Karen Armstrong entered a convent when she was a teenager. She started as a postulant, then became a novice and then took the vows of a nun, prostrating herself fully and saying "This is the beginning of death," as the mantle that would one day cover her coffin covered her body. When she entered her holy service in England in the early 1960s, the Roman Catholic Church imposed severe discipline on those who took vows of celibacy and poverty. Armstrong described her painful seven years in the convent in two spiritual memoirs: *Through the Narrow Gate* and *The Spiral Staircase*. She then left to pursue an academic career, but not without an attendant sense of guilt and desperation. She concluded: "I had failed to make a gift of myself to God."

Armstrong found a different, more expansive faith only when she left the narrow gates she had once embraced, and this gave her a portal into the universal impulse to create community around belief. "Sometimes it's the very otherness of a stranger, someone who doesn't belong to our ethnic or ideological or religious group, an otherness that can repel us initially, but which can jerk us out of our habitual selfishness, and give us intonations of that sacred otherness, which is God."

By letting go of one truth, she found many. "Religion is not about accepting twenty impossible propositions before breakfast, but about doing things that change you."

What leadership setback was eventually liberating?

✦ DAY #236 ✦

ON CONTRACTION

Tzimtzum in Hebrew means "contraction" and refers to the way in which we make ourselves smaller. Kabbalah, Jewish mysticism, uses this term to describe a mythical way in which God created the world: a spiritual big bang theory. When God created the world, God had to contract in order to make room for human life. Since divine power is so strong, the intense "vessels" in which it resided shattered, resulting in what one writer has called a cosmic catastrophe. In contracting, God spread divinity everywhere and into everything.

Rabbi Abraham Isaac Kook (1865–1935), the first chief rabbi of what was then Palestine, described the impact of this shattering:

"We cannot identify the abundant vitality within all living beings, from the smallest to the largest, nor the hidden vitality within inanimate creation. Everything constantly flows, vibrates and aspires. . . . Everything teems with richness, everything aspires to ascend and be purified. Everything sings, celebrates, serves, develops, evolves, uplifts, aspires to be arranged in oneness."

In 1974, Rabbi Eugene Borowitz wrote an article, "*Tzimtzum:* A Mystic Model for Contemporary Leadership," in which he adapted this framework for leadership. Look for the spark in all. Contract yourself to make room for those you lead.

> **Think of the most difficult person you**
> **work with. Identify three divine sparks—**
> **redeeming qualities—of that individual.**

✦ DAY #237 ✦

ON EQUALITY

There is the Rudyard Kipling (1865–1936) view of equality: "All the people like us are We, and everyone else is They." We feel comfortable extending equality to those we deem like us, be it in terms of gender, color, faith, sexual orientation or socioeconomic class.

There is the Bertrand Russell (1872–1970) view of equality in the United States: "In America everybody is of the opinion that he has no social superiors, since all men are equal, but he does not admit that he has no social inferiors, for, from the time of Jefferson onward, the doctrine that all men are equal applies only upwards, not downwards."

There is the W. C. Fields (1880–1946) view of equality: "I am free of all prejudices. I hate every one equally."

Then there is the Joss Whedon view. Whedon cowrote *Toy Story* and was asked why he creates such strong female characters in his movies:

"Equality is not a concept. It's not something we should be striving for. It's a necessity. Equality is like gravity. We need it to stand on this earth as men and women, and the misogyny that is in every culture is not a true part of the human condition. It is life out of balance, and that imbalance is sucking something out of the soul of every man and woman who's confronted with it. We need equality. Kinda now."

**Use your leadership influence to take one
small step toward greater equality today.**

✦ DAY #238 ✦

ON ADAPTABILITY

Scholar of mysticism Gershom Scholem (1897–1982) believed that certain conditions need to exist for divine mystery to flourish. It represents, as he wrote in *Major Trends in Jewish Mysticism*, "a certain stage of religious consciousness."

The first stage of the historical development of religion is the presence of many gods; humans encounter them everywhere. The second period or stage represents the emergence of organized religion. Instead of the unmediated relationship people have with gods or spirits, formal hierarchies, rituals and structures are introduced. Prayer takes the place of direct conversation. The priest or clergy takes the place of direct communication. Sacred texts replace unmediated experiences.

"Mysticism does not deny or overlook the abyss; on the contrary, it begins by realizing its existence, but from there it proceeds to a quest for the secret that will close it in, the hidden path that will span it. It strives to piece together the fragments broken by the religious cataclysm, to bring back the old unity which religion has destroyed."

We rarely think of religion as the structure that kills the spirit, and yet the moment we institutionalize any ideals, we damage the soul of them. In *Christianity after Religion: The End of Church and the Birth of a New Spiritual Awakening*, Diana Butler Bass wrote that today a spiritual awakening is taking place. People today are feeling tired of structure. They want spirit: "a spiritual space beyond institutions, buildings, and organizations, a different sort of faith."

**Begin a more direct and intimate
conversation with your faith.**

✦ DAY #239 ✦

ON AUTHORITY

The Talmud says that "authority buries the one who owns it." Some commentaries believe that this is to be taken literally. People with power shorten their lives. The responsibility they shoulder and the burden they carry shaves years off their existence.

Others understand this to mean that leaders shorten the quality of their lives by replacing pleasure with the heaviness of leading others. They take on the suffering of others as their own.

The Talmud substantiates this view by remarking on the human condition: "He was naked when he entered [into power], and he will be naked when he leaves it. If only his exit would be like his entrance—without sin and iniquity."

Few people enter the world with any power. Not even kings are born wearing ermine capes. And when they exit this world and their positions of power, kings will once again be naked, but this time sin and iniquity will have to be removed. Power changes people.

If you're not careful, it will change you.

**Identify a quote, a verse from a sacred text or a question
that keeps you aware that your authority is fragile.**

ON HUMILIATION

The French abbot Bernard of Clairvaux (1090–1153) knew a thing or two about humiliation. The pope assigned Bernard a role in the Second Crusade. He failed. He wrote a letter of apology to the pope for disappointing him and failing in his mission.

He learned critical wisdom that can only come from a certain response to failure.

"Many of those who are humiliated are not humble. Some react to humiliation with anger, others with patience, and others with freedom. The first are culpable, the next harmless, the last just."

Humiliation is not a choice. It is a response to losing, to compromising our best selves, to withdrawing our energies, to acting badly, to making someone else suffer. The humiliated can respond with anger, creating protective shields against shame. Some hold on and wait to get on the other side; and the last, according to Bernard, feel liberated by the embarrassment. It feels strangely redeeming.

When humility teaches you to be wise, your wisdom can be shared. Many employees and followers can never believe that those who lead them were ever humiliated, ever lost, ever insecure. We help those we lead when we are vulnerable enough to share our moments of humiliation because we would not be able to lead without them.

**Think of a professionally humiliating moment and find
a way to share it with someone who needs to hear it.**

ON LIBERTY

PROCLAIM LIBERTY THROUGHOUT ALL THE LAND
UNTO ALL THE INHABITANTS THEREOF LEV. XXV. V X.

BY ORDER OF THE ASSEMBLY OF THE PROVINCE OF
PENSYLVANIA FOR THE STATE HOUSE IN PHILAD
PASS AND STOW
PHILAD
MDCCLIII

This famous biblical verse, copied letter-for-letter from Philadelphia's Liberty Bell, signals the exuberance and public nature of liberty. When freedom finally arrives, it cannot be contained. It must
burst out and gather momentum. It is the verse that freed slaves in
the Jubilee year, when ownership of property and people had to be
relinquished.

The drafting committee wrote to Robert Charles in 1751 to
order the bell, requesting a weight of about two thousand pounds
for the sum of a hundred English pounds. Placing the verse on a
bell was a way to make the words ring, quite literally, in the ears of
the people. Legend has it that it cracked after its first use to gather
legislators and lawmakers to order. In 1846, the hairline crack appeared, becoming an iconic aspect of the bell, making it instantly
recognizable. It was also associated with the antislavery movement.

The bell was placed right near Abraham Lincoln when his body
lay in state in Philadelphia, with its inscription near his head. Paying one's last respects to the assassinated president also provided a
fresh encounter with what he stood for and gave his life for—liberty
across the land.

**Does your view of liberty have any hairline fractures,
like tolerating racism in jokes or comments?**

✦ DAY #242 ✦

ON FAVORITISM

The book of Genesis is riddled with favoritism. God favored Abel
over Cain. Cain kills Abel. Abraham favored Isaac over Ishmael.
Abraham's two sons—although friends in their lifetime—went on

to father nations that continually fought with each other until this very day. Isaac gave his blessing to Jacob instead of Esau, the oldest. The two of them fought in the womb and long beyond it. Leah and Rachel fought for the love of Jacob. The twelve sons who evolved into the twelve tribes are virtually all named after the rivalry between Rachel and Leah. Jacob favored Joseph above his other eleven sons. The other sons threw Joseph into a pit.

How is it that one generation failed to learn from the mistakes of the previous generation, especially when favoritism had such pernicious and life-threatening consequences, often making brothers and sisters into enemies?

Leadership thrives on favoritism. Many leaders have been groomed for leadership from a young age. Chosen for awards and responsibilities as youngsters, they continue to collect trophies and certificates; they get chosen because they *were* chosen. Favoritism is terrible in families but usually excellent in creating leaders.

If you could pick a leadership favorite
to groom, who would it be?

✦ DAY #243 ✦

ON COVENANT

A covenant is a contract, a binding commitment, a guarantee, a warrant, a pledge, a promise. It adds an element of what is binding, a sense that you answer to a higher authority when you keep your word.

This may feel constricting and unpleasant, but, as Russell Nelson has reminded us, "A covenant made with God should be regarded not as restrictive but as protective." A covenant ultimately protects our most treasured commitments. For Nelson, this "social contract" is seen as honoring the humanity of every person.

Nelson's own vocation demonstrates a covenant he made with God and society. The fourth most senior apostle in the Quorum of the Twelve Apostles of the Church of Jesus Christ of Latter-Day Saints, he is a cardiothoracic surgeon who was one of the initial team members to create the first heart-lung machine.

When you freely enter a covenant, you become a partner. In partnerships, we create expectations of each other and ourselves. That is why it is critical to know thyself before entering any enduring contract: "Your life will be a blessed and balanced experience if you first honor your identity and priority."

Nelson admonished us to keep covenants supple enough to embrace those outside of your inner circles: "Every religious group, while perhaps a majority somewhere, is also inevitably a minority somewhere else. Thus, religious organizations should and do show tolerance toward members of other religious denominations."

> Describe a covenant—
> a firm, binding commitment—
> that you freely entered.

✦ DAY #244 ✦

ON FELLOWSHIP

Two are better than one, the Bible tells us.

We become a soul-searching community when we stand together with something powerful above us.

Christian preacher A. W. Tozer (1897–1963), in *The Pursuit of God*, took two and multiplied them. When a hundred worshipers meet and all look to God, Tozer wrote that they are "in heart nearer to each other than they could possibly be, were they to become 'unity' conscious and turn their eyes away from God to strive for closer fellowship."

Leaders have to work hard to turn a group into a community,

but, as George Eliot reminded us in *Adam Bede*, this is the best way to exist:

"What greater thing is there for two human souls, than to feel that they are joined for life—to strengthen each other in all labor, to rest on each other in all sorrow, to minister to each other in all pain, to be one with each other in silent unspeakable memories at the moment of the last parting?"

Create stronger bonds of fellowship at work today.

✦ DAY #245 ✦

ON LIVING SMALL

Calvin Trillin grew up in Kansas, where he picked up quips like "I haven't had so much fun since the hogs ate my little sister." In *Messages from My Father*, he wrote that his father's Midwestern ethics taught him that "proper behavior was modest behavior." Gratitude and admiration were responded to with a "no big deal" attitude.

"Even the words to live by that I always associated most strongly with him—'You might as well be a mensch'—lacked grandiosity. The German word *Mensch*, which means a person or human being, can take on in Yiddish the meaning of a *real* human being—a person who always does the right thing in matters large or small, a person who would not only put himself at serious risk for a friend but also leave a borrowed apartment in better shape than he found it."

Trillin added: "I also knew he had a contempt for people who felt the need to pump up their own importance." This he also used a Yiddish expression to describe: big *k'nocker*, from the German word for *crack*, "the one who cracks the whip"—in other words, a big shot. He didn't care for people who drove flashy cars, displayed their intelligence overtly or needed to lord their triumphs over others. "These were big *k'nocker*s."

Most people, Trillin's father believed, do not leave a lasting impression. A mensch does.

**Stop being a *k'nocker*. And make
sure to be a mensch today.**

✦ D A Y #246 ✦

ON THE OTHER

"When two people relate to each other authentically and humanly, God is the electricity that surges between them." Martin Buber (1878–1965), an Austrian-born philosopher who resigned from his university position when Hitler came to power and eventually moved to Israel, thought a great deal about the role of self and other in dialogue. As the author of *I and Thou*, Buber believed that something remarkable happens when two people connect with each other as subjects rather than viewing each other as objects, which he called an I–It relationship.

"When I confront a human being as my Thou and speak the basic word I–Thou to him, then he is no thing among things nor does he consist of things. He is no longer He or She, a dot in the world grid of space and time, nor a condition to be experienced and described, a loose bundle of named qualities. Neighborless and seamless, he is Thou and fills the firmament. Not as if there were nothing but he; but everything else lives in his light."

Buber confessed that, given the choice between books or people as company, he would have chosen books as a young man. As he aged, he claimed he met fewer delightful people than delightful books—but that he learned much more from people than he did from written words on a page.

**How would an outsider know that you
have I–Thou relationships with those you
lead, rather than I–It relationships?**

ON REDEMPTION

"Now there is a final reason I think that Jesus says, 'Love your enemies.' It is this: that love has within it a redemptive power. And there is a power there that eventually transforms individuals. . . . Just keep being friendly to that person. . . . Just keep loving them, and they can't stand it too long. Oh, they react in many ways in the beginning. . . . They react with guilt feelings, and sometimes they'll hate you a little more at that transition period, but just keep loving them. And by the power of your love they will break down under the load. . . . There's something about love that builds up and is creative. There is something about hate that tears down and is destructive. So love your enemies."

In his "Loving Your Enemies" sermon delivered at Dexter Avenue Baptist Church, Martin Luther King Jr. (1929–1968) described the slow and patient process of redemption, the act of saving ourselves and others and gaining absolution from sin, error, evil and hate. Sustained love chisels away at enmity. It takes a long time to achieve redemption.

Redemption has a financial meaning. It is the act of regaining possession for payment. We also use the term to describe clearing a debt. When we pay what we owe, it is more than clearing our name in the eyes of others. The relief turns into a sense of personal accomplishment, a small but significant victory in the everyday battle we fight with the universe.

**Think of one small way you can redeem yourself
today and have the discipline to do it.**

ON BEING UNSETTLED

There are losses in our lives that shake us to the core, that make us question our existence, our relationship with God—or if there is a God—and what purpose exists for our suffering.

If you're a leader, you may suffer with an audience. Others are counting on us to be strong, to be stable, to be a guide through the ambiguity of living. And we don't always feel safe to say "I feel unsettled myself."

Anne Lamott observed in *Stitches: A Handbook on Meaning, Hope and Repair* that, as we mature, we realize that there are very few ways to protect ourselves from being unsettled outside of stitching together the moments of bliss and purpose that help us get through what seems at times unbearable loss.

"Only together do we somehow keep coming through unsurvivable loss, the stress of never knowing how things will shake down, to the biggest miracle of all, that against all odds, we will come through the end of the world again and again—changed but intact (more or less). Emerson wrote, 'People wish to be settled; only as far as they are unsettled is there any hope for them.'"

The tidings are not all bad. "The good news is that if you don't seal up your heart with caulking compound, and instead stay permeable, people stay alive inside you, and maybe outside you, too, forever."

**When, in a leadership role, did you
publicly admit to being unsettled?**

ON GETTING STARTED

In 2002, Blake Mycoskie finished racing around the world for the reality show *The Amazing Race*. After thirty-one days, he lost by four minutes. It was one of the great disappointments of his life.

You may not recognize his name, but you will probably know the company he created: TOMS Shoes. That wasn't the work of a loser but the enterprise of a winner. Mycoskie was vacationing in Argentina and noticed everyone wearing *alpargatas*, soft canvas shoes. He also met a woman who explained to him how many children do not own shoes in developing countries.

"Yes, I knew somewhere in the back of my mind that poor children around the world often went barefoot, but now, for the first time, I saw the real effects of being shoeless: the blisters, the sores, the infections—all the results of the children not being able to protect their young feet from the ground."

He continued: "I'd been playing around with the phrase 'Shoes for a Better Tomorrow,' which eventually became 'Tomorrow's Shoes,' then 'Toms.' (Now you know why my name is Blake but my shoes are TOMS. It's not about a person. It's about a promise—a better tomorrow.)"

Start something remarkable and pay it forward. "The first step to starting the journey is simply to put on your shoes—that's all."

**How can you, in your leadership position,
make something new and wonderful
happen for someone in need?**

✦ DAY #250 ✦

ON BRAVERY

"There are so many ways to be brave in this world. Sometimes bravery involves laying down your life for something bigger than yourself, or for someone else. Sometimes it involves giving up everything you have ever known, or everyone you have ever loved, for the sake of something greater.

"But sometimes it doesn't.

"Sometimes it is nothing more than gritting your teeth

through pain, and the work of every day, the slow walk toward a better life.

"That is the sort of bravery I must have now."

These are the words of Tris, a character in the third of Veronica Roth's Divergent trilogy, *Allegiant*. Roth has won awards for her science fiction writing for young adults. She wrote *Divergent*, the first in her trilogy, while a senior in college.

Bravery, in Roth's words, can involve the intrepid boldness we need to steel ourselves for difficult challenges ahead, the big, principled moments that transform us and others as leaders. But, as Roth gently reminds us, bravery can also be the patience and strength to put one foot in front of another after loss, pain and anguish and take a slow walk toward a better life.

"I'll say it one last time: Be brave."

**Name a leadership moment that required
real bravery on your part.**

✦ DAY #251 ✦

ON REPUTATION

John Wooden (1910–2010) was named one of the best basketball coaches of all time. Despite his awards and his celebrated career, Wooden knew that basketball was not his ultimate game. "Be more concerned with your character than your reputation, because your character is what you really are, while your reputation is merely what others think you are."

He was constantly surrounded by talent and wild success, but as he reminded his players: "Material possessions, winning scores, and great reputations are meaningless in the eyes of the Lord, because he knows what we really are, and that is all that matters." And in a field dominated by large egos, he understood that your reputation is linked to the contributions of others: "The main ingredient of stardom is the rest of the team."

Wooden was fiercely faithful to his wife, Nellie. After she died, he had a custom of visiting her grave on the twenty-first day of every month, then writing a love letter and leaving it on her pillow, stacked with the letters of all the previous years.

This man spent a lifetime mentoring and servicing others.

Think of a time when you were so wrapped up in concern for what others thought about you that you lost your grounding.

✦ DAY #252 ✦

ON SELFLESSNESS

Gretchen Rubin devoted one year to happiness, a goal that resulted in a book, *The Happiness Project*, which, she confessed, made her a happiness bully.

The thought was easier than the execution. "It was time to expect more of myself. Yet as I thought about happiness, I kept running up against paradoxes. I wanted to change myself but accept myself. I wanted to take myself less seriously—and also more seriously. I wanted to use my time well, but I also wanted to wander, to play, to read at whim. I wanted to think about myself so I could forget myself. I was always on the edge of agitation; I wanted to let go of envy and anxiety about the future, yet keep my energy and ambition."

She also discovered the relationship between anger and happiness. Expressing anger did not lead to relief and serenity: "Studies show that aggressively expressing anger doesn't relieve anger but amplifies it. . . . Not expressing anger often allows it to disappear without leaving ugly traces." The opposite was true, as Tolstoy noted: "Nothing can make our life, or the lives of other people, more beautiful than perpetual kindness."

Seeking happiness, like dieting or exercise, is not a onetime event. "What you do every day matters more than what you do once in a while." And say "yes" whenever you can. "Say 'no' only when it really matters."

Fight your inclination to say "no" and instead say "yes" to someone today.

✦ DAY #253 ✦

ON ESCAPE

Ever been on the road and felt overwhelmed when you passed an exit ramp for an airport and wondered to yourself, *Hmmm, how crazy would it be for me to take that ramp, fly somewhere really remote right now where there are palm trees, hammocks and girlie drinks, and disappear?*

For some leaders, this is an everyday dilemma: Stay or escape. Breathe in. Exhale. Stay.

In *Growing Up Amish*, Ira Wagler traced his childhood as a member of the Older Order Amish. No cars, no electricity—not in the house or outbuildings—no telephones in the house. Formal schooling until eighth grade and then a future of manual labor. Communities are tight, prayerful and supportive. Restrictions are constant limitations aimed at trying to achieve holiness and simplicity. Wagler ran away at age seventeen: "I could not know that night of the long hard road that stretched before me. That I was lost. I could not know of the years of turmoil, rage and anguish that would eventually push me to the brink of madness and despair."

He came back and left again several times and then one final time. "For the first time, I was not running in frantic despair into some wild and dangerous horizon. For the first time, I was leaving with a clear mind, quietly focused on faith, not fear."

What is the difference between an escape and an exit in your leadership?

ON RECOVERY

"Nearly every elite athlete we have worked with over the years has come to us with performance problems that could be traced to an imbalance between the expenditure and the recovery of energy. They were either *overtraining* or *undertraining*. . . . We achieved our breakthroughs with athletes by helping them to more skillfully manage energy—pushing themselves to systematically increase capacity in whatever dimension it was insufficient, but also to build in regular recovery as part of their training regimens."

Jim Loehr and Tony Schwartz spent twenty-five years working with great athletes, and in *The Power of Full Engagement*, they shared recommendations that have shaped the careers of these individuals. The goal was to identify the sources of their strength and energy and to build greater capacity, in particular achieving a balance between stress and recovery.

"Balancing stress and recovery is critical not just in competitive sports, but also in managing energy in all aspects of our lives. When we expend energy, we draw down our reservoir. When we receive energy, we fill it back up."

They identified this pattern of expending and saving energy as oscillation and claimed that "it represents the fundamental pulse of life." To fill yourself as a leader, you need to draw on four separate but related sources of energy: physical, emotional, mental and spiritual. "The most fundamental source of energy is physical. The most significant is spiritual."

Of these four sources of energy, which do you most often recover and which do you too often neglect?

ON INERTIA

The book of Proverbs takes a practical rather than a spiritual view of inertia.

"I went past the field of the lazy man, past the vineyard of the man who lacks judgment; thorns had come up everywhere, the ground was covered with weeds, and the stone wall was in ruins. I applied my heart to what I observed and learned a lesson from what I saw: A little sleep, a little slumber, a little folding of the hands to rest and poverty will come on you like a bandit and scarcity like an armed man" (24:30–34).

Proverbs understands the seduction of inertia, the appeal of lying in a warm bed for a few extra minutes. But it also knows the price of self-preservation. Two chapters later, we are offered this portrait.

"The lazy man says, 'There is a lion in the road, a fierce lion roaming the streets!' As a door turns on its hinges, so a lazy man turns on his bed. The lazy man buries his hand in the dish; he is too lazy to bring it back to his mouth" (26:13–15).

Inertia has morphed into an extreme, into a lion that is ignored, a dish that feels so heavy that the lazy man does not lift it and, therefore, takes in no nourishment.

When does inertia get in the way of your best leadership?

ON SPIRITUALITY

We have all heard people make the declaration "I am not a spiritual person."

Pierre Teilhard de Chardin (1881–1955) would have disagreed with this declaration. This Jesuit scholar, who was both philosopher and scientist, made his own famous declaration:

"We are not human beings having a spiritual experience. We are spiritual beings having a human experience."

We are not people who chose to have a spiritual outlook or experience. We live in the spirit, and this frames our human experience. Teilhard struggled with notions of religion that bifurcated the sacred from everyday experience.

The world for him was inherently mysterious, containing moments of great transcendence and possibility: "He that will believe only what he can fully comprehend must have a long head or a very short creed."

In Teilhard's words: "The universe as we know it is a joint product of the observer and the observed." As a religious man and a scientist, he observed the world and understood that we select the way we view it.

"Our duty, as men and women, is to proceed as if limits to our ability did not exist. We are collaborators in creation."

As a leader, you are a unique collaborator in creation.
So what is limiting you from being a more spiritual person?

✦ DAY #257 ✦

ON INSULTS

"We are a people who need to be among people. The problem is that once we are among them, we feel compelled to sort ourselves into social hierarchies." One of the ways we sort ourselves into these hierarchies, claimed William B. Irvine, is to insult each other.

Irvine wrote *A Slap in the Face: Why Insults Hurt—and Why They Shouldn't*. Of course insults hurt. Irvine began studying insults while researching the Stoic philosophers.

An insult is a barb, a stab, a little prick in the tender way we think about ourselves. Irvine argued that those with a "wealth of self-esteem" can afford the insult in the sense that the damage that is done is minor. People can only really hurt us if we allow them entrance. If we feel confident about ourselves, then that will not be changed by someone else's insensitivity, poor attempt at humor, or bad decision to put us in our place.

"We all want other people to know and appreciate how wonderful we are, . . . and one way to accomplish this is by making them realize how relatively insignificant they are."

This occupational hazard poses a particular danger for leaders. Be careful. You do not know the pain you may inflict.

Spend today catching yourself when you could say something mean, and couch it more lovingly.

✦ DAY #258 ✦

ON BODY LANGUAGE

Leaders are sometimes blind to the power of their body language to communicate rejection, boredom, disinterest, anger or pleasure. They may roll their eyes at a board meeting, yawn while a staff member is presenting a report or sit with their legs and arms crossed during a difficult conversation. They may be saying very little but their bodies are actually screaming.

Daniel Goleman, a pioneer of emotional intelligence studies, reported in *Primal Leadership*—with his coauthors Annie McKee and Richard Boyatzis—just how important body language is in leadership. They based their findings on a dissertation by Anthony T. Pescosolido submitted to Case Western Reserve University called "Emotional Intensity in Groups."

"Leaders typically talked more than anyone else, and what they said was listened to more carefully. Leaders were also usually first to speak on a subject, and when others made comments, their remarks most often referred to what the leader had said than to anyone else's comments. Because the leader's way of seeing things has special weight, leaders 'manage meaning' for a group, offering a way to interpret, and so react emotionally to, a given situation. But the impact on emotions goes beyond what a leader says. In these studies, even when leaders were not talking, they were watched more carefully than anyone else in the group. . . . In a sense, the leader sets the emotional standard."

Leaders set the standard, and they can determine, even when they say nothing, the emotional reaction of others to events and news.

**Think of an instance when your body language
spoke too loudly to those you lead.**

✦ DAY #259 ✦

ON MINDSIGHTS

"Mindsight is a kind of focused attention that allows us to see the internal workings of our own minds. It helps us to be aware of our mental processes without being swept away by them."

Daniel Siegel, a professor of psychiatry at UCLA School of Medicine and executive director of the Mindsight Center, wrote these words in *Mindsight: The New Science of Personal Transformation*. Siegel asked us to step out of ourselves and to "see what is inside, to accept it, and in the accepting to let it go, and finally, to transform it."

Standing outside ourselves and judging seems like this mindsight lens. But it isn't, according to Siegel. "Reflection requires an attunement to the self that is supportive and kind, not a judgmental stance of interrogation and derogation. Reflection is a compassionate state of mind."

One important mirror lens in life is the way that we experience loss. Siegel helped us understand the process through mindsight: "Loss rips us apart. Grief allows you to let go of something you've lost only when you begin to accept what you know you have in its place." Loss happens to us on so many levels. Death is far from our only loss. Divorce, estrangement from a family member or a friend, job loss, loss of youth, identity loss through retirement: All change is a form of loss.

Accept something you've done wrong; let it go.

ON BULLYING

Bullying is not only about middle school playgrounds. It also happens in cubicles, offices and corporate cafeterias. It happens in adult e-mails and supervisory relationships. It happens because some people relish the power they have over others.

Karla Miller, a work-advice columnist for the *Washington Post*, got a letter from a person who was sick and tired of her office bully. He was charming and funny, which masked the fact that he often gave off body language that was intimidating. He also sent the correspondent unpleasant e-mails, making sure to copy others. Colleagues called him a bully so this was not her opinion alone.

Miller advised asking him an innocent question next time she got the stare: "Do you need something?" This would alert others to his behavior, show him that the recipient of these stares was unfazed and "alert him to the fact that he suffers from chronic resting derpface."

She also advised this office worker to keep a written record of interactions, with copies of nastygrams, so that she could report the behavior to his supervisor if necessary.

Leaders should be in the business of creating places where exciting work gets done in safe spaces. Don't be the last to know. Today that is not an excuse. It is an admission of guilt.

Find out who is the office bully.
How are you going to stop it?

ON RESONANCE

When we think of resonance we think of something that is deep and full and reverberates within us. "That resonates with me," we might say when we hear a good idea or we meet someone for the first time but feel we've known that person for a lifetime. Resonance happens when we read a beautiful poem that articulates a feeling we've held on to but didn't have words to express.

In their book *Resonant Leadership*, Richard Boyatzis and Annie McKee made the case that leadership needs to communicate benevolence, mindfulness, compassion, optimism and hope. We want leaders to resonate with us, not to feel remote and distant. Resonant leaders are "exciting and get results," they wrote.

"These leaders are *moving* people—powerfully, passionately and purposefully. And they do so while managing the inevitable sacrifices inherent in their roles. They give of themselves in the service of the cause, but they also care for themselves, engaging in renewal to ensure they can sustain resonance over time."

Resonance takes constant and intentional work.

"People who think they can be truly great leaders without personal transformation are fooling themselves. You cannot inspire others and create resonant relationships that ignite greatness in your families, organizations, or communities without feeling inspired yourself, and working to be the best person you can be."

Resonant leaders are inspired and inspiring.

Who is the most resonant leader you know?

✦ DAY #262 ✦

ON PERSONAL
RESPONSIBILITY

"Blaming others or outside conditions for one's own misbehavior may be the child's privilege; if an adult denies responsibility for his actions, it is another step towards personal disintegration." Bruno Bettelheim (1903–1990) wrote these words in his book *The Informed Heart: Autonomy in a Mass Age*. Bettelheim was born in Austria and moved to the United States in 1939 after leaving a concentration camp. He did groundbreaking work on Freud and the world of emotional disturbances in children, focusing on fairy tales in *The Uses of Enchantment.*

As we mature, we hope that we have the courage to own our mistakes. Leaders often have to suck up responsibility for the errors and failures of others simply by virtue of being leaders.

This point is made in weighty prose in the Talmud:

"Anyone who has the capability to protest the sinful conduct of his household and does not protest, he himself is liable for the sins of the members of his household. If he could have protested the sins of the people of his town but did not, he is held liable for the sins of the people of his town. If he is in a position to protest the sins of the whole world and does not do so, he is liable for the sins of the whole world."

What was the most serious wrongdoing of your organization for which you took personal responsibility?

✦ DAY #263 ✦

ON VANITY

"The greatest magnifying glasses in the world are a man's own eyes when they look upon his own person."

The word *vanity* has seemingly contradictory meanings. The most common understanding of *vanity* is self-absorption, an excessive concern with one's appearance or achievements, as in the Alexander Pope quote above. A person who is vain looks at himself again and again. Every look, every comment is directed within, usually in self-admiration. But vanity doesn't always appear that way to others. It may look like insecurity.

"How do I look?"

"What did you think of my speech?"

"How many people were in the audience?"

The compassion that surfaces to allay another's anxiety just feeds the beast of vanity:

"You look fabulous."

"You spoke beautifully."

"Everyone in the room heard you. They were transfixed."

The monster ego was hungry, and it supped.

The other meaning of *vanity* is nothingness, as in the oft-repeated line from Ecclesiastes: "Vanity, O vanity, all is vanity." All leads to nothing. Nothing is worth anything. Some scholars have translated the Hebrew word for *vanity—hevel—*as "breath." All is an empty breath: invisible, impossible to grasp, unable to manipulate.

But maybe the two competing meanings are really one. The grab at self-attention is meaningless. It is futile because the lust for adoration can never be sated. Put the mirror down.

**What do you do to catch yourself when
you find your own vanity surfacing?**

✦ DAY #264 ✦

ON FLOW

When was the last time you were "in the zone" at work? Ideas flowed freely. Thinking through problems came easily. You were totally engaged. You lost total track of time. Hours went by like minutes. The sense of why you do what you do was apparent. It did not even require articulation.

Mihaly Csikszentmihalyi, a Hungarian-American psychologist, called this feeling "flow" in the 1970s, when he began with a study of artists who lose themselves in their work. Flow describes what it is like to be wholly immersed in what we are doing, so fully engaged that, in Csikszentmihalyi's words, "nothing else seems to matter." Rapture wraps us in flow.

You are not doing your job. You *are* your job.

Athletes call this feeling a zone. Some people describe it as being on fire, being in the moment, highly attuned, hyperfocused, or exceptionally present. Our work seems almost effortless, natural.

We feel our minds and bodies to be aligned and that we are truly alive and living out our calling.

These times can pass quickly. It's wonderful when we can recognize them, savor them and feed off them, even when their intensity dissipates. No one wants these moments to go away. The poet Rainer Maria Rilke wrote his own little prayer for flow: "May what I do flow from me like a river, no forcing and no holding back."

Describe your last flow moment in leadership.

⬧ DAY #265 ⬧

ON CHANGING THE WORLD

"Some people may be lucky.

"They will know exactly what they want to change.

"But for many it's uncertain. There are so many problems, and so many ways to deal with them. Surprisingly often, we find ourselves impaled on a paradox: We desperately want to do something, but have no idea what it may be."

In John-Paul Flintoff's *How to Change the World: Social Entrepreneurs and the Power of New Ideas*, he recognized the drive to do something big. But what?

How can we change the world when it is so hard to change the smallest thing about ourselves? The arrogance of it can seem astounding. Flintoff turned to Mother Teresa at her most inspiring and wrote: "I never look at the masses as my responsibility. I look at the individual. I can only love one person at a time, just one, one, one."

One plus one. You and another. And then maybe another.

"The question we are looking at is not 'What is the meaning of life?' but 'How can I make my life meaningful?' And the answer to that requires action." We are not going to solve it all, not even a little piece of it. We give back to the world that put us here one day at a time.

**What do you feel is the most meaningful small way
you have changed the world since you've arrived?**

◆ DAY #266 ◆

ON BURNOUT

We all know burnout. Sometimes we're on intimate terms with it. Or we can see it on the horizon, coming closer and closer.

American author and philosopher Sam Keen, in *Fire in the Belly: On Being a Man,* described burnout visually: "Burnout is nature's way of telling you, you've been going through the motions but your soul has departed; you're a zombie, a member of the walking dead, a sleepwalker. False optimism is like administrating stimulants to an exhausted nervous system.

"Our inner dialogue is frequently composed of old tape loops that we run again and again. . . . So we play the old movies with their stale fears and their unrealistic hopes until we become bored enough to risk disarmament and engagement."

Burnout does not have to be a state of disintegration. It might just be intense boredom. I work in a job I hate that enables me to have another life outside of work, which brings me pleasure. Keen had something to say about this deal with the devil: "A society in which vocation and job are separated for most people gradually creates an economy that is often devoid of spirit, one that frequently fills our pocketbooks at the cost of emptying our souls."

There has to be more. There is. But it requires us to expect more of work and expect more of ourselves. Otherwise burnout is just around the bend.

"Freedom is an inside job."

**Describe what burnout feels like to you and write
down every adjective you associate with it.**

ON STOPPING

"Life is similar to a bus ride.

"The journey begins when we board the bus.

"We meet people along our way of which some are strangers, some friends and some strangers yet to be friends.

"There are stops at intervals and people board.

"At times some of these people make their presence felt, leave an impact through their grace and beauty on us fellow passengers, while on other occasions they remain indifferent."

Indian writer Chirag Tulsiani added a twist to the journey metaphor above. We do not often walk on a path alone, an image many of us hold. We are, instead, on a bus with others. We may know some of those others, but most are strangers. People will get on and off that bus that is our lives. There will be many stops.

Jim Collins, in *Good to Great,* offered the oft-quoted image of the corporate bus. Get the right people on the bus, the wrong people off, and then let the right people decide on the bus's direction together.

Unless you actually own a bus, there aren't always right or wrong people with you. They are just a collection of friends, neighbors and strangers who happen to want to go to the same location or stop along the way.

When is the last time you rode on public transportation? Get out a little. See other worlds.

ON SELF-DELUSION

There are vital lies we tell ourselves. We call these self-delusions because they are the lies that help us maintain the images we have of ourselves. Not every self-delusion is positive. Sometimes we doom ourselves to failure without realizing how successful we are. Sometimes we put ourselves down without due cause.

"Self-delusion is a powerful trap indeed, skewing our attempts to assess ourselves. Because of it, we give more weight to what confirms our distorted self-image—and ignore what doesn't." Daniel Goleman, Richard Boyatzis and Annie McKee offered this warning in *Primal Leadership* to show leaders how to harness emotional intelligence and lead more effectively.

Not everyone will chip away at our self-delusions, bolster our insecurities or praise us for who we are not. They withhold these comments because of "fear of the leader's wrath," not wanting to be marginalized and wanting to be seen as team players.

This can have disastrous consequences. "Most leaders are deprived of important feedback. Often the reason is simply that it makes people uncomfortable to give candid feedback on someone else's behavior. Few people want to intentionally hurt another person's feelings—but often they don't know how to deliver feedback in a productive, rather than hurtful, way. They therefore often swing too far in the other direction, making enormous efforts to 'be nice.'"

The more senior you are, the more intimidating you seem, the less approachable you become.

What are you going to do about that?

✦ DAY #269 ✦

ON SANITY

"I am going crazy."

"I am going to lose my mind."

"This place is making me insane."

In our more overwhelming moments, we may find ourselves thinking, if not saying, these things in the halls of our offices or when the door is closed. We question our sanity.

Psychoanalyst and writer Philippa Perry explained in *How to*

Stay Sane that mental health needs vary from person to person. "For every one of us who needs to take the risk of being more open, there is another who needs to practise [she's English] self-containment. For each person who needs to learn to trust more, there is another who needs to experiment with more discernment." The list goes on.

"When we practice self-observation, we learn to stand outside ourselves, in order to experience, acknowledge and assess feelings, sensations and thoughts as they occur and as they determine our moods and behaviour. The development of this capacity allows us to be accepting and non-judgmental. It gives us space to decide how to act and is part of us that listens to and brings together our emotions and logic. In order to maximize our sanity we need to develop self-observation to increase self-awareness. This is a job that is never finished."

Re-forming helps us reform when life feels out of control.

Practice the art of watching yourself respond and react to situations. How do you make yourself crazy?

◆ DAY #270 ◆

ON ADVICE

Leaders are often called upon to give advice. And many leaders love giving it.

In *The Getaway Car: A Practical Memoir about Writing and Life*, Ann Patchett shares that requests for her advice got so bad, she had to put it all down in one place: *"Look, it's here, I wrote it all down."*

No matter. At dinners and parties she was accosted: "My story will be a true blockbuster, a best-selling American original. Unfortunately, my busy schedule does not afford me the time to write it myself."

At a family reunion, after having too many drinks, a woman approached her and said that everyone has at least one great novel in them. Normally Patchett would have smiled, nodded in agreement and moved on. But she had been there too long. She was bored and tired. She pointed to a large floral arrangement.

Does everyone have a great floral arrangement in them?

One algebraic proof?

One Hail Mary pass?

One five-minute mile?

The absurdity of it brought the truth about advice to the surface. If we are sufficiently humble, the most we can do is what Patchett attempted: "This isn't an instruction booklet. This is an account of what I did and what has worked for me." I can tell you what I did. I cannot, however, really ever tell you what you should do because I respect the complexity of each human life. And I am not you.

**Share a piece of professional advice
you once gave that backfired.**

✦ DAY #271 ✦

ON HONESTY

"So many times I've heard people say "We never addressed the real issue, never came to terms with reality." Or "We never stated our needs. We never told each other what we were really thinking and feeling."

Susan Scott, in *Fierce Conversations: Achieving Success at Work and in Life, One Conversation at a Time*, describes the illusions we sometimes feed on that lead us astray. We are not being dishonest. We are just not being honest enough.

We do not have the psychic energy to do the hard work of an honest conversation.

When we think of the word *fierce*, we tend to focus on images of aggression. Scott, however, searched her thesaurus and came up with these synonyms: *robust, intense, strong, powerful, passionate, eager, unbridled, uncurbed, untamed*. "In its simplest form, *a fierce conversation is one in which we come out from behind ourselves into the conversation and make it real*."

She continued: "*The conversation is the relationship*. If the conversation stops, the relationship stops, all of the possibilities for the relationship become smaller and smaller and all of the possibilities for the individuals in the relationship become smaller and smaller, until one day we overhear ourselves in midsentence, making *ourselves* smaller in every encounter."

Where is the honesty in that?

**What fierce conversation have you
as a leader been avoiding?**

✦ DAY #272 ✦

ON NATURE

"The future will belong to the nature-smart—those individuals, families, businesses, and political leaders who develop a deeper understanding of the transformative power of the natural world and who balance the virtual with the real. The more high-tech we become, the more nature we need."

Robert Louv, in *The Nature Principle: Reconnecting with Life in a Virtual Age*, advocated strengthening children's relationship with nature, something he has called the "leave no child left inside" movement. He also coined the term "nature deficit disorder." According to research, only 6 percent of children regularly play outdoors.

Louv acknowledged the risks of being outside, but then he showed us the risks of being indoors, what he called "virtual protective house arrest." These dangers include "threats to their independent judgment and value of place, to their ability to feel awe and wonder, to their sense of stewardship for the Earth—and, most immediately, threats to their psychological and physical health."

Maybe you're reading Louv's words while you sit in front of a computer, walled in by windows, seeing an outdoors behind glass that *you* aren't enjoying.

Louv wrote his next book for adults: "Time spent in nature is the most cost-effective and powerful way to counteract the burnout and sort of depression that we feel when we sit in front of a computer all day."

When was the last time you felt the awe and wonder of nature at work? Go outside.

✦ DAY #273 ✦

ON REGRESSION

"We can see in each person his own (weak) tendencies to grow toward self-actualization; and also descriptively, we can see his various (weak) tendencies toward regressing (out of fear, hostility, or laziness)." Abraham Maslow (1908–1970) created a polarity of growth and regression in *Religions, Values, and Peak-Experiences*.

Maslow looked at the psychological and emotional states of individuals who choose growth over regression. And he made a large claim: "If a person could himself see all the likely consequences of growth and all the likely consequences of coasting or of regression, and if he were allowed to choose between them, he would always choose the consequences of growth and reject the consequences of regression."

Regression can look very attractive. Actualization can seem hard, overwhelming, demanding.

Leaders can model what it means to move up the ladder of self-actualization and strive for the highest priorities in the hierarchy of human needs, or leaders can regress. There are two directions on this and on every ladder. Stasis does not get you anywhere.

Ralph Waldo Emerson wrote: "God offers to every mind its choice between truth or repose. Take which you please. You can never have both."

Do you find yourself gravitating more to professional growth or more to professional regression?

ON SCARCITY

"I routinely will interrupt an interesting face-to-face conversation to answer the ring of an unknown caller. In such a situation, the caller has a compelling feature that my face-to-face partner does not: potential unavailability. If I don't take the call, I might miss it for good."

The good news is that if you call the psychologist Robert Cialdini—who wrote this in *Influence: The Psychology of Persuasion*—he might interrupt whatever important thing he is doing to pick up your call.

This fear of missing out (FOMO) has come to be a major distraction of a high order. We see this fear being manipulated in all kinds of marketing ploys. A course advertises limited seating. An expiration date on a gift card looms large in our minds. Access to someone is on a first-come-first-serve basis.

"The idea of potential loss plays a large role in human decision making. . . . People seem to be more motivated by the thought of losing something than by the thought of gaining something of equal value." FOMO is a powerful drug indeed. Its power lies in exactly what is most frustrating about it: You will never know if you've really missed out.

What about FOLWYH—fear of losing what you have?

**When have you lost something of value because
you feared potentially losing something else?**

ON ANXIETY

Sometimes anxiety feels like the invasion of the body snatchers, viscerally overtaking us with perspiration, knee knocking, rapid breathing and nausea. Jodi Picoult compared it to a rocking chair: "It gives you something to do, but it doesn't get you very far."

This may explain the preacher Max Lucado's great story. A man who suffers anxiety decides to subcontract his worries. He hires someone else to do all the worrying for him. He offers a salary of $200,000 to do this job, finds someone and gives him the work. The first question this employee asks his boss is this: "Where are you going to get the $200K?" To which the boss responds, "That's your worry."

The Bible offers us its good word on this bad feeling. "Anxiety in a person's heart weighs him down, but a kind word cheers him up" (Proverbs 12:25).

The Talmud interprets this verse differently based on the different meanings of the word *yashkhenah*—translated loosely here as "weighs him down." It actually has three possible meanings: (1) to suppress, (2) to ignore, (3) to articulate.

You can overcome worry by suppressing it, ignoring it or articulating it. The Talmud prefers the third. Speak through your worries. Any other method of dealing with them will just postpone the inevitable. They'll be back. If you speak them through and give language to them, they may dissipate because of their absurdity or impossibility.

**Name an anxiety you are carrying right
now and speak through it.**

✦ DAY #276 ✦

ON MISFORTUNE

On the upper Missouri River, Ontopanga or Big Elk (1770–1853), lived the chief of the Omaha Native Americans. He led his tribe through many transitions and hardships: smallpox, the approach of warring American whites and conflicts with the Sioux. The process of accommodation, assimilation and battle with neighbors was shaking the foundations of his tribe. Two of his daughters married

Europeans who became absorbed in the Omaha tribe. Big Elk made some critical decisions to trade with the Americans and become allies. Eventually these negotiations resulted in a reservation for the Omaha tribe in northern Nebraska.

Big Elk had what so many leaders today need: the gift of passionate oration.

"Do not grieve. Misfortunes will happen to the wisest and best of men. Death will come, always out of season. It is the command of the Great Spirit, and all the nations and people must obey. What is past and what cannot be prevented should not be grieved for. . . . Misfortunes do not flourish particularly in our lives—they grow everywhere."

Big Elk can help us manage difficulties by learning to diminish their uniqueness. Misfortune is not special to you. It is owned by us all. It grows and spreads and ripens everywhere.

**Think of a time when you felt that misfortune
flourished in your life. How did you get perspective?**

✦ DAY #277 ✦

ON STATUS

"All see, and most admire, the glare which hovers round the external trappings of elevated office. To me there is nothing in it, beyond the lustre which may be reflected from its connection with a power of promoting human felicity."

George Washington wrote this in 1790 in a letter to Catherine Sawbridge Macaulay Graham (1731–1791). She was an English historian who described herself as a trivial girl until she picked up a book of history at age twenty. She believed that the weakness of women lay only in their poor education, which she tried to rectify with her writing and her political advocacy. She stayed at Mount Vernon with President Washington's family in 1785 and continued correspondence with the president on the ideal republic and other aspects of politics.

In the passage above, President Washington disabused Graham of the lure of status that often accompanies high office. He understood full well that people find the baubles of power irresistible, but he had no trouble resisting them himself.

Being the first president of the United States was a job not only with status but, at his time, a position without precedent. He set a precedent of service because he removed his ego needs from the leadership equation.

**What part of leadership status do you
have that you cannot stand?**

✦ DAY #278 ✦

ON BEING A SPIRITUAL ACTIVIST

In *Letters to a Young Activist*, Todd Gitlin warned that advocacy for those you love can create an inner circle of concern and leave everyone else outside the ring. "Love of your own, of people like yourself, people with whom you share an identity (or, more precisely, people with whom you decide to share an identity and overlook differences), slides easily into what Erik Erikson called *pseudospeciation*—the belief that your tribe, clan, family, class, race, nation, ethnicity, religion is the whole of humanity."

One of the first spiritual activists we have on record is Abraham fighting God for the people of Sodom and Gomorrah: "Will you sweep away the righteous with the wicked? What if there are fifty righteous people in the city? . . . Far be it from you to do such a thing—to kill the righteous with the wicked, treating the righteous and the wicked alike. Far be it from you! Will not the Judge of all the earth do right?" (Genesis 18:22–25)

Abraham stood his ground and negotiated downward: "'May the Lord not be angry, but let me speak just once more. What if only ten can be found there?' He answered, 'For the sake of ten, I will not destroy it.' When the Lord had finished speaking with Abraham, he left, and Abraham returned home."

Identify a person who is not like you but for whom you have advocated.

✦ DAY #279 ✦

ON LOSING IT

We all have days when we lose it. We should have kept quiet. We shouldn't have used that word, that tone. We should have walked out of the room before exploding. We should have explained that there was a lot going on at home. We didn't.

We're not alone.

"So Moses took the staff from the Lord's presence, just as he commanded him. He and Aaron gathered the assembly together in front of the rock, and Moses said to them, 'Listen, you rebels, must we bring you water out of this rock?' Then Moses raised his arm and struck the rock twice with his staff. Water gushed out, and the community and their livestock drank" (Numbers 20:9–11).

Rebels? When you start to call your followers names, when you label them as dissenters—even if they are—your new level of disrespect signals that your leadership has come to an end. You cannot lead people for long and through difficult terrain if you no longer believe in them.

God reproached Moses immediately: "Because you did not trust in me enough to honor me as holy in the sight of the Israelites, you will not bring this community into the land I give them." All that travel, all that vision and hardship dissipated in a moment. His punishment: he could not cross over into the Holy Land.

Before you lose it, try to catch yourself and ask: "What will I *really* lose if I lose it?"

Describe the last time you lost it and the cost.

ON RELIGION

"I could say a thousand things to you, if I had leisure. I could dwell on the importance of piety and religion, of industry and frugality, of prudence, economy, regularity and even Government, all of which are essential to the well-being of a family. But I have not time. I cannot however help repeating piety, because I think it is indispensable. Religion in a family is at once its brightest ornament and its best security."

This was the advice of Samuel Adams (1722–1803) to his future son-in-law.

Religion is both ornament and anchor, a sparkling centerpiece and a life insurance policy for the family. Having a structure of morals, rituals and a communal language of kindness can help families bond and grow.

We can dismiss Adams the way many today dismiss religion. He lived a long time ago. Religion, too, is old. It's the opiate of the masses; it's for people who are unsophisticated and needy. Many who toss religion out this way have minimal acquaintance with its teachings.

"He who is void of virtuous attachments in private life is, or very soon will be, void of all regard for his country. There is seldom an instance of a man guilty of betraying his country, who had not before lost the feeling of moral obligations in his private connections."

**What nouns would you use to describe the role
of religion in your life and in your leadership?**

ON THE "SLASH"

Remember Gail Sheehy's *Passages*? The self-help classic helped us navigate the stages we move through in adulthood. In *New Passages*,

Sheehy observed that professional life can be most economically secure and meaningful when we don't limit ourselves to one job.

"A single fixed identity is a liability today. It only makes people more vulnerable to sudden changes in economic conditions. . . . Recent research also suggests that developing multiple identities is one of the best buffers we can erect against mental and physical illness."

Pushing this notion of multiple work identities, Marci Alboher wrote *One Person/Multiple Careers* to help us think more holistically about the way we spend most of our daylight hours.

Alboher interviewed dozens of people who "live in the slash." "Listening to their stories," she said, helped her realize that "people who have figured out how to add slashes to their lives are an incredibly fulfilled bunch, both in what they think of as work and what they think of as 'life.' What's more, they seem to have found the answers to some of the most vexing issues in working life today, from job insecurity to career burnout to work/life balance."

When we were kids, we often explored and discovered many talents and areas of interest: sports, music, art, politics, theater. As we age our world narrows. We aren't expected to master many arenas. We look dilettantish if we do. And thus we become smaller and smaller.

Name your slash.

◆ DAY #282 ◆

ON RITUAL

Think of your rituals. Which dictionary definition most aptly describes them?

Ritual: (1) The prescribed order of a religious ceremony. (2) The body of ceremonies or rites used in a place of worship. (3) The prescribed form of conducting a formal secular ceremony: the ritual of an inauguration. (4) The body of ceremonies used by a fraternal organization. (5) A book of rites or ceremonial forms. (6) Being part of an established routine: a ritual glass of milk before bed. (7) A detailed act or series of acts carried out by an individual to relieve anxiety or to forestall the development of anxiety.

Spiritual traditions place rituals at key points of change to "forestall the development of anxiety." Rituals provide cushions.

But sometimes the rituals become tired. What then? Blu Greenberg tackled this problem in *How to Run a Traditional Jewish Household*:

"But how . . . can one perform ritual without perfect and pure intent? Is it not a sham? The answer might be, 'Once more, with feeling.' Even so, should ritual or rite happen to be devoid of inner spirit at any given moment, it does not mean that it is devoid of meaning. Sometimes, in ritual, we simply feel part of the community, and that is enough. Sometimes, ritual serves to generate a sense of self, and that is enough. Sometimes it strengthens the family unit, and that is enough. And sometimes, it connects us to the Divine, and that is enough."

What professional rituals do you observe?

✦ DAY #283 ✦

ON BEING REPLACED

Calling Jesus a CEO seems a bit of a stretch. But he is a very high-ranking executive of religion.

Laurie Beth Jones said that the idea for her book *Jesus, CEO: Using Ancient Wisdom for Visionary Leadership* came to her when she was living in the mountains and thinking about different leadership styles that she had both witnessed and experienced. She saw "invaluable human energy and intelligence untapped and underutilized" and "multiple examples of corporate abuse, neglect and violence." But in her spiritual life, she saw the opposite. Jesus trained twelve disciples who went on to influence the world in simple and humble ways that could be incorporated and implemented by anyone who was open to "divine excellence." She came to believe that the workplace is "indeed very holy and fertile ground."

Jesus, she contended, was intent upon training people who could replace him: "'Greater things than I have done shall you do,' he promised. Jesus did not hoard or guard the power of his office. He kept teaching and sharing and demonstrating it to team members who would learn that they, too, had the power to do what he had done."

Jones claimed that Jesus could be generous with his power because he was extremely secure: "He never doubted that, when it was all over, he would be sitting at the Head Table. His job was to fill that table and make sure others were sitting with him.

"Jesus trained his replacement."

Who are your disciples?

✦ DAY #284 ✦

ON EXCELLENCE

Excellence does not come in a one-size-fits-all package, nor do we all mean the same thing when we use the term. Here are four different ways to understand excellence with the help of four famous people:

Relative excellence: We are probably not excellent, but we're a lot better than any other game in town. Dolly Parton: "It's hard to be a diamond in a rhinestone world."

Instrumental excellence: We're not committed to excellence for its own sake but for the sake of efficiency. John Wooden: "If you don't have time to do it right, when will you have the time to do it over?"

Aspirational excellence: We set our standards so high that they become unattainable. Vince Lombardi: "Perfection is not attainable, but if we chase perfection we can catch excellence."

Focused excellence: We cannot accomplish every goal, so we need to determine what we can really do best and be laser-focused. Steve Jobs: "We don't get a chance to do that many things, and every one should be really excellent. Because this is our life."

**Which understanding of excellence describes
your own view of the term and what you strive
for when you are working at your best?**

ON HOSPITALITY

In his book *Setting the Table: The Transforming Power of Hospitality in Business*, Danny Meyer made the case for hospitality:

"Hospitality is the foundation of my business philosophy. Virtually nothing else is as important as how one is made to feel in any business transaction. Hospitality exists when you believe the other person is on your side. The converse is just as true. Hospitality is present when something happens *for* you. It is absent when something happens *to* you. These two simple prepositions—*for* and *to*—express it all."

He offered a key distinction between service and hospitality and knowing the difference between the two:

"Understanding the distinction between service and hospitality has been at the foundation of our success. Service is the technical delivery of a product. Hospitality is how the delivery of that product makes its recipient *feel*. Service is a *monologue*—we decide how we want to do things and set our own standards for service. Hospitality, on the other hand, is a *dialogue*. To be on a guest's side requires listening to that person with every sense, and following up with a thoughtful gracious response. It takes both great service and great hospitality to rise to the top."

Service is what you expect. Hospitality is everything we do not expect that makes an experience worthwhile, that makes us want to return again and again. Hospitality is what distinguishes average service from legendary service.

**What hospitality legends can you create
through your leadership?**

ON PRIVACY

Voltaire once said: "What a heavy burden is a name that has become too famous." One of the heaviest burdens of success is the lack of privacy.

Think for a moment of a DO NOT DISTURB sign in hotels. As Garret Keizer wrote in *Privacy*: "We make a clear choice for privacy whenever we hang the PRIVACY PLEASE sign on the outside of a hotel room door. . . . We hang out the sign because we are not prepared to leave the room, because we are not prepared to have someone come into the room and because, at least until checkout time, we have some claim to call the room our own. We are not aiming for secrecy. Secrecy and privacy are not the same thing."

Keizer asked whether anything says so much about the times we live in as the fact that the word *sharing* has almost everything to do with personal information and almost nothing to do with personal wealth.

By privacy, we mean solitude, intimacy, anonymity, or seclusion. We are aiming for integrity in preserving bodily privacy and privacy in expression.

Granting privacy is a deep way in which we acknowledge and honor the dignity of the spiritual boundaries between us and others.

Sometimes we want to put that DO NOT DISTURB sign on our office doors but know that it would just create a murmur of intrigue.

Sometimes in leadership we want to put that DO NOT DISTURB sign around our necks.

When have you craved privacy recently?

ON CARING

A sign-language interpreter in a hospital, Clara Huerta, explained that her most important work has little to do with signing and everything to do with caring: "Some of my greatest moments occur when I am doing little more than being present with patients and their families. It is in those inactive moments that patients draw a great deal of strength and comfort."

Huerta shared this insight in Joseph Michelli's book on the UCLA health system approach to customer service: *Prescription for Excellence*.

Another nurse observed: "Most service comes down to your presence during an important life event and how much that means to the person served. Patients remember your being there. . . . If there is a reason for me to cry about something, I cry with the family. If there is a reason to be happy, I am happy with them. I just allow myself to be present and involved."

Many leaders are accused of being aloof and uncaring because staff members or board trustees undergo major milestones and small life tremors without an acknowledgment from a leader. Babies are born. Spouses get sick. Parents die. Children graduate. And all of it passes by with hardly a nod.

We are whole beings who need to know that we matter.

What can you do today to show you care to someone who may feel a bit neglected?

ON JUDGMENT

It's hard to be around people who we feel constantly judge us. They form opinions—not necessarily well considered—about our work, our lives, our personalities, our contributions. They make us feel insecure and uncomfortable. Most often, we are our own worst judges.

Eckhart Tolle, in *A New Earth,* asked: "Can you look without the voice in your head commenting, drawing conclusions, comparing, or trying to figure something out?"

Probably not.

As we judge ourselves, we find ourselves increasingly diminished. The voice of judgment is crushing and limiting: "If small things have the power to disturb you, then who you think you are is exactly that: small."

He added: "Discontent, blaming, complaining, self-pity cannot serve as a foundation for a good future, no matter how much effort you make."

**Stand in front of a mirror and tell yourself out loud
everything that you are doing right now that *is*
working. Make no reference to the past or the future.
Just speak in the present tense without judgment.**

✦ DAY #289 ✦

ON FLOURISHING

Martin Seligman is a psychologist and professor who has been called the father of positive psychology.

He popularized the notion of "learned helplessness," an underlying cause of depression among those who suffer a pervasive sense of powerlessness. Learned helplessness occurs when someone is exposed to aversive stimuli again and again and believes that this is the nature of his or her life, such that even when presented with an escape route from the emotional mess, the victim will take no action. If you can learn to be helpless, Seligman said, you can also learn to be hopeful.

Seligman made a bold claim in the very first sentence of *Flourish: A Visionary New Understanding of Happiness and Well-being*: "This book will help you flourish. There, I have finally said it." Seligman surprised himself with this sort of written money-back guarantee (he didn't actually go that far).

Seligman claimed to hate happiness and said he detests the word. It is "so overused that it has become almost meaningless." He was saddled with the word in the title of his book before *Flourish* because his publisher felt it would sell more books. Instead he has turned to the word *flourish*: a combination of positive emotion, engagement and meaning.

Describe a day when everything is working
well for you and you are totally flourishing.
Invite today to look like that.

✦ DAY #290 ✦

ON CONFUSION

We live in a confusing world. It is hard, some days, to get clarity. As we get older, we might find ourselves responding to more questions with "I don't know" until it feels less like an admission of ignorance and more like an existential state.

The confusion that is not-knowing is not a comfortable place of curiosity but a persistent, nagging sense that age does not necessarily bring wisdom and that wisdom may mean knowing less than you knew before about life's mysteries.

"Accepting that the world is full of uncertainty and ambiguity does not and should not stop people from being pretty sure about a lot of things," wrote Julian Baggini, the author of many books that popularize philosophy. He coedits the *Philosophers' Magazine*

"Happiness," Baggini insisted, "is not the same as life satisfaction, while neither are identical to what we might call flourishing." Sometimes we think that when we wade through the confusion and get to the other side, we will flourish and prosper. But like snakeskin that sloughs off in intermittent cycles, we shed confusion for clarity and then thrive for a while and then enter the tunnel of confusion again, only to repeat the cycle endlessly. With each shedding, we emerge more secure and ennobled until we become humbled by all we will never know and reenter the surety of confusion.

Describe a leadership situation that's deeply confusing.

ON RECEPTIVITY

"Why do you speak to the people in parables?" Jesus's disciples asked him (Matthew 13:10). Jesus told his students that not everyone is given the capacity to absorb esoteric knowledge. A parable is a safe way to communicate a truth that can be understood on many levels.

Jesus went on to compare receptivity with good soil, a parable farmers could comprehend and value. "The one who received the seed that fell on good soil is the man who hears the word and understands it. He produces a crop, yielding a hundred, sixty or thirty times what was sown" (Matthew 13:23).

In this parable there is roadside soil—soil that was seeded from the trampling of feet on paths. Seeds fall here but can never sprout. There is rocky soil, where seeds can germinate but cannot develop deep roots. In the summer, these fledgling plants cannot reach far enough into the earth for moisture and they die. There is congested soil that looks good on the surface but contains many weeds that compete with the seed for sun and nourishment and cut off the seed from growth. And then there is good soil, deep and plowed, which is able to produce multiples of the yield of others.

Out of Matthew's four types of soil, which most closely matches your listening receptivity skills as a leader?

ON IMPOSSIBILITY

"You don't think I get bored writing?" Philip Roth said in an interview in *Vanity Fair*.

Roth was seventy-seven at the time. He described a simple, almost monastic existence:

"I do the same things every day. I work, I write. I read every night. . . . I like my days of being by myself. I don't see people, except on weekends. That's the way I live."

The interviewer prodded: "Do you find writing difficult?"

"I find it arduous and un-doable. It's laden with fear and doubt. It's never easy—not for me. The ordeal is part of the task, and the satisfaction usually comes at the end. You stood up to it, you endured it! You achieved the unachievable—for you. But the next time out, I find it impossible all over again."

The interviewer was bewildered that an award-winning author of so many books found writing impossible. But Roth found it simple. Every book is a new book, a new adventure into the unknown that poses problems he has never seen before. It seems impossible, but then it happens.

Leaders can minimize the creativity of each project. Been there. Done that. But if we approach each task as a distinct piece of art that must be mastered, perhaps we will fall in love with the impossibility of it all over again.

Name your most impossible act of leadership.

ON PAUSING

Mark Twain (1835–1910) wrote "How to Tell a Story" in 1897 after he was himself well practiced. He was a journalist, a novelist, travel writer, riverboat pilot, lecturer, inventor and entrepreneur.

Twain liked stories with twists and turns. "Another feature is the slurring of the point. A third is the dropping of a studied remark apparently without knowing it, as if one were thinking aloud. The fourth and last is the pause."

Let's pause on the pause, since Twain did. "The pause is an exceedingly important feature in any kind of story, and a frequently recurring feature, too. It is a dainty thing, and delicate, and also uncertain and treacherous; for it must be exactly the right length—no more and no less—or it fails of its purpose and makes trouble. If the pause is too short the impressive point is passed, and [if too long] the audience have had time to divine that a surprise is intended—and then you can't surprise them, of course."

His advice: "You can practice with it yourself—and mind you look out for the pause and get it right."

Tell a story today that uses a pause as a way of building attention or drama and adding a verbal exclamation to your remarks. It can become addictive.

+ DAY #294 +

ON DEFEAT

"He is a great fish and I must convince him, he thought. I must never let him learn his strength nor what he could do if he made his run."

One of the great battles of literature was between a great fish and an old man. Ernest Hemingway wrote *The Old Man and the Sea* in 1951 in Cuba. Santiago fights a marlin far out at sea in his small boat. The old man had not caught a fish for eighty-four days. He suffered bad luck: *salao*. His young novice was forbidden to fish with a mentor who had caught nothing for so long.

On the eighty-fifth day, a marlin goes for his bait, dragging him for two days and nights in his little skiff.

"The old man had seen many great fish. He had seen many that weighed more than a thousand pounds and he had caught two of that size in his life, but never alone."

He finally caught the fish. Santiago's greatest catch was eaten by sharks on the trip back. But the skeleton of the fish remained for all to see that Santiago would not be defeated. His young friend ran to take care of the exhausted fisherman: "We will fish together now for I still have much to learn."

"But man is not made for defeat," Santiago said. "A man can be destroyed but not defeated."

As a leader, name a time when defeat
became your best teacher.

✦ DAY #295 ✦

ON PRESENTATIONS

Time for another conference. Time for the usual wash of boredom at the plenary, the keynote lecture, the breakout sessions, the "helpful" power-points. Snooze time.

"One keynote speaker can't change the world. But one speaker with the right message, the right tools, and the right delivery can make an audience understand why their world needs to change, and then not only show them how to do it, but how to get inspired to do it well."

Katrina Smith, CEO of Keynote Speakers Inc., in an interview about the worth of keynote speakers for *Forbes*, said: "It's not realistic to expect that a speaker can come in for forty-five minutes and fix a long-standing problem the company has been facing, a problem that perhaps the executives have been struggling for years to overcome. . . . But it is a powerful delivery technique for new ideas, practical explanations, memorable examples, and inspiration about why the whole thing is important in the first place."

Keynote speakers are given temporary authority by an organization to put out a message and create electricity. Most don't.

When we demand so little, we get even less.

Who was the last truly great speaker you heard? Describe the magic. Replicate it.

✦ DAY #296 ✦

ON FINISHING

"The day is short, the task is great, the workers are lazy but the reward is great, and the boss is pressing."

These observations are over two thousand years old. Rabbi Tarphon, in *Ethics of the Fathers,* offered us this gem and continued: "It is not upon you to finish the work but neither can you exempt yourself from it entirely" (2:20–21).

Contemplating just how much we have to get done can overwhelm us to the point of paralysis. Why even bother starting if you will never finish? It is a fair question, and one that displays the curl of fatigue that travels with resignation. The finish line feels so far away—*too* far—so we decide not to cross the start line at all.

Ethics of the Fathers goads us on, not through guilt or the burden of obligation, but through a realistic understanding of what we can be responsible for. We cannot finish every project. We can make a decent start and perhaps even a dent on a good day. We don't have to finish.

We are here to improve the universe, not to finish it.

Think of a leadership undertaking that you will never finish.

ON PERSPECTIVE

"Every man makes some mistakes in his first compositions, and he who knows them not, cannot amend them. But you, knowing your errors, will correct your works and where you find mistakes amend them, and remember never to fall into them again."

In *The Notebooks of Leonardo da Vinci*, the Italian artist and inventor (1452–1519) tried to present rules for painting and drawing that would create an error-free understanding of vision and how to capture it on paper.

"There are three branches of perspective; the first deals with the reasons of the diminution of objects as they recede from the eye, and is known as Diminishing Perspective. The second contains the way in which colors vary as they recede from the eye. The third and last is concerned with the explanation of how the objects ought to be less finished in proportion as they are remote."

In other words, perspective is understanding how close something is to you and its relation to other objects within that visual field. When we say that someone has lost perspective we mean that he or she has failed to understand the relationship of something to something else.

Da Vinci believed you could master perspective.

Describe a loss of perspective you struggle with right now.

ON MOTIVATION

"Motivation on the job too often is taken for granted; we assume people care about what they do. But the truth is more nuanced: Wherever people gravitate within their work role indicates where their real pleasure lies—and that pleasure is itself motivating.

Although traditional incentives such as bonuses or recognition can prod people to better performance, no external motivators can get people to perform their absolute best."

Daniel Goleman, Richard Boyatzis and Annie McKee shared this insight in *Primal Leadership* and asked us to consider what motivates us to lead.

Why not motivate with bonuses, commissions or other awards? They help, but only short term. Daniel H. Pink, in *Drive: The Surprising Truth About What Motivates Us*, focused on why external motivators will never create genuine pride of professional ownership. He called his seven reasons "Carrots and Sticks" or "The Seven Deadly Flaws":

1. They can extinguish intrinsic motivation.
2. They can diminish performance.
3. They can crush creativity.
4. They can crowd out good behavior.
5. They can encourage cheating, shortcuts, and unethical behavior.
6. They can become addictive.
7. They can foster short-term thinking.

In the rush to beat the competition and win that trip/gift/recognition, we might just take the kind of shortcuts that hurt the quality of our work or undermine genuine collaboration.

What have you found to be an effective motivator?

✦ DAY #299 ✦

ON DISCOMFORT

Bless the days when things go wrong.

Some days feel that they are snowballing out of control. We can't find a parking space. We're late. The deal we were counting on did not go through. The receptionist just quit.

And that's exactly what should be happening, because if everything went right all of the time, there would be no need for leadership. Discomfort challenges us. It prevents us from becoming complacent.

Fix it.

Manage it.

Slow it down.

Speed it up.

Create perspective.

If everything is going swimmingly, we don't need to build spiritual capacity. We can avoid tensions, but then we avoid anything great prompted by discomfort, like productivity, creativity, reflection and kindness.

Psychologists often compare this low-lying unease to a pebble or sand in one's shoe. You can still walk, but with every step there is slight discomfort. You can't take a step and not feel that little annoyance. It's inconvenient to have something stuck where you can feel it, so it surfaces as a choice: Do you stop and take the pebble out, or do you keep moving?

**What pebble is in your shoe today, and
what will you be doing about it?**

✦ DAY #300 ✦

ON TALENT

Are leaders born or made?

Many leaders believe that they are made. Many followers believe leaders are born.

"The most dangerous leadership myth is that leaders are born—that there is a genetic factor to leadership. This myth asserts that people simply either have certain charismatic qualities or not. That's nonsense; in fact, the opposite is true. Leaders are made rather than born."

Warren Bennis, a pioneer in the field of leadership, could not have been more clear. "Leaders must encourage their organizations to dance to forms of music yet to be heard." Leaders must not only grow their own talent but bring others into the dance. "Good leaders make people feel that they're at the very heart of things, not at the periphery."

No one was born to do that.

Leaders do that through experience, being mentored, reflecting on failures, learning and creating a network of allies that offer wisdom and advice.

"Excellence is a better teacher than mediocrity. The lessons of the ordinary are everywhere. Truly profound and original insights are to be found only in studying the exemplary." If you want to maximize your talent, study excellence and imitate it until you and it are inseparable.

Bennis remarked: "Failing organizations are usually over-managed and under-led." Is your organization under-led because you are not exerting your talent to the max?

✦ DAY #301 ✦

ON DYING

Jim Fannin, life, business, and sports coach, had a childhood best friend, Brian, who discovered he had a life-threatening disease when they were both delivering newspapers. His best friend discovered a lump, and eventually died from it in Fannin's arms: "I made up my mind that day that I would never have a bad day again."

Fannin wrote in *Esquire* about his life advice and, of course, his attitude toward death. Research shows that high achievers generally have more angst about their mortality. If you're driven, you're livin'. Every day. Every minute.

Fannin wrote about that terrible day that helped him have no more bad days.

"I visualized my death at his funeral. I went to the end of my life, saw everybody happy, saw me happy. I saw myself having an awesome life. And I've never had a bad day since." He faced tragedy. He lost both of his parents. He's been disappointed, but he's eliminated the idea of a bad day in favor of a promising life.

Fanin revealed how he's going to go:

"You know what's gonna be on my tombstone? 'Next!'"

**What's going on your tombstone? Take
a few minutes to write it out.**

ON ADVENTURE

"Live, Travel, Adventure, Bless, and Don't Be Sorry."

Jack Kerouac (1922–1969) wrote *On the Road* in bursts of feverish imagination and actually typed it continuously—without any natural breaks in the paper—by taping 120 sheets together. The method cohered with the mind—it expressed his stream-of-consciousness ruminations on his life and life in general.

"There was nowhere to go but everywhere, so just keep on rolling under the stars," Kerouac wrote, celebrating his directionless path. "Nothing behind me, everything ahead of me, as is ever so on the road." He called the empty sky his witness, and beneath it he intended to live life fully, "for life is holy and every moment is precious."

His break from the world was a relief. "I was surprised, as always, by how easy the act of leaving was, and how good it felt."

Kerouac had crazy, talented friends, "the ones who never yawn or say a commonplace thing, but burn, burn, burn like fabulous yellow roman candles exploding like spiders across the stars." And explode he did. Kerouac died from complications of chronic alcohol abuse but not before becoming an overnight success. "What is that feeling when you're driving away from people and they recede on the plain till you see their specks dispersing?—it's the too-huge world vaulting us, and it's good-bye. But we lean forward to the next crazy venture beneath the skies."

Lean forward today into an unexpected adventure.

ON INTENSITY

"The works must be conceived with fire in the soul but executed with clinical coolness." To create great art, passion must be tempered by reason.

Joan Miró (1893–1983) was a Spanish painter and sculptor who worked in a modernist style and dismissed art he felt was too conformist. Art was not meant to comfort but to challenge the eye and the mind. Large odd shapes are joined by thin black lines in splotches of color.

There is something about his work that pulses with life, even though a canvas is two-dimensional. "For me an object is something living. This cigarette or this box of matches contains a secret life much more intense than that of certain human beings."

Miró aimed for intensity: the saturation of color, the push and pull of shapes and lines, the placement of objects. "I feel the need of attaining the maximum of intensity with the minimum of means. It is this which has led me to give my painting a character of even greater bareness."

The artist takes you into the process and evolution of the work: "Throughout the time in which I am working on a canvas I can feel how I am beginning to love it, with that love which is born of slow comprehension." The intensity would mount as Miró became more emotionally involved in the painting.

Intensity is a path to greatness. Intensity can be all-consuming, propulsive, frightening.

Would you describe yourself as intense?

ON DELEGATION

Is it possible to have stress-free productivity? David Allen thinks so. He believes it is an art form, as he wrote in *Getting Things Done*. On a deeper level, when productivity involves too much stress, we pull back from investing the totality of our minds and hearts in our work. The soul price is too high to pay.

Allen wrote that, to heighten efficiency, we need to approach every action with three possible responses:

Do it: if it takes fewer than two minutes.

Delegate it: if you are not the appropriate person or there is someone just as capable or more capable of taking it off your plate.

Defer it: the pending category, which will have to be noted and handled later.

We might tell ourselves that nothing takes only two minutes, but you'd be surprised at how much we can squeeze out of 120 seconds: a quick handwritten thank-you or a card with praise, a brief memo, an e-mail response to an easy question. Get it done and out. "If the next action is going to take longer than two minutes, ask yourself, 'Am I the best person to be doing it?'"

Maybe we don't delegate more because we are not trusting enough of others. It's our problem. Not theirs.

Maximize your divinely given talents by shelving tasks and responsibilities that can be taken care of by others.

Name three tasks that you can delegate right now and then delegate them today.

ON SEEING

At the age of forty-eight, John Hull became completely blind. A professor of religious education in England, Hull described his three-year descent into blindness in a journal that was eventually published as *Touching the Rock: An Experience of Blindness*.

The neurological and emotional impact of Hull's trial was described by Oliver Sacks in *The Mind's Eye*: "The sense of objects having appearances, or visible characteristics, vanished." Hull was distressed. He could no longer conjure an image of his wife or children, places he loved or familiar landscapes.

He soon entered a state of deep blindness, described as "an authentic and autonomous world, a place of its own. . . . Being a whole body seer is to be in one of the concentrated human conditions."

Hull shifted his center of gravity to other senses and discovered a new state of intimacy. Blindness was "a dark, paradoxical gift." It was not, as Sacks observed, a question of compensation for loss of sight. Hull had entered a whole new order of being.

"His teaching at the university expanded, became more fluent; his writing became stronger and deeper; he became intellectually and spiritually bolder, more confident. He felt he was on solid ground at last."

John Milton and Jorge Luis Borges wrote their greatest poetry only after becoming blind.

Sit at your desk and close your eyes for one timed minute. Describe what happens to your mind in that minute. Open your eyes. What do you see that you did not see before?

ON CHOICES

Oscar Wilde (1854–1900) loved dichotomies.

"There are only two tragedies in life: one is not getting what one wants, and the other is getting it."

"There is only one thing in life worse than being talked about, and that is not being talked about."

"The only difference between the saint and the sinner is that every saint has a past, and every sinner has a future."

Putting stark and extreme choices in front of oneself can lead to clarity or confusion. The hardest aspect of decision making is usually the recognition that making choices involves loss. One option has to be dropped to pursue another, and it feels desperately hard at times to let go of that potential.

Wilde was wildly funny. He sparkled, dressed like a dandy and loved to be the center of attention. Wilde's witticisms are often repeated, and he himself confessed: "I am so clever that sometimes I don't understand a single word of what I am saying."

He offered this advice: "I won't tell you that the world matters nothing, or the world's voice, or the voice of society. They matter a good deal. They matter far too much. But there are moments when one has to choose between living one's own life, fully, entirely, completely—or dragging out some false, shallow, degrading existence that the world in its hypocrisy demands. You have that moment now. Choose!"

**What choice stands before you now that requires
a deep look in the mirror of authenticity?**

ON BEING A WORKAHOLIC

"The very notion of time management is a misnomer. For we cannot manage time. We can only manage ourselves in relation to time," wrote Alec Mackenzie and Pat Nickerson in *The Time Trap*. "We cannot control how much time we have; we can only control how we use it. We cannot choose whether to spend it, but only how. Once we've wasted time, it's gone—and it cannot be replaced."

Marilyn Machlowitz, in *Workaholics*, defined *workaholic* as "one whose desire to work long and hard is intrinsic and whose work habits almost always exceed the prescriptions of the job they do and the expectations of the people with whom and for whom they work."

Doesn't that describe every leader you know?

But Machlowitz warned us that often workaholics are not efficient, and that is why they work the hours they do.

She devised a little workaholic test to see if we can turn down work intensity and drive:

Do you get up early, no matter how late you go to bed?

If you are eating lunch alone, do you read or work while you eat?

Do you find it difficult to do nothing?

Are you energetic and competitive?

Do you work on weekends and holidays?

Do you work anytime and anywhere?

Do you find it hard to take a vacation?

Do you dread retirement?

How did you do?

**Identify one area of improvement
in your time management.**

ON FLIGHT

"All the world is made of faith, and trust, and pixie dust."

"There is a saying in the Neverland that every time you breathe, a grown-up dies." J. M. Barrie (1860–1937) was born and raised in Scotland. His works became timeless, and he seemed ageless himself. "To die will be an awfully big adventure" became "To live will be an awfully big adventure" in the movie *Hook*.

His most famous work continues to delight audiences the world over, and because Barrie gave the rights to the Great Ormond Street Hospital, his writing has benefited the world in more than one way. But perhaps he never left us; as he wrote in *Peter Pan*: "Never say goodbye because goodbye means going away and going away means forgetting."

Barrie pointed us again and again to the world above us and the world within us:

"When the first baby laughed for the first time, its laugh broke into a thousand pieces, and they all went skipping about, and that was the beginning of fairies."

"Second star to the right and straight on 'til morning."

"Fairies have to be one thing or the other, because being so small they unfortunately have room for one feeling only at a time."

Can you fly? "The moment you doubt whether you can fly, you cease for ever to be able to do it."

Yes you can. "The reason birds can fly and we can't is simply because they have perfect faith, for to have faith is to have wings."

**Describe a moment when your leadership
had wings and you were flying.**

ON PROCRASTINATION

Why do we procrastinate? If we have to get something done, we should just do it. But somehow moving from idea to actualization rarely works out that way.

"In a nutshell, you procrastinate when you put off things that you should be focusing on right now, usually in favor of doing something that is more enjoyable or that you're more comfortable doing." This is the simple answer found in "Overcoming Procrastination" on MindTools.com. We're not doing it because we don't want to. We love doing what we love.

"Procrastinators work as many hours in the day as other people (and often work longer hours) but they invest their time in the wrong tasks. Sometimes this is simply because they don't understand the difference between urgent tasks and important tasks, and jump straight into getting on with urgent tasks that aren't actually important."

Virtually every guide on time management advises us to do what we like least first.

And then there's the other side of the procrastination equation: What are the consequences of not doing what we know we have to do? Meditating on these unpleasant outcomes can often be a great motivator. The only way to fight the demons of procrastination is to invite the angels of honesty to take their place.

Identify what is urgent right now and what is important.

ON INGRATITUDE

Why is it so hard for some people to say thank you? Two little one-syllable words seem to stymie some people. A senior leader at a large high-tech firm once confessed that he never says thank you to his employees. "They get paid. That is their thank-you."

Shakespeare (1564–1616) absolutely detested ingratitude and found it incomprehensible, as Viola put it in *Twelfth Night*: "I hate ingratitude more in a man than lying, vainness, babbling, drunkenness, or any taint of vice whose strong corruption inhabits our frail blood."

Turning to the universe of modern psychology, we find this observation by Robert C. Solomon in the introduction to the anthology *The Psychology of Gratitude*: "The neglect of gratitude is, in itself, interesting. . . . We do not like to think of ourselves as indebted. We would rather see our good fortunes as our own doing. . . . Like the emotion of trust, it invokes an admission of our vulnerability and our dependence on other people."

If I thank you, is it in some way an admission that I need you, that I cannot exist or function—at least in some capacity—without your help? Yes. It does mean this. We are limited beings. A personal, deeply felt thank-you is one of the most beautiful ways we acknowledge our fragility and dependence on others.

**Take five minutes now to write a note to
a parent or a mentor to acknowledge
what they've meant to you.**

✦ DAY #311 ✦

ON COMPLETION

How do you ever know when you are finished with a project or a paper or a presentation or a major leadership decision?

Ask Rembrandt.

"A painting is finished when the artist says it is finished" is one statement commonly attributed to Rembrandt (1606–1669). Or, more eloquently: "A painting is complete when it has the shadows of a god." In the first instance, completion is determined by the artist. In the second, there is some external, almost divine sense that a painting has achieved its transcendence and then is ready to be shared.

A contemporary artist once said that she signs her paintings precisely so that she can let go of them. Until then, they never seem complete. Another artist whined about completing a painting: "I find that at about the point when I no longer want to rip the canvas apart and smash the stretcher, then it's probably about finished!"

"The paintings I love most," said another artist, "are those where there is still a mystery, ending, or question that I provide from my own experiences. Paintings tell stories but should leave something to the imagination of the observer." In this last description, the painting is only truly finished by the onlooker.

As long as what we do has enduring impact, it will always keep speaking and singing and living. It will never really be finished.

**Create a ritual to acknowledge that
you have completed something.**

✦ DAY #312 ✦

ON LOSS

Part of human development is coming to terms with loss. As we move deeper into our adult lives, we experience more loss, what Judith Viorst has called "necessary losses." The subtitle of the book speaks its truth: *The Loves, Illusions, Dependencies, and Impossible Expectations That All of Us Have to Give Up in Order to Grow*. We lose parents, friends, hair, money, position. Our children leave home. We age, and the loss of our physical vitality plagues us. Suffer enough loss, and we may lose our bearings.

Viorst described the way we advance and retreat, how we progress and regress:

"Somewhere slightly before or after the close of our second decade, we reach a momentous milestone—childhood's end. We have left a safe place and can't go home again. We have moved into a world where life isn't fair, where life is rarely what it should be."

Viorst's own path was not linear. She is perhaps best known as a writer of children's books, like *Alexander and the Terrible, Horrible, No Good, Very Bad Day*; then she studied Freudian psychology for decades.

"Growing up means letting go of the dearest megalomaniacal dreams of our childhood. Growing up means knowing they can't be fulfilled. Growing up means gaining the wisdom and skills to get what we want within the limitations imposed by reality—a reality which consists of diminished powers, restricted freedoms and, with the people we love, imperfect connections."

Name an adult loss that turned into
leadership wisdom for you.

◆ DAY #313 ◆

ON SELF-PROTECTION

You are your most important asset. Since you probably protect your assets well, what are you doing to protect yourself?

Ronald Heifetz and Marty Linsky offered a guide for self-protection in their article "A Survival Guide for Leaders."

"When people attack someone in a position of authority, more often than not they are attacking the role, not the person. Even when attacks on you are highly personal, you need to read them primarily as reactions to how you, in your role, are affecting people's lives."

When we take the message too personally, we leave ourselves too vulnerable emotionally.

"You need to distinguish between your personal self, which can serve as an anchor in stormy weather, and your professional role, which never will." This is hard to do. "It is easy to mix up the two. And other people will only increase the confusion: Colleagues, subordinates, and even bosses often act as if the role you play is the real you. But that is not the case, no matter how much of yourself—your passions, your values, your talents—you genuinely and laudably pour into your professional role."

And they warned us of another related cost: "When you take

'personal' attacks personally, you unwittingly conspire in one of the ways you can be taken out of action—you make yourself the issue."

This is about your role, not your being.

Describe a "personal" attack and a professional response.

ON EMPATHY

"The word *attention* comes from the Latin *attendere*, meaning 'to reach toward.' This is a perfect definition of focus on others, which is the foundation of empathy and of an ability to build social relationships."

In the *Harvard Business Review*'s "The Focused Leader," Daniel Goleman offered the empathy triad, dividing up empathy into distinct emotional expressions:

cognitive empathy: the ability to understand another person's perspective;
emotional empathy: the ability to feel what someone else feels;
empathic concern: the ability to sense what another person needs from you.

What happens when leaders are accused of lacking self-awareness or the ability to show compassion? They can achieve it, or at least get closer to achieving empathy, through meditative techniques like deep diaphragmatic breathing and detachment, observing themselves from a distance, and noticing what is happening as they interact with others. Observe body language, eye contact, breathing, impulsive reactions, movement away.

Lack of empathy is a way we protect ourselves from pain. Protect yourself too much and you might lose your capacity to connect with others.

Of the three types of empathy identified above, which comes easy to you and which is more challenging?

ON CHARISMA

Charisma is that magical combination of charm, intelligence and personal energy that is often tied up with good looks. It's a compelling kind of attractiveness that draws people in with adoration and devotion.

Charisma comes from the Greek word *charisma*, or "divine favor," a gift of the gods. Charisma often inspires intense loyalty.

"He can ask me to do anything."

"I would jump through fire for her."

But charisma brings its fair share of problems with it. In 1997 Jim Collins wrote an article titled "The Death of the Charismatic Leader," all about the seduction and the liability of charisma.

"Almost by definition, an enduring great company has to be built *not* to depend on an individual leader, because individuals die or retire or move on. What's more, when a company's identity can't be separated from the identity of its leader, it can't be known for what it stands for. Which means it sacrifices the potency of being guided by its core purpose. . . . A charismatic leader is not an asset; it's a liability companies have to recover from. A company's long-term health requires a leader who can infuse the company with its own sense of purpose, instead of his or hers, and who can translate that purpose into action through mechanisms, not force of personality."

Charisma draws us in but must be met with substance and humility to really work well for enduring leadership.

What can you do to strengthen or
temper your personal charisma?

ON BREATHING

Breathing is involuntary. It happens if we are conscious of our breathing or not. And yet so many mystical and meditative traditions center on breathing precisely because of its involuntary nature. Thich Nhat Hanh, in *Stepping into Freedom: Rules of Monastic Practice for Novices*, wrote: "Feelings come and go like clouds in a windy sky. Conscious breathing is my anchor."

The happiness, power and simplicity of a simple breath is captured majestically in a psalm that has become a joyous form of prayer, filled with instruments, song and delight, but ending with the simple breath.

"Praise the Lord. Praise God in his sanctuary; praise him in his mighty heavens. Praise him for his acts of power; praise him for his surpassing greatness. Praise him with the sounding of the trumpet, praise him with the harp and lyre, praise him with tambourine and dancing, praise him with the strings and flute, praise him with the clash of cymbals, praise him with resounding cymbals. *Let everything that has breath praise the Lord. Praise the Lord*" (Psalm 150).

We all need praise. We all need *to* praise. Praising should become as natural and involuntary to us as breathing. With every exhalation, we shape our breath into words that buoy, uplift, inspire and aspire.

> **For the next few minutes, focus on your breathing and its rhythm and watch what happens. Later, turn your breath into praise.**

ON SELF-DISCIPLINE

"In reading the lives of great men, I found that the first victory they won was over themselves. . . . Self-discipline with all of them came first."

Harry S. Truman (1884–1972) was the thirty-third president of the United States and a master of wit, who once said: "I never gave anybody hell. I just told them the truth and they thought it was hell." He had a simple past. He grew up in Missouri and worked as a farmer and, later, a haberdasher. He distinguished himself through his military service during World War I on the Western Front, and then as president bookended his immersion in world wars by officially concluding World War II. The physical and mental stamina and self-discipline involved in this surfeit of conflict was remarkable.

"Men make history and not the other way around. In periods where there is no leadership, society stands still. Progress occurs when courageous, skillful leaders seize the opportunity to change things for the better."

Truman seized many opportunities to stretch himself beyond his background and capabilities. He is the only president in recent history not to have earned a college degree. He was turned down by West Point. He was turned down initially by his wife, Bess Wallace. But he persisted, and through self-discipline he achieved success in virtually every arena where he had first met failure.

On a scale of 1 to 10, with 1 being poor and 10 being outstanding, how would you rate your self-discipline?

✦ DAY #318 ✦

ON GOOD NEWS

There are so many days when our souls crave good news, when the daily catalog of woe that leaks out our optimism is too much to bear.

The book of Proverbs offers us a gorgeous entry into the importance of good news. "What brightens the eye gladdens the heart, and good news puts sap on the bones" (15:30). Good news fattens the bones; it puts a bit of meat on us at a time of scarcity. It fills us.

This verse has been dissected by Bible commentators for

centuries. Medieval Jewish commentators were primarily intrigued by the first part of this verse: What visual would gladden the heart? An eleventh-century scholar, Rabbi Solomon Yitzhaki, explained that nature generates happiness.

Two centuries later Gersonides, a French philosopher, took a more cerebral approach. He wrote that the light of the eyes refers to an idea; intellectual illumination makes us happy.

A German scholar, Rabbi David Altschuler, argued this verse is about the resolution of a plaguing difficulty: "There is no happiness like the resolution of doubt." Hanging in the ether of ambiguity eats away at us. Make a decision, and you will feel better.

Proverbs throws us happiness possibilities: immersing in nature, delving into ideas and resolving problems—internal ways in which we pursue greater tranquillity. Every once in a while, happiness is thrown at us from outside.

It comes in the form of good news.

Deliver good news in your leadership role today.

◆ DAY #319 ◆

ON TRADITION

It's hard to put your finger on what tradition is: If ritual is an act that we repeat, tradition seems to be the way that we pass on those rituals from one generation to another, cementing elements of our family culture or ethnicity. Organizations also have rituals.

Even if we do not know their meaning or origins, traditions are valued simply because they have existed and stood the test of time.

Tevye, the famous milkman in *Fiddler on the Roof*, captured both the mystery and the irrationality of tradition in the song of that name, sung while a fiddler is actually on the roof playing, a precarious thing. Sing if you feel you need to.

Tevye: A fiddler on the roof. Sounds crazy, no? But in our little village of Anatevka, you might say every one of us is a fiddler on the roof, trying to scratch out a pleasant, simple tune without breaking his neck. It isn't easy. You may ask, "Why do we stay up here if it's so dangerous?" We stay because Anatevka is our home. And how do we keep our balance? That I can tell you in a word—tradition.

Villagers: (Enter, singing) Tradition, tradition—tradition. Tradition, tradition—tradition.

Tevye: Because of our tradition, we've kept our balance for many, many years. Here in Anatevka we have traditions for everything—how to eat, how to sleep, how to wear clothes.

**Name a work tradition that
helps anchor and center you.**

✦ DAY #320 ✦

ON JUSTICE

"God is in the slums, in the cardboard boxes where the poor play house. . . . God is in the silence of a mother who has infected her child with a virus that will end both their lives. . . . God is in the cries heard under the rubble of war. God is in the debris of wasted opportunity and lives, and God is with us if we are with him. . . . It's not a coincidence that in the Scriptures, poverty is mentioned more than 2,100 times."

These aren't the words of a preacher. They're the words of a rock star: Bono. When addressing the National Prayer Breakfast in 2006, he asked everyone to join him in praying that he didn't say something that everyone would regret.

"If you're wondering what I'm doing here, at a prayer breakfast, well, so am I. I'm certainly not here as a man of the cloth, unless that cloth is leather. It's certainly not because I'm a rock star. Which leaves one possible explanation: I'm here because I've got a messianic complex."

He had them laughing, but not long after, he had them crying.

"It's not about charity, it's about justice. And that's too bad.

Because you are good at charity. We like to give, and we give a lot, even those who can't afford it. But justice is a higher standard."

Bono ended his prayer with one compelling sentence:

"History, like God, is watching what we do."

Name an injustice you are fighting right now.

+ DAY #321 +

ON PRODUCTIVE
NARCISSIM

Freud identified three main personality types: erotics, obsessives and narcissists. Erotics want to love and be loved. Obsessives crave order and improvement. Narcissists need admiration.

In *The Productive Narcissist: The Promise and Peril of Visionary Leadership*, Michael Maccoby identified key narcissistic personality traits that can grow into great leadership. Freud wrote of narcissists: "They are especially suited to act as a support for others, to take on the role of leaders, and to give a fresh stimulus to cultural development or damage the established state of affairs." He also believed they were the hardest personalities to analyze.

Maccoby wrote that destructive narcissists can hurt themselves and others through intensity, aggression, stress and often paranoia. But if narcissism is channeled well it can produce remarkable leaders who are "gifted and creative strategists who see the big picture and find meaning in the risky challenge of changing the world and leaving behind a legacy. Indeed, one reason we look to productive narcissists in times of great transition is that they have the audacity to push through massive transformations that society periodically undertakes. Productive narcissists are not only risk takers willing to get the job done but also charmers who can convert the masses with their rhetoric."

As a leader, is it more important for you to be loved, to be in control, or to be adored?

ON DARKNESS

"My Lord God, I have no idea where I am going. I do not see the road ahead of me. I cannot know for certain where it will end. . . . I trust you always though I may seem to be lost and in the shadow of death. I will not fear, for you are ever with me, and you will never leave me to face my perils alone."

This touching confession is almost painful to read. It takes us into the dark search for divine redemption. Trappist monk Thomas Merton (1915–1968) offered this prayer, inviting us into his own confusion, to make our way into the light.

When it comes to confronting inner darkness, Merton shared this observation: "The more you try to avoid suffering, the more you suffer, because smaller and more insignificant things begin to torture you, in proportion to your fear of being hurt. The one who does most to avoid suffering is, in the end, the one who suffers most.

"Our job is to love others without stopping to inquire whether or not they are worthy. That is not our business and, in fact, it is nobody's business. What we are asked to do is to love, and this love itself will render both ourselves and our neighbors worthy."

We should fight our demons, not by searching for the light switch inside that is hard to find, but by being drawn to the light of others.

Whose light helped you shed your own darkness?

ON DETERMINATION

Paul Tough wanted to know how to help children be smarter and behave with stronger moral fiber. In *How Children Succeed*, Tough summed up the most important quality kids today need to make it in a complex, fast-paced world. Mixing together stubborn resilience and determination, he came up with one word: grit. Kids today, and arguably adults, need grit, a combination of courage and resolve to get it done and get it done well.

"We can't get better at overcoming disappointment just by working harder at it for more hours."

Tough admonished us: "We have been focusing on the wrong skills and abilities in our children, and we have been using the wrong strategies to help nurture and teach those skills." We need more persistence, self-control, curiosity, conscientiousness, self-confidence and grit.

We can teach people to love grit, in the words of actor Daniel Day Lewis: "I like things that make your teeth grit. I like tucking my chin in and sort of leading into the storm. I like that feeling. I like it a lot."

Describe what your face looks and feels like when you are determined.

✦ DAY #324 ✦

ON SERVANT LEADERSHIP

Are those you work with wiser, freer and more capable of acting from an expanded consciousness because of your leadership?

That's what Robert Greenleaf, creator of the servant leadership concept, wanted to know. Greenleaf's ideas were picked up by Christian and other spiritual movements because he hit a deep chord with foundational religious thought. But Greenleaf was not a preacher. He was an employee who worked at large corporations and saw the way they could swallow the best of an individual and make that person a conformist, a cog.

He knew it did not have to be that way. Leaders could develop visions that would help people evolve and mature, develop and thrive, if they thought of their own leadership as servantship.

Servant leadership requires involved, engaged listening, curiosity and the desire to make others better.

Some people find the concept too submissive, and the term *servant* too servile and humble. Greenleaf felt that it was descriptive of a particular way of approaching the world and those within it. *I am not here to lead, which is presumptuous. I am here to serve, which is the least I can do.*

Act in service to others today.

+ DAY #325 +

ON ANONYMITY

Patrick Lencioni writes leadership fables to illustrate dilemmas and how to overcome them. In *The Three Signs of a Miserable Job: A Fable for Managers (and Their Employees)*, Lencioni advised managers to pay careful attention to the signs of flagging energy. Employees who feel anonymous and irrelevant or who cannot measure their productivity can quickly spiral into unhappiness at work.

Lencioni kept his recommendations blunt and simple: Take time to sit with employees and ask them what's going on in their lives. "Some managers reflexively avoid this because they've been taught that it is illegal to ask that kind of question during job interviews. Somehow they forget that what may be illegal when selecting a candidate is actually a basic form of human kindness once someone has been hired."

People who have no idea of the impact of their work are also at risk of despair. If they think their work has no impact whatsoever, Lencioni wrote, "they begin to die emotionally."

Finally, when leading others, make sure their work counts by giving them something to count. Lencioni argued that people in sales are often much more satisfied at work than those who cannot tangibly measure any outcomes. He calls it "immeasurement," which may not be a word, but it is certainly descriptive of a central problem in work that is abstract to the point of frustration. It is "an employee's lack of a clear means for assessing his or her progress or success on the job."

Eliminate these "three signs" for someone today.

ON ENTHUSIASM

Winner of the Nobel Prize for Literature, V. S. Naipaul knew at age eleven that he wanted to be a writer. He tracked this desire in *Reading and Writing: A Personal Account.*

"I liked to be given a fountain pen and a bottle of Waterman ink and new ruled exercise books (with margins), but I had no wish or need to write anything; and didn't write anything, not even letters: There was no one to write them to. I wasn't especially good at English composition at school; I didn't make up and tell stories at home. And though I liked new books as physical objects, I wasn't much of a reader."

Naipaul wrote more than forty works of nonfiction and twelve novels.

He credited his career to his father's enthusiasm for reading. Naipaul's father was a journalist and a great storyteller. "He read many books at once, finishing none, looking not for the story or the argument in any book but for the special qualities or character of the writer."

His father shared lots of convoluted and sophisticated novels, ones that he failed to properly understand. "But somehow—no doubt because of the enthusiasm of my father—I was able to simplify everything I listened to. In my mind, all the pieces took on aspects of the fairy tale."

Name how someone else's passion translated into your own. Don't curb your enthusiasm.

ON OPENING DOORS

"All profound distraction opens certain doors. You have to allow yourself to be distracted when you are unable to concentrate."

Argentine novelist Julio Cortázar (1914–1984) presented different views of distraction in *Around the Day in Eighty Worlds*. In this first view, something that has the capacity to distract us enough is also telling us something. Pay attention, even when you think you shouldn't. Something important is happening inside, and you cannot keep papering it over with other ideas, thoughts and emotions that you think you are "supposed" to have. Resign yourself to the distraction and see where it takes you. Let it open a door.

But Cortázar also had a harsher view of the subject: "That's what Idiocy is: the ability to be enthusiastic all the time about anything you like." Be wary about every door.

Unmeasured enthusiasm for everything can seem out of proportion and unbalanced. Enthusiasm is a filter by which we understand where to put our energies.

**Give in to deep distraction today and
see if it opens any doors.**

ON THE COMIC SPIRIT

What's missing in corporate life today?

"Having fun in the office. I don't think I've ever run into a leader who didn't have a good sense of humor that seemed to get better when times got tough," said Warren Bennis to economist Robert M. Townsend in conversation. Humor doesn't seem to make it on any lists of great leadership behaviors and characteristics.

Bennis observed: "I think it's very important. Before writing my last book, I consulted with a friend of mine who was a gag writer for Bob Hope and Johnny Carson. He's been writing gags for years, and I wanted him to instruct me on developing a sense of humor and also on joke telling. I paid my friend something like a hundred dollars an hour for six months until he finally decided I was hopeless."

Why is fun and laughter so important but increasingly so absent from the workplace today? It's hard to laugh with people when they are working remotely through technology. We laugh when we feel safe around others. It's hard to laugh with people when you're afraid that your job may be on the line.

Townsend came back into the conversation: "George Meredith called it 'the comic spirit,' the ability to laugh at things even when they're painful. He thought it was humanity's saving grace."

Humor soothes and smoothes, distracts and saves face, unifies and creates lightness and laughter.

When is the last time you had a really good laugh?

✦ DAY #329 ✦

ON PLACE

"Where is there a place for you to be? No place. . . . Nothing outside you can give you any place. . . . In yourself right now is all the place you've got."

In *The Writer's Desk*, photographer Jill Krementz captured a wonderful shot of Flannery O'Connor (1925–1964) at her desk. The desk is large. The room is very orderly.

For O'Connor, place was important but could not substitute for the anchor that is the self. We have enough inside to carry us and ground us, as she quipped in her book of prose *Mystery and Manners*: "Anybody who has survived his childhood has enough information about life to last him the rest of his days."

She said: "I write to discover what I know."

It is all there—that place inside. It is not always an easy place, and O'Connor was churlish about the truth. "The truth does not change according to our ability to stomach it." As a result, she could be too honest at times: "Everywhere I go I'm asked if I think the university stifles writers. My opinion is that they don't stifle enough of them. There's many a best-seller that could have been prevented by a good teacher."

Take a picture of your desk and study it.

✦ DAY #330 ✦

ON REINVENTION

"Everyone has talent at twenty-five. The difficulty is to have it at fifty."

Ouch. That hurts.

But Degas meant it. Edgar Degas (1834–1917) studied painting from the time he was a child. As he aged, he had to keep reinventing the artist within so that he could maintain mastery. He did this through pure diligence and repetition: "One must do the same subject over again ten times, a hundred times. In art nothing must resemble an accident, not even movement."

Degas did not reinvent himself as an artist by trying different styles but by approaching the same subjects with the same techniques from every possible angle—again and again and again. "No art," Degas observed, "is less spontaneous than mine. What I do is the result of reflection and the study of the great masters." This colluded with his observation that painting only gets more difficult over time: "Painting is easy when you don't know how, but very difficult when you do."

As he aged, he gave more of himself to his art to the point that he cut himself off from many friends and family members. Renoir complained about how difficult Degas was: "What a creature he was, that Degas! All his friends had to leave him; I was one of the last to go, but even I couldn't stay till the end."

How have you reinvented yourself?

ON MAKING MAGIC

One day at a Disneyland resort in Anaheim, a little boy lost a tooth. His mother washed his mouth off in a water fountain and, by accident, lost the tooth. The boy was devastated. The Tooth Fairy would not come.

A Disney employee—called a Cast Member (spelled with capital letters)—witnessed this and had the drain opened. They didn't find the lost tooth, but they did ask the family to meet them that afternoon at Guest Services. When the family came, Tinker Bell presented this little boy with his tooth in a beautifully wrapped box. How is that for a Tooth Fairy? The maintenance team never found the tooth but made a fake tooth in their shop.

Lee Cockerell loved working at Disney so much that he vowed to write a book about it when he retired. He told the tooth story and said that while making teeth is not in the job description of Disney employees, they always go "the extra mile" because "that's what people of character do. They are fully committed. . . . As all Cast Members are told, it is not magic that makes Disney work; it is the way that the Cast works that makes Disney magical. The Cast Members . . . created magic for the Guests whose lives they touched, and don't think that doesn't matter when their families plan their next vacation or recommend a destination to a friend."

Describe a way that you made magic for someone else through your leadership.

ON INTENTION

Pablo Picasso (1881–1973) was a Spanish painter and one of the founders of the Cubist movement. He spent most of his artistic life in France, experimenting with color and technique and trying, in his art, to return to the imagination of a child. "The artist is a receptacle for emotions," Picasso wrote, "that come from all over the place: from the sky, from the earth, from a scrap of paper, from a passing shape, from a spider's web."

Picasso created a breathtaking legacy, more than 50,000 pieces of art: sculptures, ceramics, lithographs, linocuts, drawings, even tapestries.

"What one does is what counts. Not what one had the intention of doing."

Intention is critical. Picasso, an engine of inspiration, said: "Action is the foundational key to all success. Inspiration exists, but it has to find us working."

Picasso as a child showed talent—but, more than talent, he showed the drive to succeed by doing and doing again and doing differently. When he was young, his mother said to him:

"'If you are a soldier, you will become a general. If you are a monk, you will become the pope.' Instead, I was a painter, and became Picasso."

**In your leadership, when did you last
experiment with something new?**

◆ DAY #333 ◆

ON THE GOOD FIGHT

"I have not yet begun to fight."

These are some of the most immortal words of leadership to ring in history.

On September 23, 1779, a British commander yelled from his ship to John Paul Jones, commander of the ship *Bonhomme Richard*, asking if he was ready to surrender. Jones's ship was nearly destroyed. Morale was low. The skirmish seemed over. The British officer was close enough to have his voice heard over the water and the fighting.

He called out to Jones to give up, to resign himself and his sailors to capture.

But Jones saw this ending as merely a beginning. You fight when you have a lot of fight in you. When you have a reason. When you have the drive. When you've created the momentum. When you have nothing left to lose. And Jones meant what he said: "I wish to have no connection with any ship that does not sail fast; for I intend to go in harm's way."

For the next three hours, Jones manned what little he had left of his ship and its sailors, and in the end it was the British who surrendered.

It was a glorious and exhausting finish.

Everything about it proved John Paul Jones's philosophy of war: "It seems to be a law of nature, inflexible and inexorable, that those who will not risk cannot win."

**Describe a good fight that you thought
you would lose and won instead.**

✦ DAY #334 ✦

ON DEVOTION

"Try to do something for your people—something difficult. Have pity on your people and love them. If a man is poor, help him. Give him and his family food, give them whatever they ask for. If there is discord among your people, intercede.

"Take your sacred pipe and walk into their midst. Die if necessary in your attempt to bring about reconciliation. Then, when order has been restored and they see you lying dead on the ground, still holding in your hand the sacred pipe, the symbol of peace and reconciliation, then assuredly will they know that you have been a real chief."

This powerful Winnebago leadership lesson in devotion is found in Kent Nerburn's collection, *The Wisdom of the Native Americans*. The Winnebago tribe is also known as the Ho-Chunk.

The leader holds the sacred pipe, or calumet, and dies with it in his hand. The pipe was smoked at special ceremonies as a means of communication between human and sacred beings. The inhalation and exhalation represented a way of moving with the spirits. Intricate movements are part of the ritual, as in smoking it in the six directions—the four compass directions and then toward the sky and the earth.

Sometimes, but only if you are willing to give up everything while holding the pipe in hand, your followers will understand how important reconciliation is.

What is the most you have sacrificed as a leader to communicate a critical message?

✦ DAY #335 ✦

ON EXITS

In *Exit: The Endings That Set Us Free*, Sara Lawrence-Lightfoot claims that we are a society where beginnings are praised and celebrated, but leave-takings often go unmarked. "Our exits are often ignored and invisible. They seem to represent the negative spaces of our life narratives. There is little appreciation or applause when we decide (or it is decided for us) that it is time to move on."

Lawrence-Lightfoot quoted the work of sociologist Helen Rose Fuchs Ebaugh, author of *Becoming an Ex: The Process of Role Exit*, who identified four distinct stages of disengagement—a process that includes entertaining "first doubts," weighing "role alternatives," and coming to a "turning point" at which the person makes the move, often announcing it publicly as a way of deterring retreat. However, Ebaugh's fourth stage—"creating an ex-role"—is a subtle recognition of life's messiness.

"During this fourth and final stage, people struggle with incorporating their 'hangover identity' into their future identity; seeking to find a balance between who they were and who they are becoming . . . struggling to establish themselves in their new role while they continue to disentangle themselves from the social expectations of their previous one."

Think of a professional exit you made that needed more acknowledgment than you or others gave it. What can you do now to mark it?

✦ DAY #336 ✦

ON FREE WILL

"A puppet is free as long as he loves his strings."

Think of a decision you're facing. Now read this from Sam Harris's *Free Will:*

"Take a moment to think about the context in which your next decision will occur: You did not pick your parents or the time and place of your birth. You didn't choose your gender or most of your life experiences. You had no control whatsoever over your genome or the development of your brain. And now your brain is making choices on the basis of preferences and beliefs that have been hammered into it over a lifetime—by your genes, your physical development since the moment you were conceived, and the interactions you have had with other people, events, and ideas. Where is the freedom in this? Yes, you are free to do what you want even now. But where did your desires come from?"

Only when we contemplate the role of genetics, chemical determinants, our place of birth, income, parents, fashions, trends, education and our sources of information do we begin to realize how really minimal our own input is. Lest this frighten us, we turn to Harris again.

"Losing a belief in free will has not made me fatalistic—in fact, it has increased my feelings of freedom. My hopes, fears, and neuroses seem less personal and indelible. There is no telling how much I might change in the future."

Do you find this perspective frightening or liberating?

ON LOYALTY

"We are a family, and the loyalty of the family must come before anything and everyone else."

"You're my older brother and I love you. But don't ever take sides against the family."

"The strength of a family, like the strength of an army, lies in its loyalty to each other."

"Friendship is everything. Friendship is more than talent. It is more than the government. It is almost the equal of family."

Meet Don Corleone, the infamous Godfather, and his creator, Mario Puzo (1920–1999). Puzo grew up in New York and was born into a poor Italian family that had immigrated to America. He wrote *The Godfather* in 1969 to make money.

"You cannot say 'no' to the people you love, not often. That's the secret. And then when you do, it has to sound like a 'yes.'" Don Corleone was not someone people said no to often.

Loyalty was loyalty until it wasn't, and then it turned into cement shoes. You can leave the gun and pick up the cannoli, but it doesn't mean that you won't be picking up the gun again later.

Some of the most difficult ethical issues leaders will ever have involve loyalty versus quality, allegiance to company versus allegiance to people, love of excellence versus love of others. Loyalty to something can mean disloyalty to something else.

**Take a few minutes to thank the most
loyal person in your life.**

ON MODERATION

Western civilization exists in the shadow of the Aristotelian golden mean. Between two extremes is a place of moderation and rationality.

Thomas Paine (1737–1809) wrote in *The Rights of Man:* "A thing moderately good is not so good as it ought to be. Moderation in temper is always a virtue; but moderation in principle is always a vice."

We desire moderation in the way that we interact with others. But moderation, when it comes to our principles—what we stand for—can become a vice. In *The American Crisis*, Paine admonished those who "expect to reap the blessings of freedom" but not "undergo the fatigue of supporting it."

And even there, Paine was cautious: "Society in every state is a blessing, but government, even in its best state, is but a necessary evil; in its worst state, an intolerable one." In *Common Sense*, Paine asked us to engage our common sense and understand the limitations of institutions.

Paine came to his commonsense theories through hard work with no intellectual moderation. Born in England, Paine was an inventor and a corset-maker before coming to America at the age of thirty-seven. His writing furthered the cause of American independence, but despite his immense wisdom Paine died poor and isolated.

Moderation in character. Passion in action.

Would people describe you as moderate?

ON SAFETY

Many of the most well-loved children's books begin with a parent's death or abandonment. Only by embracing the nightmare that there is no protector does the protagonist become interesting and independent. The release from safety propels the plot, as it does for Harry Potter in *The Half-Blood Prince*:

"And Harry remembered his first nightmarish trip into the forest, the first time he had ever encountered the thing that was then Voldemort, and how he had faced him, and how he and Dumbledore had discussed fighting a losing battle not long thereafter. It was important, Dumbledore said, to fight, and fight again, and keep fighting, for only then could evil be kept at bay, though never quite eradicated. . . .

"And Harry saw very clearly as he sat there under the hot sun how people who cared about him had stood in front of him one by one, his mother, his father, his godfather, and finally Dumbledore, all determined to protect him; but now that was over . . . the last and greatest of his protectors had died, and he was more alone than he had ever been before."

**Describe the loneliest moment of your leadership,
when you realized that no one could protect you.**

✦ DAY #340 ✦

ON RELATIONSHIPS

"Take short views of human life—never further than dinner or tea." This advice from Reverend Sydney Smith ends John Bayley's anguished memoir of life with his literary wife, Iris Murdoch (1919–1999), *Elegy for Iris*. He was a professor of English at Oxford. She was alive at the time he wrote it, but it was a different she. He had lost the famous writer and philosopher, author of over thirty books. They were married for forty-two years. In her last four years, Murdoch seemed lost; she repeated herself, asked the same questions again and again, watched children's television shows.

Murdoch eased into Alzheimer's in 1995. She thought it was writer's block.

Over time, Bayley taught himself to love this "other" woman.

"Life is no longer bringing the pair of us 'closer and closer apart,' in the poet's tenderly ambiguous words. Every day we move closer and closer together. We could not do otherwise. . . . Purposefully, persistently, involuntarily, our marriage is not getting somewhere. It is giving us no choice—and I am glad of that."

A relationship is the way in which we are emotionally connected to another person over time, when contexts and conditions change. Sustaining meaningful relationships can be hard for leaders because they manage so much change that identifying who and what is core and essential to identity can come under question.

**What anchor relationship needs your
love and attention right now?**

✦ DAY #341 ✦

ON HOPE

"When the way seems dark before me, give me grace to walk trustingly:

"When much is obscure to me, let me be all the more faithful to the little that I can see clearly.

"When the distant scene is clouded, let me rejoice that at least the next step is plain.

"When what Thou art is most hidden from my eyes, let me still hold fast to what Thou dost command.

"When insight falters, let obedience stand firm.

"What I lack in faith let me repay in love."

This is from the evening prayer for the twenty-seventh day in John Baillie's small treasure, *A Diary of Private Prayer*, first published in 1936. Baillie (1886–1960) wrote a morning and evening prayer for one month of Christian devotion and added two additional prayers to be used at one's discretion.

Baillie was a Scottish theologian and professor of divinity at the University of Edinburgh, and his book identified him as "chaplain to the King." In that capacity, there was a lot to pray for, and—no doubt—one of the things he prayed for often was that hope would not leave him.

"And if I still cannot find Thee, O God, then let me search my heart and know whether it is not rather I who am blind than Thou who art obscure, and I who am fleeing from Thee rather than Thou from me."

**When was your hope strengthened by
renewed intimacy in a relationship?**

✦ DAY #342 ✦

ON ACHIEVEMENT

Leadership drive, the sheer ambition required for leadership, can mystify those who stand at a distance. When leaders reach goals, they move the goalposts. Isn't it enough?

The answer to that question for most successful leaders is no. It is actually not enough. There is so much more to do. There is so much potential waiting to be actualized. There is so little time.

In this continuous acceleration forward, it is worth pausing and breathing for a moment to ask how we define success so that there are moments when we can step back and say: "Yes, it's enough."

A dictionary definition of *success* offers us this:

1. achievement of intention: the achievement of something planned or attempted;
2. impressive achievement, especially the attainment of fame, wealth, or power;
3. something that turns out well: something that turns out as planned or intended;
4. somebody successful: somebody who is wealthy, famous, or powerful because of a record of achievement.

The Latin origin of the word—from *succedere*, to "go after" or "give way"—substantiates the way achievement works in our typical understanding, but to "give way" makes us wonder what gives way in our drive to achieve and what we give up to be successful.

**Circle one of the four definitions that
best describes your drive.**

◆ DAY #343 ◆

ON SETTING A
PERSONAL VISION

Steven R. Covey, in *Principle-Centered Leadership*, wrote: "Constancy of vision cannot exist in strategic road maps that are obsolete almost before they are handed down. In a world of such tremendous global change, what is needed is a compass in the hand of each associate."

We all need a compass, even if it too becomes obsolete.

A personal vision statement is a portrait of you in the future, written in the present tense. Create a total picture of your life: personal, spiritual and professional.

Just write a few sentences and describe where you are physically when you write this. Put this on a card and put it away for safekeeping so you can take it out and look at it periodically and see where you are.

Let this vision statement be your compass.

**Write a vision statement about where you
are five years from now that begins,
*I am . . .***

ON LOVING

"Is love an art?" psychologist Erich Fromm wrote in the opening lines of *The Art of Loving*. If so, he continued, "it requires knowledge and effort. Or is love a pleasant sensation, which to experience is a matter of chance, something one 'falls into' if one is lucky?"

Fromm came down on the side of art when most people think love is a matter of chance. "Most people see the problem of love primarily as that of *being loved*, rather than that of *loving*, of one's capacity to love." The problem, then, is how to be loved or lovable rather than examining our own deficiencies in delivering love.

Many leaders want to be loved. They confuse love and adoration. If they are successful or popular or attractive or powerful, they will be more loved. But in order to be loved, one must give love. This, Fromm, suggested, goes hand in hand with another fallacy about love. It is the problem of an object rather than a faculty: *I am the object of love or I am not; it is not that I have the capacity for love and I maximize it*. If it is about an object, there is little to learn. If it is about character and a faculty, then there is much to learn.

"*Love is an art,* just as living is an art. . . .

"Love is the only sane and satisfactory answer to the problem of human existence."

What will you do today to master the art of loving?

ON SALVATION

"Human salvation demands the divine disclosure of truths surpassing reasons," wrote Thomas Aquinas (1225–1274). Aquinas understood that for human beings to believe in salvation—that their humanity can be redeemed even from great darkness—they must step outside the boundaries of normal reality.

Aquinas is best known for his *Summa Theologica*. "Three things are necessary for the salvation of man: to know what he ought to believe; to know what he ought to desire; and to know what he ought to do." Deliverance from sin, destruction or evil, according to this medieval theologian, requires knowledge on three different levels: the doctrines that would save you, the desire to be saved and the practical knowledge of how to save yourself.

"The soul is like an uninhabited world that comes to life only when God lays His head against us." It's an endearing image: God resting his head on us, joined together with us in a sweet moment of affection and dependency.

This affection is captured in a prayer Aquinas wrote: "Bestow upon us also, O Lord our God, understanding to know you, diligence to seek you, wisdom to find you, and a faithfulness that may finally embrace you."

**When it comes to support, whom
do you lay your head on?**

✦ DAY #346 ✦

ON FULFILLMENT

"The thought once occurred to me that if one wanted to crush and destroy a man entirely, to mete out to him the most terrible punishment, one at which the most fearsome murderer would tremble, shrinking from it in advance, all one would have to do would be to make him do work that was completely and utterly devoid of usefulness and meaning."

Roman Krznaric chose these words of Fyodor Dostoyevsky to begin his small, potent book, *How to Find Fulfilling Work*. And we understand this dark sentiment because we assume that a murderer does his work quickly, while a job bereft of meaning involves the slow and tortured death of the soul, day after day after day.

Describing himself as a lifestyle philosopher, Krznaric set out to help people question why they work: what needs are fulfilled and how one prioritizes the need for money with the need for meaning and satisfaction. He followed Aristotle's advice: "Where the needs of the world and your talents cross, there lies your vocation."

Sometimes we ask ourselves why we need to find fulfillment at work. "The desire for fulfilling work—a job that provides a deep sense of purpose, and reflects our values, passions and personality—is a modern invention."

**Name five characteristics of work that
you need to thrive as a leader.**

✦ DAY #347 ✦

ON DECEIT

Young American poet Criss Jami observed: "Just because something isn't a lie does not mean that it isn't deceptive. A liar knows that he is a liar, but one who speaks mere portions of truth in order to deceive is a craftsman of destruction." When a simple lie is crafted into something more complex, nuanced and credible, it becomes an act of deceit.

To avoid feeling betrayed and duped, we might do the hard work for liars: We let ourselves be deceived by them. Susan Forward, in her book *When Your Lover Is a Liar: Healing the Wounds of Deception and Betrayal*, wrote: "Allowing the lies to register in our consciousness means having to make room for any number of frightening possibilities." These possibilities include: (1) my partner isn't who I thought he was; (2) I have no idea what to do because this relationship feels so out of control; and (3) this relationship is over.

Because we do not want to face these terrifying possibilities, we often go along with deceit and become its accomplice. We begin to rationalize deceit and even confess our contribution to it. "In fact, many of us are willing to rewire our senses, short-circuit our instincts and intelligence, and accept the seductive comfort of self-delusion."

Someone else's deceit makes life much more complicated.

Name a lie that trapped you.

✦ DAY #348 ✦

ON VIRTUE

Matthew Kelly, in *The Seven Levels of Intimacy*, wrote that in our most important relationships, we believe others are helping us become better versions of ourselves.

The most basic level is characterized by unoriginal interactions: We say: How's it going? Have a good one. Weather's fine today. Level two: We move on to shared facts. We know things about people and they know things about us. Level three is knowing another's opinions. Moving up the ladder of intimacy, level four involves knowing the hopes and dreams of another with the safety to reveal your own. Level five involves the same understanding but a deepening of feelings. Level six is more vulnerable because it involves confessing faults, fears and failures. The seventh level is expressing legitimate needs. You are able to share your physical, emotional, intellectual and spiritual needs with someone without restraint and you are able to know and sometimes satisfy those of another.

The basis of this highest level of intimacy with others, Kelly wrote, is a shared commitment to virtue.

"Virtue makes all respectful relationships possible. Two patient people will have a better relationship than two impatient people. Two generous people will have a better relationship than two selfish people. Two forgiving people will have a better relationship than two people who decide to hold grudges and refuse to forgive. . . . Two disciplined people will always have a better relationship than two undisciplined people."

Which of the seven levels of intimacy have you achieved with a partner in your leadership?

✦ D A Y # 3 4 9 ✦

ON CONSISTENCY

One of the most important ways leaders build trust is through consistency. People know what to expect from a leader, and that leader delivers. Leaders who are unpredictable in their responses or moods can frighten us. We don't trust them, sometimes even when they are being nice, because we are not sure that streak of friendliness will last.

Consistent behavior engenders trust. Stephen M. R. Covey, in *The Speed of Trust*, identifies thirteen behaviors that develop what he calls "high trust." Consistency is the building block because people can only judge us on behavior, not intent.

To build trust, Covey suggests creating a trust account. Remember that (1) withdrawals are always bigger than deposits, and (2) what may be perceived as a deposit into one person's account may actually be a withdrawal in the way they perceive it. Covey explains that in order to create what he calls (and actually trademarked) high trust, you need to exhibit thirteen behaviors.

1. Talk straight.
2. Demonstrate respect.
3. Create transparency.
4. Right wrongs.
5. Show loyalty.
6. Deliver results.
7. Get better.
8. Confront reality.
9. Clarify expectations.

10. Practice accountability.
11. Listen first.
12. Keep commitments.
13. Extend trust.

Covey also wrote that redundancy, politics, bureaucracy, high turnover, disengagement and, at its worst, fraud create atmospheres of low or no trust.

**What is one thing you can do right now
to increase your trust account?**

✦ DAY #350 ✦

ON HOSTILITY

One of the hardest challenges any leader faces is dealing with difficult people. But since we all define what is difficult behavior to manage, it is hard to have any one formula for managing criticism, deeply ingrained stubbornness, deception, hostility, negativity or downright cruelty. *Not all difficult people are alike in the way that they are difficult.* David D. Burns, in his *Feeling Good Handbook*, shared some thoughtful and counterintuitive advice.

When you react with defensiveness in managing the unmovable stubbornness or arrogance of someone else, you are essentially giving that person power over you. In virtually every instance of handling these types of people, Burns asks us to acknowledge the feeling or kernel of truth in another person's view, no matter how hostile or irrational. Ignoring or resisting will only escalate responses that are dogmatic and furious. Only then can you call attention to the way you are being treated, and you must.

"People who are judgmental and critical often have a lot of unexpressed anger or dissatisfaction. . . . You will contribute to this problem if you are argumentative and defensive. Instead, encourage the other person to say everything bad they can think of about you. If they open up and tear you to shreds, don't defend yourself.

Instead, find the truth in what they say. Acknowledge how they feel. Urge them to tell you more. This can work wonders."

The next time someone rips you apart, respond with one initial, humbling question: "Is that all?" It really works.

✦ DAY #351 ✦

ON THIN PLACES

When the Roman Empire came to a final decline in the fifth century, Church power moved away from Rome to places on the margins of that once spiritual stronghold. New expressions of Christianity emerged, one of them in Ireland. Celtic Christianity, infused with the energy of missionaries like Saint Patrick, moved to a less hierarchical expression of faith and to a more community-based model.

Celtic Christianity, among many other contributions, gave us the expression *a thin place*. A thin place is any location where the wall between the divine and the human or material is very thin. Ordinarily, we might think of these places as particularly vulnerable. But in this model, a thin place provides a very close glimpse of what is holy and majestic. Our material world becomes so thin that transcendence seems almost touchable. We have encountered the holy.

Luke described the baptism of Jesus as a moment when "the heavens opened." In opening the firmament, those on earth found themselves in a thin place.

For some of us, a thin place is just that: an actual place where we have heightened experiences of being in God's presence or feel the extraordinary pull of the sacred very strongly.

Few people would call an office a thin place. But every once in a while, we create a magic moment at work, and the barriers between the ordinary and the extraordinary seem to almost disappear.

Describe a thin place in your leadership that you created.

ON SERENITY

"Win it, or it's start all over around here." Even if you win it, you will be starting all over again, because every victory and triumph means another challenge will come your way, harder than the one before. This isn't a reference to corporate leadership. It's about winning the Super Bowl.

It would be unusual to turn for guidance on serenity to an NFL athlete, but Troy Vincent, a former football player, has shared how he achieved peace in the middle of a game. If you can find it there, you can pretty much locate serenity anywhere: in the midst of hard pushes, human pyramids, head butts, immense pressure and intense scrutiny. You have to learn to make your own silence.

"Everyone has a different way of finding peace. As for me, I listened to gospel music and read the Bible before every game. Once I was out on the field, I didn't hear any boos. I didn't hear any cheers. I didn't worry. I just played."

There is so much noise in leadership, so much oversight, criticism, distraction, drama and trauma. The consequences of failure can be extremely costly. The pleasure can seem far-off or nonexistent.

Perhaps Vincent is onto something about the secret of playing hard. Find the kernel and serenity in the noise and expand it so that you cannot hear anything but your own proud, beating heart.

Describe your serenity zone at work.

ON FOCUS

Focus. Stop and take a good, hard look around. What do you actually see? Notice everything for only a few minutes.

The novelist Roxana Robinson, in an article in the magazine

Real Simple, wrote beautifully about the way we can sometimes move through a day—maybe even through a life—without feeling grounded.

"It's easy to drift through the day, to move without thinking from one activity to the next. Our lives are so crowded, and we do so many things, often at the same time. We're caught in a web of tiny threads, all tugging at our attention. We're on the street or in the car, on the phone, with the radio on, already late, distracted, our minds leaping ahead, worrying away at the knot of obligation and expectation and urgency that binds us. . . . Often it seems there's no way to slow down."

There is a larger purpose to Robinson's accentuated noticing. "I want to remember what it's like, being human, right now."

It's the same power of concentration that Paulo Coelho was referring to when he said that whenever we want to achieve something, we have to keep our eyes open: "Concentrate and make sure you know exactly what it is you want. No one can hit their target with their eyes closed."

Open your eyes and spend two timed minutes writing down everything you see at this very moment in time.

✦ DAY #354 ✦

ON FEAR

In the preface to *The Inspired Life: Unleashing Your Mind's Capacity for Joy*, by Susyn Reeve and Joan Breiner, we are invited into the world of the spirit with a dash of speed: "The fastest way to the realization of your own highly inspired life is to ride the wave of that which the Great Spirit is already seeking to bring forth into human experience, fully surrendering your life, to be used in service to this great and glorious unfolding."

We never enter the unknown without hesitation and small, timid steps. The idea of opening a parachute to an inspired life or surfing a fast-moving wave is hardly a welcoming induction.

The authors wrote that that which holds us back from an inspired life is what sabotages us. An uninspired life, in their words, is a prison—"each bar cemented into a foundation of 'I can't. I'm afraid, nothing works for me. I'm not enough.'" Fear, they argue, is like a set of high-performance brakes. It's time to take your foot off the pedal.

Fear is a powerful emotion. Instead of minimizing it or sidestepping it, step into fear and harness its considerable strength. "While fear can automatically stop you in your tracks, it can serve as a powerful wake-up call."

Take a few minutes to move through a fear you have in your leadership, but do so as a strong, powerful agent of change who can step into the emotional danger and emerge whole and energized.

✦ DAY #355 ✦

ON MEANING

The Book-of-the-Month Club voted *Man's Search for Meaning* one of the most influential books of the last century. Viktor Frankl (1905–1997) was a psychiatrist and Holocaust survivor who developed a form of treatment called logotherapy based on his experience in concentration camps. "Everything can be taken from a man but one thing: the last of the human freedoms—to choose one's attitude in any given set of circumstances, to choose one's own way."

When we understand what we are prepared to suffer, we understand what gives our lives meaning. "In some ways suffering ceases to be suffering at the moment it finds a meaning, such as the meaning of a sacrifice."

During World War II, Frankl and his family were transported to the Theresienstadt ghetto, where Frankl practiced psychiatry and confronted firsthand shock.

Frankl was liberated in 1945, after three years of being controlled by the Nazi regime. He went back to Vienna, where he wrote his most famous treatise, but he went back with no one left but his sister.

"Ultimately," Frankl wrote, "man should not ask what the meaning of his life is, but rather must recognize that it is he who is asked. In a word, each man is questioned by life; and he can only answer to life by answering for his own life; to life he can only respond by being responsible."

**In one sentence, capture what
gives your life meaning.**

✦ DAY #356 ✦

ON DESPAIR

The Pulitzer Prize–winning American author Studs Terkel wrote in his book *Working: People Talk About What They Do All Day and How They Feel About What They Do:* "Most of us have jobs that are too small for our spirit."

Terkel was a free spirit and a noted ham. He was, through his directness and his honesty, also able to capture the soul of the everyday worker—from waitress to corporate warrior, from farmer to valet parker. He detailed the existential anguish of work at times and its impact in creating "the walking wounded among a great many of us."

He also understood that small exchanges of kindness and generosity were able to offer meaning and dispel despair at work.

"Work is about a search for daily meaning as well as daily bread, for recognition as well as cash, for astonishment rather than torpor; in short, for a sort of life rather than a Monday through Friday sort of dying. He wrote:

"I think it's realistic to have hope. One can be a perverse idealist and say the easiest thing: 'I despair. The world's no good.' That's a perverse idealist. It's practical to hope, because the hope is for us to survive as a human species. That's very realistic." But you have to work at it. "I want, of course, peace, grace, and beauty. How do you do that? You work for it."

**What do you do to overcome
moments of despair?**

✦ DAY #357 ✦

ON TIME

Haruki Murakami observed in *Dance Dance Dance*: "Unfortunately, the clock is ticking, the hours are going by. The past increases, the future recedes. Possibilities decreasing, regrets mounting." This view of time is choking. And yet it aptly describes what most leaders feel acutely. Time chokes us: the marching approach of deadlines, the punishing hands of the clock indicating that another day has passed and another project is past due.

Time can pass quickly in exhilaration or slowly in tedium, but it is moving ahead, with or without us.

Take apart the usual components of a workday, and fill in the blanks.

I can make meetings fly by _____

I can make presentations fly by _____

I can make phone calls fly by _____

I can make answering e-mails fly by _____

ON INNOVATION

Steve Jobs wrote: "The mark of an innovative company is not only that it comes up with new ideas first but also that it knows how to leapfrog when it finds itself behind."

How do you leapfrog? You see things others don't see.

"Some people say, 'Give the customers what they want.' But that's not my approach. Our job is to figure out what they're going to want before they do. I think Henry Ford once said, 'If I'd asked customers what they wanted, they would have told me, 'A faster horse!' People don't know what they want until you show it to them. That's why I never rely on market research. Our task is to read things that are not yet on the page."

Innovation often comes from connecting people and ideas in unusual ways. But if we continue to do the same thing, we can't expect a different result.

**As a leader, are you creating something
new—or building a faster horse?**

ON TRANSPARENCY

Science fiction writer Vera Nazarian, in *The Perpetual Calendar of Inspiration*, wrote: "In the kingdom of glass everything is transparent, and there is no place to hide a dark heart." Imagine you are living in a glass house. Everyone can see everything. There can be no secrets. Your life is open to spectators, strangers. Anyone can comment on what they see to the larger, broader world. On some level, if you are a leader, you do live in a glass house.

Earlier we spoke about the importance of trust in leadership, of trusting others and being a trustworthy person. Perhaps there is no greater obstruction to trust than the failure to be transparent. Leaders are trusted with a great deal of confidential information. Spilling it engenders suspicion. You can't say everything. You can't show everything. But when leaders can be transparent with information, they must. Secrets are a way of controlling people and situations. The spiritual goal of being one with the universe cannot take place in an environment of outward hostility or unnecessary secrecy, politics or other obstructionist behaviors.

Rollin King, founder of Southwest Airlines, described his business model in this way: "We adopted the philosophy that we wouldn't hide anything, not any of our problems, from the employees."

That is a big commitment.

That is transparency.

**Think of a leadership moment
when you were more transparent
than you initially thought wise.
What were the results?**

✦ DAY #360 ✦

ON THE ENVIRONMENT

In the Garden of Eden, Adam was assigned two tasks: to work the garden and to watch it. These are two separate acts of stewardship. We can work and overwork land, but we cannot do it exclusively. We also have to step back in a posture of absolute wonder and think about what it means to have a garden, what it means to be a good, caring gardener.

No one asked us to steward our planet. It doesn't matter, we think.

Without an invitation, many may regard this as someone else's job. It isn't.

You might think that, as a leader, you have better things to do—leave recycling and picking up trash on the office floor to someone else. Please don't think that.

Green leaders role-model from the top what it means to be environmentally sensitive. Green leaders ask difficult questions about office systems that are not efficient when it comes to using natural resources more responsibly.

Pope John Paul II asked us not to be hypocrites when it comes to our precious world: "The earth will not continue to offer its harvest, except with faithful stewardship. We cannot say we love the land and then take steps to destroy it for use by future generations."

Do you love the land? Show it in the way you set a high environmental standard for your shared indoor space.

**Name one small change you could
make today to be visibly more
environmentally friendly.**

✦ DAY #361 ✦

ON ACTION

"Waking up this morning, I smile. Twenty-four brand new hours are before me. I vow to live fully in each moment and to look at all beings with eyes of compassion."

This is the way Thich Nhat Hanh has committed to waking up, ready to face a day where actions matter. Nhat Hanh is a Buddhist monk who has written over a hundred books.

In *Understanding Our Mind: 50 Verses on Buddhist Psychology*, Nhat Hanh offered us an unusual way to think of what we own: "My actions are my only true belongings." The notion of the impermanence of the material world for Buddhists makes this approach to action not surprising but refreshing. We own our actions. When we make a mess, we must clean it up. When we do good, we can own that too. At the end of a life, our legacy is what we do, not what we have.

Nhat Hanh reminds us, however, that we can never own others. "If your love is only a will to possess, it is not love." The desire to possess someone else constitutes self-love.

Let go.

**What have you done as a
leader that you do not own?**

✦ DAY #362 ✦

ON MONOTONY

There are days, many of them, when we tire of the same routine, the same dramas, the same faces. We seek adventure. We wish we could just do the same things we enjoy again and again, with intensity and pleasure. The sky outside the office window is overcast, and the grayness settles inside us, and all becomes a blur.

It is this despondency that David Eagleman draws our attention to in *Sum: Forty Tales from the Afterlives*. Eagleman is a neuroscientist and writer.

"In the afterlife you relive all your experiences, but this time with the events reshuffled into a new order: all the moments that share a quality are grouped together. You spend two months driving the street in front of your house. . . . You sleep for thirty years without opening your eyes. For five months straight you flip through magazines while sitting on a toilet."

Get it?

Eagleman continued with the hours, days, months and years spent cutting your nails, showering, thinking, being bored, suffering heartbreak. A life goes on, "where episodes are split into tiny swallowable pieces, where moments do not endure, where one experiences the joy of jumping from one event to the next like a child hopping from spot to spot on the burning sand."

What gift has monotony given you?

ON PAYING ATTENTION

Pay attention. The job of a poet is to pay attention and articulate the ordinary, making it universal and transcendent through the mastery of language.

The *New York Times* called Mary Oliver a best-selling poet—not an expression often heard in the literary world. Oliver rarely gives interviews, nor does she give out her address: "One time a stranger came to the house and asked if I was Mary Oliver. . . . And I said, 'No, I'm not Mary Oliver.'"

Oliver pays attention to exquisite details, often in the very same place. "Ten times a day something happens to me like this—some strengthening throb of amazement—some good sweet empathic ping and swell. This is the first, the wildest and the wisest thing I know: that the soul exists and is built entirely out of attentiveness."

Pay attention. Wisdom lives all around us. Holiness is close by. Knowledge is ours for the taking, but sometimes we're blind to it.

In order to get us to pay attention, Oliver tells a sad story to make our heart "break open and never close again to the rest of the world."

To whom should you open your heart to today?

ON DREAMING

Biff: He had the wrong dreams. All, all wrong.
Happy: Don't say that!
Biff: He didn't know who he was.
Charley: Nobody dast blame this man. You don't understand:

Willy was a salesman. And for a salesman, there is no rock bottom to life. . . . He's a man way out there in the blue, riding on a smile and a shoeshine. And when they start not smiling back—that's an earthquake. And then you get yourself a couple of spots on your hat, and you're finished. Nobody dast blame this man. A salesman is got to dream, boy. It comes with the territory.

By now, we recognize the scene. It's from the last act of Arthur Miller's *Death of a Salesman*. Willy Loman's two sons, Biff and Happy, are talking to their neighbor Charley after the death of their father. Biff feels his father had the wrong dreams and, therefore, was never successful. Happy cannot face this truth. Charley, Willy's only friend in life, tells the boys that they are mistaken. Salesmen like Willy live on dreams. They sell dreams.

Every dream comes with its risks. It may be too ambitious, too disconnected from reality, a shadow of the truth.

The harsh and flawed salesman of Miller's imagination reflects the harsh and flawed reality of always pushing a fiction, a vision that will never match a reality.

Dream big but make sure those dreams are not too far, far away.

What dream have you made real?

✦ DAY #365 ✦

ON GRACE

Grace is hard to define. It is that ephemeral quality—like a piece of lace or a cloud—that overlays what we do with a patina of gratitude. Grace is getting something we do not deserve and, as a result, paying forward the abundance and blessings in our lives.

Horst Schulze, cofounder and past president of the Ritz-Carlton Hotel Company, began his tenure in the hotel business as a busboy at age fourteen. His mother took him to the hotel and said, "We could never go to this hotel. This is only for important people. For important, fine people." She told him he was lucky and sent him off to wash his hands. That day, his mother's words were confirmed by the hotel's general manager, who said to Horst and his mother that they would never be like the hotel guests: "So don't ever get jealous. This is for Ladies and Gentleman—very important people."

Schulze had the best revenge—the revenge of grace. In the words of an essay he penned as a young man studying the hotel business, he created a hotel for "Ladies and Gentleman serving Ladies and Gentlemen." Today this is the service motto of the Ritz-Carlton.

There are many hardworking and talented human beings who never achieve the power or position that you have. It was an act of grace that put you where you are.

You are a fortunate one.

As a recipient of grace, how are you paying it forward?

CLOSING MEDITATION

This is only a temporary end. There really is no happy ending, not because there is nothing happy but because there is no ending. This is not a story. It is *your* story in one year of small inspirations and challenges. A deep breath. A little shove forward. A quiet push inward. A small embrace outward. Your story continues.

This is just an arbitrary stop to an ongoing conversation that we have with ourselves. We often decide when we want to stop talking, stop working, stop engaging, stop advancing. Sometimes those ends are determined for us. We do not stop growing, however, or responding. And while the life questions we have seem to repeat themselves continually, in different variations, the life homework never seems to change. We always need to be less self-absorbed, more compassionate, more generous, more helpful, less domineering.

As leaders, these reminders often press harder upon us. Responsible for others, always watched by others, we understand the fatigue, the constant need for authenticity and moral integrity. We feel the void and the need for self-renewal. We also know that we cannot do this all alone. We need support. We need to be nurtured. We need to touch transcendence, to strive for something holy and sacred. Affirm our purpose. Feel inspired again and again.

Thanks for finishing this book with me.

There is no volume two. You can just turn back to page one. That's what I am going to do.

Affectionately,
Erica

ACKNOWLEDGMENTS

Thanks to all those at Simon & Schuster for their immense support.

Thanks to my beloved friends.

Thanks to my hardworking colleagues.

Thanks to my beautiful students.

Thanks to my loving family.

Thanks to my Creator for the moments of grace that make it all worthwhile.

ABOUT THE AUTHOR

DR. ERICA BROWN is an educator, author and consultant. She previously served as the scholar-in-residence for the Jewish Federation of Greater Washington, where she directed the Jewish Leadership Institute. She also held that position at the Combined Jewish Philanthropies. Erica was a Jerusalem Fellow, is a faculty member of the Wexner Foundation, an Avi Chai Fellow, winner of the Ted Farber Professional Excellence Award, and the recipient of the 2009 Covenant Award for her work in education and the 2012 Bernie Reisman Award (Hornstein Jewish Professional Leadership Program, Brandeis University). Erica has degrees from Yeshiva University, the University of London, Harvard University and Baltimore Hebrew University. She lectures and writes widely on subjects of spiritual interest and leadership.

Erica is the author of ten books. She writes a monthly column for the *New York Jewish Week* and has blogged for JTA, *Psychology Today* and *Newsweek/Washington Post*'s "On Faith," and tweets on one page of Talmud study a day at @DrEricaBrown. She also writes Weekly Jewish Wisdom. Access her articles at ericabrown.com.

Erica is the mother of four children and lives with her family in Silver Spring, Maryland.